MW00952763

I AM C

Urgent Messages From

God The Lord Jesus,

God The Father, and

God The Holy Spirit

Volume 1

Dictated by the Holy Spirit

To

Susan Davis and Sabrina De Muynck

FROM THE LORD JESUS AND GOD THE FATHER

DEDICATION

We dedicate this book to the Trinity: GOD THE LORD JESUS, GOD THE FATHER, and GOD THE HOLY SPIRIT.

NOTE FROM THE AUTHORS

These books were not to be created for the generation of profit but for the purpose of reaching more people through this particular medium. But certainly not to raise money through the use of these prophetic Words of the LORD. The list price of this book was set to cover only printing costs and the royalty that goes to the authors is near zero. (There may be a few cents per book due to fluctuating printing costs. Any remainder over zero is used to buy books which are given away for free.) These messages are so urgent and important that we want to ensure that the price of the book would not be an obstacle to people getting these messages.

TWO WITNESSES

(These comments about two witnesses is also in Part 24)

One morning, I, Susan, was thinking about the concept of "two witnesses" in the Bible. Then amazingly, and randomly, during the same morning, I came across references in the Bible and also another book I was reading of how GOD often uses "two witnesses" to confirm a testimony or message. This is why I believe that Sabrina and I were brought together by the LORD for this work, to be "two witnesses" in putting out the LORD's letters. Here are some verses from the Bible that speak of the importance of using "two witnesses" for confirming a message or a testimony:

Deuteronomy 19:15. One witness shall not rise up against a man for any iniquity, or for any sin, in any sin that he sinneth: at the mouth of two witnesses, or at the mouth of three witnesses, shall the matter be established.

John 8:16-17. And yet if I judge, MY judgment is true: for I am not alone, but I and the Father that sent me. It is also written in your law, that the testimony of two men is true.

Matthew 18:16. But if he will not hear thee, then take with thee one or two more, that in the mouth of two or three witnesses every word may be established.

2 Corinthians 13:1. This is the third time I am coming to you. In the mouth of two or three witnesses shall every word be established.

Luke 10:1-3. After these things the LORD appointed other seventy also, and sent them two and two before his face into every city and place, whither he himself would come. Therefore said he unto them, The harvest truly is great, but the labourers are few: pray ye therefore the Lord of the harvest, that he would send forth labourers into his harvest. Go your ways: behold, I send you forth as lambs among wolves.

ABOUT THESE PROPHECIES

Susan and Sabrina operate in the gift of prophecy. In 1 Corinthians 14:1 it states, "Follow the way of love and eagerly desire gifts of the Spirit, especially prophecy." Now we are living and supposed to be obeying God's instructions in the New Testament. Although some believe that spiritual gifts, such as prophecies, have been done away with, this is man's thinking and not God's. God has not changed His covenant. We are still living in the era of the New Covenant – which is also called the New Testament. Please understand that your first commitment should be to the Lord Jesus Christ and His Word as written in the Bible – especially the New Testament.

As always, all prophecy needs to be tested against the Bible. However, if the prophecy lines up with the Bible then we are expected to obey it. Currently God does not use prophecies to introduce new doctrines. They are used to reinforce what God has already given to us in the Bible. God also uses them to give us individual warnings of future events that will affect us.

Just like in the Old Testament, God uses prophets in the New Testament times of which we are currently in. The book of Acts, which is in the New Testament, mentions some of the prophets such as Judas and Silas (Acts 15:32) and Agabus (Acts 21:21) and there were others. The ministry of prophets is also mentioned in New Testament times in 1 Corinthians 12:28, 14:1,29,32,37 as well as in Ephesians 2:20,3:5,4:11.

Jesus chooses prophets to work for Him on earth. Among other things, Jesus uses prophecies and prophets to communicate His desires to His children. The Bible itself was written prophetically through the inspiration of the Holy Spirit.

Some people say words of prophecy are in danger of adding to the Bible or taking from it -- well the Bible speaks of prophecy as being a Gift of the HOLY SPIRIT. The way the Bible is added to or taken from is not through additional words of prophecy received by the people which the HOLY SPIRIT gives words to, but by the changing of GOD's concepts to add new unBiblical concepts from other pagan beliefs for example. But the primary work of the prophets in the Bible has always been to focus the people back to GOD's WORD, the BIBLE.

As it says in 1 Thessalonians 5:19-21, "Do not put out the Spirit's fire; do not treat prophecies with contempt. Test everything. Hold on to the good." And the way to test the messages is to compare it's content to what the Bible says.

In all the prophecies below I personally (Mike Peralta) have tested these messages and they are all in agreement to what the Bible says. But you must also test these messages, yourself, to the Bible. And if they are consistent with the Bible, then God expects that you will take them to heart and obey His instructions.

TESTIMONIALS

Sabrina, I hope it's OK, your wonderful writings have been posted on facebook. My, you cannot believe how many people are receiving these words and in total agreement. These words are a warning and many people are now seeing them and responding. Thank you so much for having a "listening" ear that hears what the Lord Jesus is saying. And then having the courage to tell us all what He has said. Yes, we pray for His soon coming but are in agreement that more souls must be won for our Lord. Your letters are a true encouragement to all of us! Thank you Sabrina. - Reader1

* * * * *

I believe that this is a Marvelous Article about the RAPTURE OF THE CHURCH which is absolutely coming from the Lord Jesus given to Sister Sabrina, for many true believers-the Bride of Christ are now already seriously preparing themselves for this Glorious Day while the rest of most Christians do not care for this special warning. My great hope is that all Christians should try to read this warning or message before it is too late for us to obey His message, for Jesus does not want us to be left behind when He returns and not to enter the Great Tribulation as told by the Lord in this special message. In the end, I have come to my conclusion about the RAPTURE OF THE CHURCH that we should take this message as our HEAVENLY GUIDANCE FROM HIM, TO LIVE ACCORDING TO HIS INSTRUCTIONS IN THESE LAST DAYS. TO BE CAUGHT IN THE CLOUDS TO MEET WITH THE LORD JESUS AT ANYTIME SOON. (1Thessalonians 4:16-17) - Reader2

* * * * *

First of all, I just want to thank you again. I laid in my bed yesterday and read yours and Susan's letters. Oh my gosh. I just was laying in the arms of Jesus. I pictured it all. I know He is coming, and I know I am going. I cannot wait to see the face of Jesus, the one Who has been preparing for me (and all the bride) all this time. I pictured His excitement as that of a child - He is just so excited and thrilled to see us. Your letters touched me, and now I am trying to determine from the Lord how He wants me to use them for those around me. I am so so sad for those that I know who won't listen and who have no idea about what is going to happen soon. I cry from the depths of my heart for them; I can only imagine the pain that Jesus feels. - Reader3

* * * * *

Hi Sabrina. Thank you for allowing yourself to be used by God to bring such warning messages from the Lord Jesus. Since I have read all the letters, my life has changed and I now emphasize the coming of the Lord in my preachings. Hope to hear from you. - Reader4

* * * * *

Hey Sabrina my friend in End Times Ministry. How I am excited to hear from you in Belgium. It let's me know I am not alone in this ministry to let the world know that The Lord is coming soon. Your letter is amazing and for God to send it around the world in different languages is something only God can do. - Reader5

* * * * *

I have just read your message from the Lord written on Nov. 10, 2010. I have gotten many confirmations from the letters. I also feel an urgency to warn others about Jesus' soon return. We can't know the day or hour but we do know the season, and that season is now. YOUR SISTER IN CHRIST. - Reader6

* * * * *

Dear sisters Sabrina/Susan – thank you so much for emailing me these very important letters! You both have blessed me beyond measure with these dear letters from our Father in heaven and His Holy Son Jesus Christ! I take these letters to heart and try to examine my spirit with each new letter to make sure that I am ready for our Lord when He comes for us. I cannot wait to meet you both in person when we are finally in heaven with our dear, sweet Lord Jesus Christ! Thank you both and God bless you! Your sister in Christ. - Reader7

* * * * *

Dear Sabrina, thank you for your courage and obedience to our Dear Lord Jesus in sending us these letters. I deeply appreciate the messages you wrote while hearing the Lord's word. Ever since I was a little girl I had this gut feeling that the end times were near. My family was in amazement that I was speaking about Times of Tribulation at such a young age. I don't need any proof that the Lord exists and I can only pray that I am worthy of His Kingdom and love. - Reader8

* * * * *

I just saw your mails recently that talk about you hearing the LORD speak to you and telling you to write letters and to warn us. I am so speechless with the way our LORD JESUS loves us and uses so many prophets to warn us. If we are left behind, we really do not have an excuse. HE has done so MUCH but still some refuse to believe. - Reader9

* * * * *

I was so heart broken to the point of tears that he actually begs us and says, "Please choose life and not death." I don't understand why He actually has to beg us on something that will benefit us and not HIM. I am still soooo overwhelmed by all of this to the point that I have lost my appetite and I can't even think straight. - Reader10

* * * * *

Dear Susan, That's a powerful message from our Father, It brought tears to my eyes. Bless you and thank you for being faithful and bold. - Reader11

* * * * *

Dear Susan, Thanks for the I am coming letters. It has really touched me and makes a big difference in my walk and relation with our Lord Jesus. I am growing in my faith and holiness. All glory to Jesus. - Reader12

* * * * *

I am so much grateful for the messages you have sent. Nothing in this world is more important than to make spiritual preparations for the rapture. Thus your letters from Jesus is really a big help for me. You know I also forward your letters to my friends in e-mail so that they will be also informed for the lateness of the hour. Thank you so much. - Reader13

* * * * *

We are even more motivated to not waste a minute while there is still light to work in reaching every single person we can with the Good News of our Lord Jesus. - Reader14

* * * * *

God bless you Sabrina and Susan, it is the End of days, the world needs to be ready for the Lords return, the signs are all around us, thank you for the Lord's words. – Reader15

* * * * *

One of the most convicting and touching messages I have seen from God the Father. Thank you Susan and Sabrina! – Reader16

* * * * *

Amen! Apostle George gives the letters to his congregation of 7,000 - your letters are truly making an impact. – Reader17

* * * * *

CONTENTS

This Volume contains Parts 1 to 32.

September 11, 2010 to December 31, 2010.

These urgent prophetic messages are recorded at the website:
http://end-times-prophecy.com

Sabrina's email is: jan.sabrina@pandora.be

and

Susan's email is: kidsmktg@sbcglobal.net

talks about the world to come and where the Bride is going.

PART 8. In this letter, JESUS talks about His bride and also talks about the evil of hell. We included the letter from Sally Richter who received a very similar message from the LORD.

PART 9. Susan just received this letter over a two-day period and it is a very serious letter given to Susan by our Lord JESUS. The Lord addresses the seriousness of the hour and also HIS anger for the lukewarm church. We have also added to it a letter given to Sally Richter from the Lord on 10-13-10 that also speaks volumes about the urgency in His voice. Also with these letters at the bottom we are including a testimony from a friend of ours (Sabrina & Susan) who has been reporting to us about having visions which started the beginning of this past summer 2010 and have been happening right up until the last couple days.

PART 10. The LORD warns people in the letter to Susan that a vile nation is forming and the people are not paying attention to what is coming. Through Sabrina's letter the LORD pleads for the people to repent and come to HIM before it is too late.

PART 11. In this letter JESUS talks about the lukewarm condition of the church, the darkness coming over the earth and the cruel master the enemy will be. Charlotte Hill's letter is included from the LORD with very similar words for the people.

PART 12. In this letter the LORD talks about the darkness coming over the earth and how little the people are paying attention to what's happening to them around them. The LORD tells how HE will see His plans through no matter whether the people are ready or not.

PART 13. This letter primarily the LORD talks about the world's descent into darkness and the people's refusal to pay attention to what's coming. In Sabrina's letter the LORD implores the people to follow HIS commandments and the importance of following them.

PART 14. JESUS pleads with the people to come to HIM now. Only

HE can save them. Repent and to turn to Him. Also for the people to stop clinging to the world.

PART 15. In Sabrina's letter from the LORD He speaks about hell and how the bride needs to be free of spots and wrinkles. In Susan's letter JESUS talks about the Bible as the standard against all other schools of thoughts. It also speaks of the evil nation forming and darkness coming over the earth.

PART 16. The letter to Susan from JESUS speaks strongly of the trouble the lukewarm church is in. In Sabrina's letter the LORD warns to listen to His prophets, He speaks of standing before Him one day and keeping HIS commandments.

PART 17. This is a letter from JESUS to Susan telling the people to listen to HIS warnings and that the people are not paying attention at all or listening to His warnings. The world is blind and not seeing what is coming. Also includes a letter from Mary of Texas who received a similar word from the LORD.

PART 18. This message has three parts. First a letter Susan received from the LORD JESUS, then second a letter Sabrina received from the LORD JESUS, and finally a word from a young 10-year-old girl who had communicated with Sabrina. The messages from the LORD are stressing the importance of following the commandments of GOD. The commandments are not obsolete as so many seem to think by their disregard of them. It is clear in this verse Revelation 12:17, a New Testament verse, that GOD's commandments are not obsolete for this generation. JESUS speaks in His letter about the many roles He can play in a person's life. Also in this letter to Sabrina, JESUS warns about not keeping His commandments including keeping the Sabbath holy.

PART 19. In the letter to Susan the LORD talks about the people being far away from HIM. HE also talks about the way the people profane HIS Holy name in this letter. Primarily this letter addresses the trivial way the people use GOD's name and HE will avenge the use of His name.

PART 20. This is a very serious word. First is a letter with words as told by the LORD JESUS to Susan. Second is a letter from the LORD JESUS as told to Sabrina. Third we have included the story about Philipa, (a young girl who is the daughter of Guinea missionaries) and the messages she has received from the LORD JESUS since contacting Sabrina. We have included the story about how Philipa came to hear the voice of the LORD and three very serious additional messages she has since received from the LORD. In this letter to Susan the LORD speaks quite a bit about the world as a cheating mistress lusting after the world. Sabrina's letter from the LORD speaks of the importance of listening to HIS warning messages.

PART 21. This message contains two letters from the LORD. The first was given to Susan about the lateness of the hour and the second letter contains a message specifically for the bride of CHRIST as told to Sabrina by JESUS. In the letter to Susan, the LORD tells the people and churches to stop building for a distant future that isn't coming and instead to get the people ready to be raptured. The letter to Sabrina is more for the Bride about what awaits her in heaven.

PART 22. In this letter the LORD speaks on those embarrassed by HIM and how He was not embarrassed when He died for them up on the cross. The next part of the letter talks about the people being in a trance over their idols. And how their idols won't ultimately rescue them.

PART 23. Now, I (Susan) want to share a testimony about the 2nd letter here below that I received from the LORD on Dec. 5. In this LETTER, our LORD JESUS makes mention of the "leaders over HIS flocks" and of the "false prophets of old" in the same section. After the LORD had finished reciting the letter to me, I asked HIM for a Scripture verse. He told me right away, "Jeremiah 23" which I immediately looked up and to my amazement this section of Scripture is all about the very same topic HE mentions in the letter regarding the "leaders over HIS flocks" and the "false prophets of old." It was an amazing confirmation because although I knew this was mentioned in the Old Testament, I sure did not know the location was Jeremiah 23 as the LORD gave me. The first part talks about not making your own plans but following JESUS' plans. He warns the lukewarm and those who lead their flocks astray.

PART 24. In this letter JESUS says He will not accept a partial commitment and to let go of future planning. He speaks of what He endured on the cross and how a lukewarm commitment will not be acceptable.

PART 25. First a letter from the LORD JESUS told to and written down by Sabrina and a second letter dictated to Susan. In Sabrina's letter the LORD makes reference to the occult and I have included a link to an article about GOD's views on the occult. In this letter the LORD says that any plans apart from HIS are not His. He tells how only the humble can hear His voice and the message He wants people to hear. He is seeking only the pure-hearted.

PART 26. Along with the letter below from the LORD is a word from the LORD to our little 10-year-old friend Philipa, whose parents are missionaries for the LORD in Guinea. Philipa began to hear from the LORD and receive visions after she communicated with Sabrina about these letters from the LORD. She expressed enthusiasm for hearing from JESUS to Sabrina and then it was right after that she did in fact hear from the LORD. The letter below was told to Susan by JESUS along with a Scripture confirmation. The last three letters Susan copied down at the dictation of JESUS, HE followed each letter with a single Scripture verse. Each time the Scripture that was given, amazingly it coordinated with some of the content HE had dictated in each letter. This letter is the same. JESUS dictated these words in this letter to me (Susan): Be HOLY as I am HOLY. Then at the end of the letter, I asked if HE had a Scripture verse to include and HE simply said LEVITICUS 19 which starts out with this verse to my amazement: 1 The LORD said to Moses, 2 "Speak to the entire assembly of Israel and say to them: "Be holy because I, the LORD your God, am holy.' (I have included the entire section of Leviticus 19 at the LORD's request below HIS letter.) So in this letter the LORD stresses that His people need to be holy. He also talks about being second to the world in the hearts of the people.

PART 27. I (Susan) would like to share an amazing story about this letter I received below from JESUS. The same morning I received this letter below, I woke in the early morning three different times and I heard very clearly the name "HEZEKIAH." Well honestly, I knew I had heard this name before and that it was probably from the Bible, but I couldn't place who it was or where I had heard of it. Well later that morning, I had been praying and I asked the LORD for a Scripture to look up and HE simply said, "MICAH." I had not yet looked up the name HEZEKIAH in the Bible yet that day, but instead I turned to the book of Micah the LORD suggested and I was amazed to discover that "Hezekiah" was actually the King reigning during the era that Micah was a prophet. Well that same morning, the LORD had dictated this letter below to me, I was stunned to discover that Micah addressed the rise of religious infidelity and idol worship as this letter also addresses and this confirmation suggests that the people still turn their backs to GOD now, just like they did during Micah's era. In this letter JESUS addresses the doubts of the people about the end coming. He speaks on hell, and the church doing things only for their benefit and not GOD's in worship.

PART 28. In this letter once again JESUS says that if you are making plans apart from HIS plans you are going to miss HIM when HE returns. He addresses how focus off of HIM will leave you behind to face the worst. This letter is about making choices and the consequences of the choices we make.

PART 29. First is a letter from the LORD JESUS as dictated to Sabrina and also a special letter to the bride of Christ specifically from her GROOM JESUS. Below it is a letter from the LORD as told to Susan. Below this letter is a Section written by the evangelist and author Charles Spurgeon about the topic: "The Form of Godliness Without the Power." Susan included this writing of Charles Spurgeon since in the letter the LORD mentions this particular phrase. Sabrina's letter speaks of the people rejecting the LORD for the world. In the letter to Susan, the LORD talks of His compassion; patience with a world that is rejecting Him, but He still wants a pure bride.

PART 30. This has one letter given by JESUS to Susan for all who will receive it. This letter speaks of lukewarm commitment and doing good works apart from GOD's consent. The world looks so normal, but it is not. No middle ground, only 100 percent commitment. There is only one path to GOD - not many.

PART 31. This was dictated by JESUS to Susan for you. Again the message here is more focus on the world than the LORD. A lukewarm commitment and following men will lead to disaster. JESUS asks do the people even wonder who created them?

PART 32. This was dictated by JESUS to Susan in the first letter for you. Then Sabrina received a letter from the LORD also for you. JESUS speaks of the stench the lukewarm church is to Him. He speaks of the path being narrow because it requires a full surrender which few are willing to give. In Sabrina's letter JESUS talks about the blood only being available in this world not the next life. HE talks about what happened on the cross and how this generation abuses HIS good name. The time of this mercy is running down.

ACKNOWLEDGMENTS

We wish to acknowledge in the first place our precious GOD, JESUS, THE FATHER, and THE HOLY SPIRIT who brought us together to write the Lord's Letters and bring them out in this last hour.

We wish to acknowledge our brother in the Lord, Mike Peralta, who gave us the idea about a book and who wrote it all out for us.

We wish to acknowledge everybody who has any part in working with these letters to bring them out in any way.

PART 1

Introduction to the Letters and Warning from JESUS that HE IS COMING and to GET READY.

September 11, 2010.

This is an urgent message from the LORD JESUS–We are but humble servants asked to do HIS work in these last days–Please read and forward to whoever you can–God bless.

Around 2007 or so, the LORD brought together two people from two different parts of the globe, one in the U.S. and the other in Belgium. Sabrina, Belgium, and I, Susan, U.S. became friends because I had posted some information about GOD online and I received an email from her about it. I was involved in church outreach at the time and she was having struggles in a very secular region of the world with outreach. I felt the LORD wanted me to support her as she and I both struggled with issues of outreach in our communities, thus began a wonderful friendship, but we did not know that GOD had bigger plans for our lives. Sabrina had the unique gift of being able to hear the voice of the LORD and I totally believed and supported her gift. Then recently she let me know that the LORD had a gift for me, I soon found out that the gift was also hearing the voice of the LORD, I started to write down letters HE gave me recently and I have been filling many notebook pages. The messages are very, very serious, the LORD told us we needed to get these messages out without delay–so here are the letters I received, you can read more about us at the bottom of this message. Please pass this message on to whomever you think needs to read this.

Then I, Sabrina, asked the LORD what about your, Susan's, letters:

"I have spoken to her so she might learn to understand MY Voice. Send the word out about MY soon coming. Don't be shy about a thing. The world must get penetrated with MY words. Everybody must know that I am coming very soon. Many do know, but are not ready. Therefore send out MY words! Send them out & don't be shy

3

about a thing."

Then the LORD said: "This refers also to you, me, Sabrina, MY daughter, don't be shy about a thing any more. Do it soon!"

Words given to Susan: 2nd Letter. September 2010.

The people should prepare. I am coming.

They need to be ready at all times. Waiting for me. Am I not worth the wait? I died for them. I wait on them long, suffering to change their hearts toward me. The day will come when I wait no more. It will be too late for them. They will suffer. Now is the time to come to me. It will happen soon. I cannot wait on their hearts. Am I not worth it? I died a horrible death for them. They do not know what torture I saw. Am I not worth it? I do everything for MY children. I spare no expense. I gave all. I gave them all of Me. I bled out. It was for them. Tell them this. Soon I will come and they will miss the greatest ride of their lives. MY love for eternity. I gave all. I give all. I am a loving God. MY heart never stops beating. It is love never ending. Sad it will be. I gave all. It was for MY children. These are MY words. Write this down MY daughter MY bride, days are getting darker. They need to turn now. I can't wait forever on their hearts. It will be too late for many soon. It will be too late. Tell them to take this seriously. Soon it will be too late. These words are true.

Everything I did was worth it. I would die again for MY children but they reject MY love, MY salvation, MY Spirit and put ME to shame again. I won't wait forever on them. They will be sad when they realize they have been left. It will be the worst moment of their lives.

4th Letter. September 2010.

Time is short. The times are progressing, it can't be stopped. I will deliver MY people.

Write it down. Cling to ME, depend on ME. Nothing else will deliver you. I am coming soon. The world will see MY wrath very soon. Nothing will save the ones who disobey. They cannot be saved if

4

they turn from ME. The hour is short, so short you can see the times changing rapidly. It will be dark, so dark for those who refuse ME. I am their only hope. People must see I am their only hope. Come to ME at this hour. There is little time left.

Destruction, darkness is coming to the earth. This hour is bleak, so bleak. So dark, people must run to ME. I will save them, I love them. They don't listen. I am their only hope, salvation. I am their salvation.

Write it down daughter, sister, MY bride. Come down now. Lay down your weapons of destruction; weapons of the tongue; evil thoughts. The world will never be the same. All will be black. They will know, and they will see it is ME. MY salvation is their only hope. I will break the tide. I will come for MY people, those who truly love ME and repent of their evil ways. Justice will be served.

You will know I am God. Time is short. Your King is coming on blinding white doves, beauty indescribable, heavenly beauty. The dawn will break over the horizon. And MY beauty is splendid, breathtaking for those who are ready. Today you choose. The choice is yours. I lay it before you: life or death. The choice is easy but you make it hard.

I love MY children. MY children know MY voice. I am calling them to come home. Come home to a safe Kingdom. Land of milk and honey, honey that drips, wine that tastes sweet. It is theirs for the taking if they surrender their hearts to ME. I am a gentle loving God, kind, a deliverer. I am strong, a strong tower supporting them.

It will be time for ME to come and I won't hesitate to move when it is time to get the bride. I won't hesitate. MY moniker is love. I love MY bride. She is waiting. I know MY bride. I know who waits. Only those who wait will be ready and taken. I know MY people's hearts. Some make ME very sad.

The hearts that are ready, they will be the ones I deliver. This is not hard, for this is truth. Have I not said it in MY word. MY word is clear and uncomplicated. I would rather you be hot or cold but you are not

5

and I must spit you out. These words are serious. It has been said by ME before, nothing is new. The world drifts from ME.

Time is short. The plagues will begin. MY people have no idea what it will be like. Life will never be the same. The hour is coming, choose life or death: simple choice. This is MY word to MY people from MY messenger. I use MY messenger to give MY words.

The beauty of MY love cannot be measured or comprehended. Men do not know what they are rejecting. This world offers them nothing but pain and suffering.

I am coming. Time is short. They will know I am God. Time is short. When I deliver MY people they will see that I am LORD. It will happen quickly. I come and then evil will rage. Soon the world will need to choose life or death. They must choose ME if they want to live. I give all for them. Didn't I die? They are disillusioned by this world. How am I to reach them? I only have to plead. They think I am a GOD who won't follow through with what I have to say. But MY word is true. It will happen. They will be amazed. Only those who are ready will go, MY precious ones who love ME. I love them and they will never see destruction. Warn them sister, MY bride.

This is your LORD. Time is short. Time is running out. The clock is ticking. I must come soon. Life will never be the same. Choose glory or destruction. You have the power to choose. Life is in your hands. I will not wait forever on MY people. This is serious. The world will stop. The destiny of the world is death. If you stay you will die. If you leave, you must leave with Me. You must choose life or death. I come quickly. MY hour is near, the hour I retrieve MY Bride. She is ready. All is ready. The hour is close at hand. Be ready. Look for ME. I cannot wait much longer for a doubting generation. Only the pure of heart will see MY face, MY beautiful face. MY heart is broken for those who will be lost.

Save yourselves, turn and surrender. The hour is close at hand. All will be dark soon, but the Bride will be safely put away. Be the Bride: turn, repent, come to ME. I am gentle. I am kind. MY words are soft and tender. I am a gentle God. MY people see, MY people know I am love. I spare no expense for MY children. Love is MY moniker. This world is going to die out soon. Soon it will all be over. Repent while you still can. Please come to ME, I am waiting. These are your last opportunities. You choose: life or death.

5th Letter. Sept. 2010.

I am coming soon. The world will never be the same. The people think they have forever. They do not. I will be here before they realize. It is coming fast.

These are MY words, true and simple. Watch for it. The people need to know I am coming soon, very soon. Very soon it will be over. People will choose. Will it be ME or the adversary? I am the choice to make if you want life and peace. Choose ME, choose life.

We have very little time left. The hour is closing in. Choices must be made. Choose love or choose death. Why is this choice hard? I offer life eternal. Please choose life. No one comes to the Father but by ME. I am the way, the truth, and the life. Your choice is simple but you choose death if you don't choose ME.

We can run, we can fly, we can live together for all eternity. Make your mind up: the hour is now and time is closing in. The world will all end, all is ending. This is the final hour. Choose life or choose death. I am life. The world is death. To live is to know ME, everything else is death. Everything else is temporal.

6th Letter. Sept. 2010.

Write it down MY dear. This is what I have to say today. Your question about 2011, this is what I have to say. You will be gone by 2011. The world will become dark. And yes, you can know the season. I had said to the LORD that you can't know the day or hour but you can know the season.

Write it down. I am coming soon, so very soon. The people do not see what is happening. They are blinded. We shall depart soon.

7

You will see. It will come quickly.

I will work everything out. You will see. It will be glorious for MY people. Many will be left. It will be a sad time for them. I have been clear about MY coming. It should not be a surprise. All is ready for the greatest banquet of all time. You are coming too MY love. This shall be a glorious time for heaven. All is ready and waiting.

The angels are standing ready. Tell the people time is up. We shall be there soon. All is getting dark. The dark clouds are forming. The darkness comes. These are dark days ahead. Warn them.

These words are true. I am waiting patiently on MY people. I won't wait forever on them. Many will find out and it will be sad for them. Some are preparing now and will be ready for ME.

I am an honest God. MY truth stands. All is ready waiting for them. Take this seriously, because when I come all will know. Sad for those left.

Tell the people it is coming. Get ready, be prepared. I won't wait. These are MY words.

Write it down. The people need to be ready. These are MY words. I am careful with MY words. Time is up. It is ready. Be ready for the greatest ride of your life. Spring beauty all year, that is what heaven is like. The angels wait for the bride. All is ready. Standing ready the heavens are breathless for MY word to come get the bride, she is ready. I am ready.

We shall be together soon. It will be glorious, so glorious. The hour is now. The season is now.

I am coming very soon. We will run, we will fly. It will be grand a sight, a spectacle for all time, when MY people come home. The heavens await the greatest sight ever. All is ready.

MY patience is up. I can wait no longer to receive MY bride, MY glorious bride. She is a beautiful sight. All is ready. I am ready. It will come like a stream flowing from heaven, when the heavenlies open up. When I come down from heaven, the Bridegroom on wings of eagles, white horse, white doves, beauty unimaginable.

Write it down. The beauty will never stop. It will never end. The days of eternity are beginning for the bride. She is glorious. We will unite and be together. Forever these are MY words. I am your Lord. I am your Lord, Maker, Keeper, God Everlasting, Truth, Strong Tower, Love Everlasting, Power over the universe. I am Maker, Lover, Father, Brother, Son. I am God. We shall run, we shall fly. You shall change. Your lives will change. It will be glorious. You will be in MY keep. I take care of MY children. MY words are true, this is truth. Write it down.

The heavenlies open up, all will see. Few will go. It is sad, so few are ready. But, I must come. It is MY hour, MY destiny to claim MY bride. I have waited for this hour. All is ready. MY bride awaits. I come for those who are waiting and ready. It will be soon. The hour is now. Now is the hour.

Many will be left. They will know it was ME. What a dark day for them. This is truth. I cannot wait forever on MY people. Tell them this. MY bride finds it worth waiting. She stands ready. I will come to receive her unto Myself. It will be glorious for both her and ME. We will fly as doves to their lattices. I will retrieve MY bride and she will be ready for ME.

They will divide Israel. You will see and you will come with ME before I pour out MY wrath on the world. Pray for your loved ones like never before. The hour is closing in. I come to take MY bride and I will put her in a safe place.

Words given to Sabrina:

Tuesday 7th of September, I was already touched greatly in the morning, so I knew the Lord would speak to me in a special way.

In the afternoon, I was reading in a book where the Lord has said to a person that first the rapture would happen and then the 7 years of tribulation.

I was like, Lord how is this possible, because You told me the last year, 2010, that we are already in the tribulation?

The Lord's answer: "The rapture is delayed. Trust on the hearing of MY Voice. The intention was that I came for MY bride just prior to the 7 years of tribulation. But MY Father has decided otherwise. The rapture is delayed for a short time."

Letter from God received on Tuesday 7th September 2010.

For Susan & me, The Lord was talking in plural form, so when He says 'You', He means you & me.

"Write it down, MY daughter. You are not crazy, you hear MY Voice and I have given you Susan as support. Encourage each other in these days with MY words. Let nothing distract you, you both hear MY Voice. I shall use you as a mighty duo in MY Hands. Much I shall reveal to you. Only listen to the hearing of MY Voice and don't let yourselves be distracted by nothing. Don't worry about a thing or human. Only act out of MY love, if you stay in MY Word & words & believe, you are walking in MY love. Don't let nothing distract you, do everything that I tell you. I have searched & I have found, MY chosen people in these last days. Please obey at the hearing of MY Voice. People do not realize how late it is. MY Father longs to give the sign, all eyes are fixed on Him. Keep your eyes only fixed on ME, don't look at the left, n'or the right, look at ME, I am Jesus, your leading man to life, the only leading man to life. Trust MY daughter, trust. I have prepared you for this. Don't look at the earthly circumstances. Keep your eyes only fixed on ME & let yourself be led by MY Spirit. He is the one who speaks. You hear His Voice, MY Words. ME & MY Spirit are one, we are a team & we want to help you both in this time. Stay close to MY Spirit, He is the most precious gift you own. If you don't have MY Spirit, you also cannot have ME. ME & MY Spirit are one. Be also you one with Us. Yes, I speak to both of you. Trust on the hearing of MY Voice. Don't doubt! I have searched & I have found, MY chosen people in these last days. I am telling you, this is the last hour. This is for both of you. Be strong & courageous. Everything comes soon to an end. I love both your hearts, keep setting it apart for ME. It belongs to ME. You belong to ME. This is Jesus."

ME: Concerning rapture 2010, what if the Father delays it again?

The Lord: "So be it! MY daughter. MY Father has all might & power. Everything lies in the Hands of MY Father. Don't worry about the day, n'or the hour. The rapture is planned for this year 2010. But the grace of MY Father is big. But there comes a day and an hour. There comes a day and an hour. Do both not worry about this fact."

Later the Lord said: "Write it down MY daughter. The rapture will happen before the great tribulation, this is in MY Word and it stands firm. I have all time under MY control. I am God, I know what I am doing."

Letter 8. Sept. 2010.

Listen to the speaking of MY voice. The days are getting darker. Soon all will be dark. The people need to see what is coming and hear MY voice. We are getting close to the end of this age. All is growing dark. These will be hard times for those left. MY love will sustain them, but it will be hard for them. All will be dark very soon.

Each day will be added upon another. The dominoes are falling, everyday will be worse than the previous. Headlines will continue to grow darker. Men's hearts will fail them. Tribulation has begun.

Write it down. Today we are much nearer to the end than a week ago, each day we draw closer, it is coming. I am coming. Life here is closing down. The people are leaving soon. It will come. It will come fast. The end is near.

ME, I had been asking if I am to release these words to the general public and email lists:

Write it down. You have MY permission to put those words out. Now is the time. Do not delay. Time is short. Lives are at stake. We are nearing the end. All is getting dark. A perverse nation is forming, the one world government.

Write it down. Warn the people. Time is short. Darkness will prevail for a brief time in history and then I will come with MY saints to destroy the enemy and all he stands for, for a time a time and a half. Anyone who wants to escape this madness needs to turn right now to ME, your Savior. There is no other way to the Father, but through ME. Don't be deceived. There is no other way. I am the Way, the Truth, the Life.

Deceptions are running amuck. The people are destroyed for lack of knowledge. They follow deception. The devil prowls like a lion looking for who he can destroy. Choose life, not death. You have a brief time left to choose. Choose ME and find freedom. freedom to fly to safety among MY loved ones to peace and love everlasting, divine love, pure love.

The people need to act now, turn before it is too late without ME. They will be lost and there will be no escape from hell. I can keep them from this destiny. Destiny to destruction. MY way is peace, wholeness, forgiveness, truth, love. MY way is righteous. With MY right hand I guide, guard, protect. I am a loving God. But to reject ME is death, eternal demise, eternal loss. There is no turning back once you have made this choice.

Don't be deceived by the world, the world is corrupt. It is an enmity to ME. I will spit it out and all it stands for. Time is short. Choose life or death. I am life. Choose ME, choose beauty, choose love, choose well.

Letter 9. Sept. 11, 2010.

Write it down MY love. You are MY love. You are faithful and loyal. I know all. I am with you. I will never forsake you. Your love is true. But you need to listen to what I have to say. These are MY words. Write them down.

I am coming soon. All is ready for ME to come. The time is drawing near. It is closing in. We will fly away soon. All is prepared. Life here is drawing to a close. The peace on earth will be lifted and exchanged for darkness, it will be utter darkness. Souls will cry out for relief. They would not follow ME when I gave them a chance. Over and over I have tried to warn them. They refuse to listen. Their worldly pursuits were more important to them. You can't have ME and the world both. MY love will never compare to this world. Their choice is a sad choice. (I think HE means that they choose the world over HIM.)

They need to run quickly to ME now, while there is time left. Soon this door will shut and all will go black. I am making MY pleas through MY humble servants, I am warning through disasters, I am putting up all the signs, and yet people will still not believe. What must I do to get through to them?

They are making their choices now. I cannot help if there will be regret later, I have given them ample opportunity to choose. The choice is theirs to make. I cannot plead forever. MY Kingdom is coming and I am ready, ready to assume MY role as King of kings and Lord of lords over all. This is MY destiny to be fulfilled.

Time is short. I will take back MY Kingdom, the people have a choice to make. MY promises will be fulfilled, all will come to pass as it is in MY Word. MY promises are being fulfilled right now, I am true to MY Word. The clock is ticking. The people must get ready, the evil nation is forming, while they stand idly by.

Allow me to rescue them or be swept away in the flood of what is coming. Please church wake up! This is the final hour. Why are you so sleepy? The people are not being warned. Read MY Word. There is nothing happening that has not been foretold. I am coming soon and it will either be a great moment or the worst moment. Choose what moment you want to live in, with ME in MY Kingdom or with the enemy in his eternal kingdom. The lines are being drawn. You must decide. Love or hate, MY ways are simple, surrender to ME or be left behind to face destruction. I love MY children, but they must choose. I gave Myself for them, I ask no less of them.

Our personal background info:

Hello. MY name is Sabrina. Let me introduce myself a bit.

13

I became a Christian in 1992.

God has done a huge job in me concerning emotional recovery. It has been an intense, difficult, painful and long journey, but it has led to an intense wonderful intimate friendship with God. God has been MY perfect counselor. He has treated me with His tender care, wisdom and especially a lot of patience.

God's heart's desire was and is intimacy with His children and this also became MY heart's desire. I learned to hunger and thirst for everything from Him. I learned to worship Him in all MY circumstances, no matter how I felt.

I learned to have a personal relationship with the Holy Spirit and I discovered that it was He who spoke to me in MY mind. I created a deep respect for Him and invited Him every day in MY prayers to fill and lead me completely. I did everything not to hurt Him.

One day in 2006 God started talking to me about His soon coming. The Lord has also told me that the fact I always hear His Voice, is His gift of grace for me. Later I understood that this gift would also be used in the prophetic and encouraging field for other people. But the principal of this gift was, that He would use me in this end-time to speak about His soon coming.

In April 2008 God told me it was important to spend much time with Him. This desire grew also in MY heart more and more and the Lord said to me that this was also His desire and His Holy Spirit's.

From then on I put a number of specific days for Him separately during the week. I filled these days with prayer, Bible reading, reading books, listening to good Bible studies on the internet, worship, etc. But it also happened that the Holy Spirit urged me to go to evangelize to someone.

Heaven is too real for me, time too short and the exhortations of the Lord too strong for something else to do.

On January 6 2010, I had a prophetic rapture dream. Though I was engaged much in these matters, I had not received many rapture dreams. This was MY second. The Lord explained that His Coming will be sudden, with great power, followed by immediate panic and chaos.

On May 25 2010, God gave me an important dream of the bride. The explanation was this: "It is important for MY Bride to prepare herself. Behold, I come quickly and then there will be no more time to make up. MY Bride must prepare now. Be ready! I am ready. "God spoke in a serious tone!

On July 9 2010, God gave me an encouraging word. Here is an excerpt from the letter: 'MY dear daughter, write it down. Know that everything here is as good as ready. There is nothing stopping ME to come for MY bride. Everything is ready. The table for the eternal marriage stands ready. The angels are on post. Everyone is rejoiced & enthusiast! Oh what a joy it will be when I come for MY bride! I want you to encourage each other with these words. It is only the grace of MY Father who holds the sound of the trumpet. Millions of people are still lost.'

In all those years, I have received many confirmations whenever the Holy Spirit talked to me, through the bible, books or other people's testimony, preaching, teachings. MY only goal is to be completely obedient to Him. MY days are completely for Him, as I don't go to work. I keep praying for everyone I witness to, take daily communion, just spent all MY time for & with the Lord. Thank you for taking the time to read all this, so you know MY walk with Him is serious. May the Lord bless you all!

Sabrina De Muynck. jan.sabrina@pandora.be

You can find more information out about me, Susan Davis, and MY relationship with the LORD by checking out the following websites:

http://end-times-prophecy.com/blog/

http://sites.advancedministry.com/lovethewhirlwind

And MY email is: lovethewhirlwind@sbcglobal.net

IMPORTANT NOTE: I am very serious about these warnings from the LORD and these testimonies so I wanted to include the following Bible verses that talk about those who speak falsely for the LORD. This is to let you know that we take this very seriously and we understand the gravity of these messages. We know how the LORD feels about people who speak on HIS behalf falsely and I wanted to point out that these messages are not contrived or made up and attributed to GOD falsely. These are very serious messages from the LORD and not to be taken lightly, so here are the verses that we have read and we confirm that we understand and know them well:

Matthew 7:15-20. A Tree and Its Fruit. "Watch out for false prophets. They come to you in sheep's clothing, but inwardly they are ferocious wolves. By their fruit you will recognize them. Do people pick grapes from thorn bushes, or figs from thistles? Likewise every good tree bears good fruit, but a bad tree bears bad fruit. A good tree cannot bear bad fruit, and a bad tree cannot bear good fruit. Every tree that does not bear good fruit is cut down and thrown into the fire. Thus, by their fruit you will recognize them.

Matthew 24:24-25. For false Christs and false prophets will appear and perform great signs and miracles to deceive even the elect, if that were possible. See, I have told you ahead of time.

1 John 4:1-3. Test the Spirits. Dear friends, do not believe every spirit, but test the spirits to see whether they are from God, because many false prophets have gone out into the world. This is how you can recognize the Spirit of God: Every spirit that acknowledges that Jesus Christ has come in the flesh is from God, but every spirit that does not acknowledge Jesus is not from God. This is the spirit of the antichrist, which you have heard is coming and even now is already in the world.

Jeremiah 14-16. Then the LORD said to me, "The prophets are prophesying lies in MY name. I have not sent them or appointed them or spoken to them. They are prophesying to you false visions, divinations, idolatries [a] and the delusions of their own minds. Therefore, this is what the LORD says about the prophets who are prophesying in MY name: I did not send them, yet they are saying, 'No sword or famine will touch this land.' Those same prophets will perish by sword and famine. And the people they are prophesying to will be thrown out into the streets of Jerusalem because of the famine and sword. There will be no one to bury them or their wives, their sons or their daughters. I will pour out on them the calamity they deserve.

Jeremiah 23:16. This is what the LORD Almighty says: "Do not listen to what the prophets are prophesying to you; they fill you with false hopes. They speak visions from their own minds, not from the mouth of the LORD.

PART 2

A second introductory letter and announcement with warnings that JESUS plans to come soon.

September 14th, 2010.

We recently posted amazing WORDS from the LORD which you can read at this website as an Urgent Message from the Lord: I AM COMING! http://end-times-prophecy.com/blog/

I have another urgent message from the LORD, but before I give you HIS letter, I have something I want to say. The fact that I am now hearing from the LORD is surprising, but I was told back in March of 2009 that I would be doing HIS end time work and to prove this to ME the LORD gave me a miraculous prayer language and a vision. So I knew that soon HE would be calling on me to do something for HIM. Also MY dear friend Sabrina, who lives in Belgium who the LORD brought us together was given the same words.

About five years ago or so, the LORD began showing me that HE was coming soon, at that time I was shocked because the only thing going on was the IRAQ war. I have since seen many things come about that the Bible said would happen and I have been amazed that it is as the LORD showed me back then.

At the time the LORD showed me five years ago that HE was coming soon, I was very busy with a family and career. Then the LORD called me away from MY career. I have since learned it was to clear the way for the work I would be doing for HIM in these last days. This past year I went for a mammogram and was greatly dreading it because I had previously had a biopsy and a lumpectomy and I was anxious about the upcoming mammogram. When the report arrived, I let it sit for four days, and when I gained the courage to open the letter it was a good report, I heard the voice of the LORD say: "I DON'T NEED YOU SICK NOW, I HAVE WORK FOR YOU TO DO." I was amazed, because I would never call

18

cancer being sick, I knew this was HIM. Later this year, we were also relieved of some financial burdens and the LORD once again told me HE was clearing the way for the work HE has me doing and HE did not want me focusing on worldly problems. I also want to add that the LORD sent many other confirmations along the way– from other people so we cannot deny what is happening. The LORD sent a woman to me who I had never met before who has a big heart for the LORD and she felt the LORD was wanting to use her and she is working with us on getting the word out through her End-Times website. The LORD has told us that HE would open many doors and HE has been true to HIS word.

Now I have experienced the wrath of GOD first hand, so honestly there isn't enough criticism to keep me from speaking the words of the LORD. I fear God much more than I fear anything people have to say about these messages. The LORD knows what HE is doing, MY job is to follow HIM and not to worry about what people say, worry is a sin. *This is what the LORD spoke to me regarding the criticism of others when I am giving HIS message out:

"MY disciples were also forbidden to speak about MY gospel. They were tortured and martyred, but they remained obedient to what I had told them to do. Therefore stay restful and calm MY daughter and you will understand the leading of MY Holy Spirit. He will guide you in everything, when to speak and with moments also to be silent. This is MY end-time work MY daughter and I have chosen you to do this work, together with many others of MY daughters. Few are willing, but I see that you are willing to do MY will. Therefore don't be surprised if many rise against you. It looks like a mountain, but it is not. Speak to this mountain MY daughter, speak MY words about MY soon coming."

One of the things that the LORD has told both Sabrina and me is that near HIS coming she would be healed. Sabrina suffers immensely and has many physical ailments. She is nearly handicapped and is in CONSTANT PAIN. I do not know how she is withstanding this pain. The LORD has promised her healing as a sign of HIS soon return. He speaks of it in this most recent letter I have included below. When she is healed, I will be singing praises for this work of the LORD because the doctors can do nothing for her now and she suffers every day, every hour. Here is the POWER behind this message: Sabrina has been telling me for over a year now that the LORD has promised to heal her just prior to HIS return and she would have a short ministry regarding her healing–well today–I heard HIS words myself that HE plans to heal her as I wrote HIS words down. I couldn't keep from weeping as I heard these amazing words knowing what this all means. We have been instructed by the LORD to release HIS words because lives are at stake.

The idea that we are in the end times is not a new concept, it is on a lot of people's minds these days, the weather reflects it; the world's sin reflects it; and the politics reflects it. The fact that few people want to believe the LORD is coming soon is completely Biblical as the LORD gave me a word about how few will be ready when HE comes and sadly how many will later turn to HIM in the great tribulation as reflected by John's words in Revelations: http://end-times-prophecy.com/blog/?p=203 Finally, here is what I have to say about these messages the LORD is telling us to release:

Here is MY position on this message, I AM Coming: I cannot speak for Sabrina, but I think she would agree with me, there is no hope if a person cannot give their complete life to the LORD, surrender all, follow HIM with all your heart, soul, mind, strength and to think you will only be met with deception or deceit from the God you seek with all your heart, soul, and mind. No, this is not the GOD I have grown to know and love. His handbook, the Bible is clear about these matters as stated in the verses below. There comes a time when GOD asks you to do something and you either worry about what people around you are going to think or you trust and obey. God knows our hearts and that is what counts. God bless. Susan.

Jeremiah 29:13. You will seek me and find me when you seek me with all your heart.

Deuteronomy 4:29. But if from there you seek the LORD your God, you will find him if you look for him with all your heart and with all your soul.

Proverbs 8:17. I love those who love me, and those who seek me find me.

Matthew 7:8. For everyone who asks receives; he who seeks finds; and to him who knocks, the door will be opened.

Acts 17:27. God did this so that men would seek him and perhaps reach out for him and find him, though he is not far from each one of us.

*Regardless as to whether you believe us or not–just do this for me: SURRENDER YOUR LIFE TO JESUS–GIVE IT ALL TO HIM–NOT JUST YOUR HEART–GIVE HIM EVERYTHING AND DON'T DELAY.

This is from Habakkuk 2:2-3, as it is plain that the LORD tells people to write things down, this is not a new thing that GOD is doing, Remember Jesus is the same yesterday, today and forever.

"Then the LORD replied: "Write down the revelation and make it plain on tablets so that a herald may run with it. For the revelation awaits an appointed time; it speaks of the end and will not prove false. Though it linger, wait for it; it will certainly come and will not delay."

Letter 12. Words given to me–Susan–by the LORD to be shared.

Write it down MY love. This is MY voice you are hearing. Write what you hear.

MY coming is close at hand. I am near. All is ready. It will happen soon. Many do not believe. They are wrong. I have been warning them. They will find out. MY words are true.

Write it down. There will be hard lessons for them to learn if this is what they have to go through to find ME. I would rather they come now. But if they resist, they will be left. MY words are true.

21

Now concerning you and Sabrina, write it down. These are MY words for you. You will find out soon what you are to do. I will reveal more in the coming days. The plan will be given to you step by step. You shall see. It will all come together. I will provide you direction. Life will change soon. Sister Sabrina will be healed. She needs to prepare. I am making ready for this great miracle. Tell her to make ready. All is ready. Susan's words: Read the description below of what she will be healed of.

These are MY words, write it down MY precious Bride. I thank you for your help in this. Sabrina is your dear sister. She has fought hard. She is MY loved one. Her healing is coming. What a great day lies ahead to be lifted of this burden. She will rejoice, it will all be worth it. Tell her it will be soon over. I will receive glory. Many will be saved. Tell the people to prepare. I am coming swiftly. Nothing can stop ME. The dominoes are falling. The plans are laid bare.

Write it down. Sabrina's healing will come soon. Your ministry will be short. Let this be a sign of MY soon coming. All is being made ready. I will come and pull MY bride out. Days are darkening. Time is short. They say I am never coming, but I am. Soon all will become dark. You must write these words down. I love you MY bride. Tell the people to make ready, prepare their hearts. These words are true. MY servants speak truth. These are MY words.

I am coming swiftly. The signs are passed. The event is coming. The greatest event of all time, MY retrieving the Bride and MY great feast. The plans are laid out. MY word is true. The earth will grow dark. The people will know they have missed it. Turn your hearts to ME now. Escape with ME. Now is the time to surrender. You must choose. If you think you have time, you don't. MY sheep hear MY voice. If you have MY Spirit, you know this is truth. You know MY words are true. You see the times. I am your Father. MY Son died for you. He is coming. Did He not say He would? There will be no excuses, all has been said. The warnings are clear. MY words are strong and full of truth. Don't be blind, open your eyes. The truth is before you. If you refuse to see it, then you cannot be helped.

Write it down. These are MY warnings. How long must I plead? I cannot plead much longer. I must come. MY heart breaks over those who will be lost, you will suffer at the hands of the enemy. It is not MY choosing that you do it this way. I will not wait forever on this lost generation. You have but a little time left. Save yourself, turn to ME. Turn from the world. It is gross. it is evil. it is dying. it is lost. I offer hope, wholeness, peace, love. I am your escape. Cling to ME. The hour is closing. The door is closing. When I come for MY bride, it will be wonderful. Won't you join us? Come meet me in the air. I am love, I will take you away to a glorious home, a heavenly home made with Holy Hands, MY precious pierced hands. I am a loving God. I will save you. Please turn now. Seek MY face, I am calling you to repent, turn, and save yourselves. These are MY words.

This is what Sabrina suffers from today as referenced above: A short summary: Pronounced Lumbar scoliosis of 20° with chronic vertebral pressure due; Chronic Fatigue Syndrome and Fibromyalgia with Spasmofilie ; Discopathy symptoms; The disc L1-L2 and L2-L3 are more pronounced narrowing ; Moderate facet degeneration L4-L5 level and L5-S1 ; At the level C5-C6 there is a wide beam discus bulge, prominent on the left, reaching down to the C6 nerve root to the left = hernia ; Continuous paralysis ; Constant pain in left knee after surgery, again torn miniscus ; Glaucoma in eyes ; Constant headaches / migraine ; total of + 66 % disability.

Matthew 12:25. Jesus knew their thoughts and said to them, "Every kingdom divided against itself will be ruined, and every city or household divided against itself will not stand."

PART 3

In this letter, the Lord is pleading to get ready and explaining that His coming is actually really soon.

September 21st, 2010.

Dear Friends of Christ:

Sabrina and I recently posted and emailed important letters, and words, we received from the LORD in a message titled I AM COMING, as seen on this blog: http://end-times-prophecy.com. I continue to receive, almost daily, letters from the LORD. Some are very personal and some, like the one below, are for public viewing. These are serious warnings and we have been instructed by the LORD to send them out. I was told to send this one out and I shared it with Sabrina first and she heard this message from HIM about the letter: Sabrina heard this from the LORD regarding MY, Susan, letter from HIM: The Lord tells me to post this word and to not be worried about what people will think and their reactions and that the ones who must receive it, will receive it. Here is the letter I copied down as the LORD dictated it to me today 9-20-10:

Susan write it down.

Susan We have work for you to do. This is what I have to say. Very soon you will be telling the people what I have to say. You will be taking your orders from ME. I will guide you with MY eye, you will see. All is prepared. All is planned. It will be glorious. The people will be amazed. This miracle will change hearts. They will come to ME. I am in control. MY plans will succeed. All is ready. You will see. We are prepared for this event to happen. You will be amazed. Many doors will open. I have prepared the way. People's hearts will be stunned. The world will stand in awe. I God can do anything. I can make the blind see. I can make the deaf hear. I can make the lame walk. I can heal Sabrina.

MY banner is Love. I am Salvation.

These are MY words. Your lives will change. Pray for comfort, for guidance, support, direction and I give it freely. Ask and you will receive. I am mighty. I am great to deliver.

Write this down. We will be going home soon. The world will be astonished because they did not believe, but MY bride will be at MY side forever more to reign and rule with ME for eternity. It will be glorious. The world will be lost in their sin. In their disgust of God, their plans will fail. All their well laid plans, gone to dust. I am the only hope for this lost world. The hour is near, all must choose: life or death. The hour is now: peace everlasting or death: a simple choice but a final choice.

Give ME your allegiance and live. Live in peace, love, comfort. Don't delay, the door is closing fast. Time is running out: life or death. Today you must choose. I have been patient, but you behave as if I will never come back. But I am coming and soon it will be too late for many.

These are MY final pleas. Soon I am coming and time will be up when the door closes it won't open again. Don't be so sure of yourself that you have all the time in the world. It will be a fatal choice. MY love is great, but I can't wait forever. Soon this world will grow dark, very dark. The time is closing, the hour is now. I won't wait forever. Choose now, make your choice. Those who call on MY name will be saved. I am JESUS, the only name that saves.

PART 4

Like the other letters, JESUS explains that HE is actually coming soon and to stop engaging with pagan idols.

September 24th, 2010.

Hebrews 6:4-6. It is impossible for those who have once been enlightened, who have tasted the heavenly gift, who have shared in the Holy Spirit, who have tasted the goodness of the word of God and the powers of the coming age, if they fall away, to be brought back to repentance, because to their loss they are crucifying the Son of God all over again and subjecting him to public disgrace.

After reading Hebrews 6:4-6, I realized that it is impossible to receive the gift of hearing the LORD's voice as I write down HIS letters and then to turn around and to become disobedient in refusing to put them out for others to read–when this is what the LORD has specifically told me to do–then to be able to continue in a close relationship with HIM if I am disobedient. Especially since this gift was given to me to support HIS end time work. So in order to maintain MY ongoing relationship with the LORD–I MUST BE OBEDIENT AND POST THE LETTERS THAT HE GIVES ME FOR ALL TO READ–Seek God while HE can still be found. HIS servant, Susan.

Letter 17. September 21, 2010.

Write it down.

I want you to write these things down. Time is short MY dear. All will know soon how very close the time is. I will give you direction. You will know what I require of you. All will happen soon. Everything is in the works. I have been patient with MY people, but the time has come to soon make our departure. The world will realize how soon it is coming.

Many things will change for those left behind. It will be their worst nightmare. I am sad for those who will be left, but this is their choice, not mine. MY choice is for them to come with ME, but they have freewill to come or stay. They are invited, but I will not force them. The choice is theirs to make. Why choose death? This is MY question. MY Spirit calls them. I cannot do this for them, they must choose. I can wait long suffering; I can invite; I can plead; I can encourage; I can argue MY position, but I won't force. No one is forced. They must decide.

All is ready. The waiting is up. The clock is winding down. The door is about to close. Many will be left. I am a patient God, I have been patient with MY children. I will lose many to the enemy. It will happen. MY heart breaks for them, but this is their choice.

They have a chance to choose. All know there is a God in their hearts. They know this, but they choose to look away. They pursue other gods. This is not MY way. I offer more than wooden idols. I am Almighty God, Creator of the universe. I am gracious with MY patience with men. I choose to be gracious. I am a loving God. I would not turn anyone away who comes to ME.

Please respond to MY pleas. I am your Father. I love you with an undying love. These are MY final offerings. I cannot wait forever. There is an opportunity to choose life, don't delay. The enemy is greedy. He wants to take many with him. He comes to kill and destroy. You can turn away from him and come to ME. Come and be safe. I will care for you eternally. What must I do to wake you up? Time is short. You must wake up to the truth. I will only wait so long, then I must go with those who will come with ME and leave behind the rest.

Do not delay in your decision making. I wait, but soon I cannot. This world is dissolving, it is dying out. It groans and wastes away in sin and darkness. Soon it will be consumed by evil. Evil will roam the earth freely unabated, unattended. MY bride will be removed and evil will consume the globe.

I am a gracious God waiting patiently, waiting quietly. I am sending warnings, but you do not heed them. What would you have Me do to draw you close?

Write it down.

I long to draw you close, but you refuse. How long must I wait? I cannot wait on you forever. Soon, very soon it will end: MY patience, MY waiting. I will move to retrieve the bride. You are hearing MY pleas, MY warnings. Please take this seriously. Many will have regrets. I am sad for the lost. It is devastating when they see the result of their choice: eternal separation from a loving God in exchange for eternal doom. Make a choice. Choose wisely, choose safety or choose disaster, death, destruction.

Some info about seeking & finding GOD:

http://sites.advancedministry.com/index.cfm?i=11265&mid=3

A very encouraging helpful website for seeking GOD:

http://seekgod.org/

PART 5

Again the LORD tells about His plan to come back for the bride, evil of the enemy and the unpreparedness of the world.

September 26th, 2010.

The 1st message here is from the LORD and was received by Sabrina, of Belgium, in regards to the letter, below, that I, Susan of the U.S. received from the LORD and HIS response given to her as to whether I should put MY letter out to people. I also want to add here that Sabrina's primary language is not English and she has to translate her messages spoken to her by the LORD into English many times and so it is her secondary language and that makes it sound a little different. But I have gotten used to the difference in her translation to MY language.

The Lord tells me, Sabrina, to send this Word through also, Susan, and not to doubt or delay, please correct if you see any type faults. I have just typed this out as He spoke to me when I wanted to answer you, I have nothing to add . Jesus is so sad.

The LORD's Words as given to Sabrina regarding 5 the message/letter below that I, Susan, received today:

"I am giving these letters because I want them sent out. You are hearing MY Voice, write it down. I am not a God of confusion. When I tell something, I will perform it. Therefore, do not take this word very lightly, as if they mean nothing to you or because you think you know it all. You know nothing, I am the Father of all truth, I am Jesus, Your saving Master who reigns on earth and in heaven for all eternity. Don't play games, MY love is too strong for you to play games. Therefore I gave you all a free choice. But the prize will be so great if you choose eternal life with ME. Don't be fooling around any longer, the time is short and many are NOT ready for MY return. I am a God of patience indeed, but also of wrath and the choice you make, has its consequences.

Please I beg you, choose wisely. The prize is too big to be lost, to be thrown away. I have many special surprises for all MY children waiting in heaven, they will be so delighted. But I want ALL of you, I want your soul, your heart, your mind, your body, your spirit, I want EVERYTHING. If you do, give ME everything, you will receive everything. If you give ME only a part of yourself, you will lose everything and suffer greatly for eternity. Take this Word very seriously, many of you do not know yet how to live a life completely separated for ME. Did I not suffer enough for you at the cross, so you can play around with your salvation? I am telling you, MY people, please listen to MY Voice, I suffered greatly, more than anyone of you can ever know, but know also, the prize for refusing MY eternal offer of salvation will be horrible. I loved you at Golgotha, I still love you now. I will love you for eternity. Please, I beg you, choose wisely! Do not play around, time is up. MY grace is forever, but time is up. This is your Lord God Jehovah speaking from heaven. Wake up earth!"

I, Sabrina tell the Lord He sounds so severe, He tells me this:

"MY heart is broken because many, very many will be left behind."

Oh the love of our Lord, the Lord is crying people, literally crying and so am I. Please I beg you too, He suffered so greatly, choose wisely as He said, give Him your all, get down on your face and cry out and weep before His Face, this is not a game! Yours, Sabrina.

Now the Letter I, Susan, received from the LORD confirmed by Sabrina to get it out to the people:

Letter 19. Saturday, September 25, 2010.

Write it down Susan. These are MY words for you. Thank you for coming to write.

Soon I will be approaching earth to remove the bride. It is coming soon. The people disbelieve just as I predicted so many years before. This generation disbelieves. I am sad for them. They are a disbelieving generation. They will know the truth soon. All is closing.

This time is closing. The hour is closing. MY patience is closing. The clock is winding down.

These are MY words. Write them down.

This world is hopeless without ME. There is no hope for them if they do not turn to ME, cling to me.

They seek and search for answers everywhere, but to ME. I am God, I have all the answers. I can solve their problems. I can save them. They refuse to follow ME.

These are MY words. I am a strong God. I am strong for MY people. Tell them to look to ME. I will care for them. They seek answers everywhere but from ME. They are a lost generation looking for answers everywhere but the Source of life.

These are MY words. Write it down. Peace is MY moniker. I am peace. I can save the people. If they just turn to ME, let ME be their Savior. I will save them. There is no help for them anywhere else. Why do they look elsewhere for solutions that can only be found in ME? They need to run to ME now. Now is the time.

I am pleading with them, but it falls on deaf ears. It falls on blind eyes. They are not paying attention. Soon they will be blind sided and they will wonder what hit them. They will be left locked out. The door will be closed to them and it cannot be opened again. They will have to come to ME the hard way and it will be tremendously difficult.

The enemy is wicked and he spares no expense in his desire to destroy and kill. He will lash out at the Christians left, those who have been lukewarm and they will die at his hand. Their torment will be great. They will face the worst. This is not MY intent that they should go through this and suffer so. But I am a patient God and I am warning them now, turn, repent, surrender all to ME now and be saved.

The hour is approaching quickly and there is very little time left to

31

make things right. I cannot continue to hold back what must happen. The plans are laid out. I am true to MY words. I will come to get MY people. Those left will see how bad it will be when MY bride is removed. You cannot see it now because you are caught up in the cares of this world, but I cannot hold back forever. The plan is put in place, I am God and I will see it through.

The time is dwindling away. You have precious little time left. You must decide. Surrender to ME or face the worst. What is your choice? These days are running out. We are coming down to the end of life as you know it. The world is evil but it is not as evil as it will be when I pull away MY hand of protection.

MY church is asleep, she sleeps, but MY bride is alert. She is awake. She sees the hour. She knows her place. She is awake and ready. She will be moved to glory and fly into the skies just as MY word promises. The enemy wants you to think this is all a fantasy. He is a liar, he is the father of lies. He comes to kill and steal. He is arrogant and ruthless.

The people are deceived. They must wake up. They must open their eyes. They are being deceived. The deception is everywhere. The time is short. Soon nothing will be the same for those taken and for those left: horror for those left; splendor for those taken.

I am a God of great love and patience, but I am ready to receive MY bride unto Myself and she is ready to be received. All is ready. The world needs to take heed. I am a God of great patience, but I am coming and the time is short.

Write it down. These are MY words. I am careful with MY words. Did I not say I was coming back to receive MY bride? I will do what I say. Don't doubt.

You do not believe, but MY word is true. The hour is at hand. All is ready. The plans are in place. Men cannot stop these plans. I am God. I will fulfill MY destiny to retrieve MY beautiful bride. She is the one who waits on ME. She is the one who longs for ME. She desires to be with ME. She puts no other gods before ME. She is the one I died for. I died for all, but MY bride receives ME without hesitation. She waits and watches. I know her and MY bride knows and loves ME. She obeys ME. She adores ME and I adore her. MY bride is surrendered and follows ME. She knows that I have answers. All others will be left.

Be part of MY wedding party and come to live with ME. Soon I am leaving with MY bride. You can be among these I take with ME. Why choose death and destruction? Come to your senses and live or be blinded and die. I am holding out MY hand for just a little bit longer. But don't think it will be forever.

Soon all will be dark and I must pull away MY hand and depart with MY bride. Choose now, the hour is waning. You have precious little time left. This is your Lord and Master Jesus speaking.

Some info about seeking & finding GOD:

http://sites.advancedministry.com

A very encouraging helpful website for seeking GOD:

http://seekgod.org/

Previous letters from the LORD can be found at this link:

http://end-times-prophecy.com/blog/

God bless and thank you to our webmaster who has also received confirmations from the LORD for our messages and wholeheartedly supports our efforts, God bless Cindy, God loves you!

Thank you and God bless to all the wonderful emails and messages we have received from around the world, your support and prayers are absolutely appreciated and needed. The enemy has challenged our lives because we choose to be obedient to our LORD JESUS, but we are in good company with those who go before us. Keep praying for Sabrina's healing. She is one of the kindest people I know and would not hurt a fly. God bless and pass the WORD on to seek JESUS right now as your undisputed LORD and Master!

PART 6

This is a letter with the LORD pleading to the people to get ready and He speaks of His sacrifice on the cross for His people.

October 1st, 2010.

I just received this letter from the LORD and I am getting it out right away because I sense the great urgency in HIS words. God bless you, Susan Davis.

Letter 21. Thursday, September 30, 2010.

Write it down. These are MY words. All is ready. I am coming so very soon.

The times are speaking of MY coming. All is evil. The world is preoccupied with itself. I am bored with this world and its preoccupation with itself. This is your Lord and Master speaking.

I know the writing is on the wall, the time is closing in. MY people need to get ready. They need to surrender their lives to ME. I, God am a powerful God. I will be sad for them. The time is drawing near. All has been said before. The hour is late. I am giving them only a little bit more time and then I must return for the bride.

What must I do to wake the people up? They sleep soundly. When they finally wake it may be too late. Then the hour will be upon them and they will be left. They cannot understand the gravity of MY nearness. The season is now. They can know the season. I am coming to bring them to MY heavenly home prepared especially for them, where they will lack for nothing. I have bled out for them and they do not believe ME. They won't listen.

Write it down. These are MY words. I am patient with these people, but I cannot wait forever. MY coming is set. I will arrive soon. The hour is closing. MY bride is ready. I am ready.

I have told you the truth, I am returning quickly to retrieve MY bride. Why do the people doubt? I am telling them the truth. It will be.

I come without delay. MY time is at hand. The time is coming for ME to remove the bride. All is set. All is established. I am ready. Soon they shall see. MY coming is appointed and no man can stop ME from returning for the bride, MY beautiful bride. We will reign on heaven and earth forever.

I will not wait on MY people forever. Why do they think that I, God, am not true to MY words? I will do as I say. I have said I am coming and I will come.

The hour is darkening. All is dark. This world is falling apart and all who seek after the things of this world. They seek base things. Their love of the world is a stench to ME. I hate their pursuit of evil, when they could have MY love. Their choice is sad and ultimately they will learn too late a horrifying truth of being apart from God for all eternity. I do not want to leave them, those who do not want ME. But they are choosing for the world and their choice is sad and fatal.

Wake 'O earth, your Lord and Creator calls you to repent and find your way home. It is not too late, but the hour is shortening. Please come to your senses. I, God, am waiting on you. Turn to ME. Repent of your sin. Open your eyes. Surrender yourselves and I will save you. All is not lost. But soon it will be too late. Remove your blinders. Open your eyes and see the truth. I am leaving soon with MY bride. These are MY last calls. I am patient only for a little bit longer. And then the shock will set in that MY bride is gone and the world will go dark.

Write it down. These are MY words. I am coming very soon. I, Jesus, am coming. I will take MY bride with ME. Many do not believe. They are wrong. They are playing a dangerous game. The hour is short. I am holding out MY hand to them. It is MY hour. They must know that I am God and I will not be mocked. I will not tolerate mocking, mocking of MY Name and MY message. MY message is clear: turn, repent, surrender. Come to safety, all will be well in MY loving arms. Turn away, and die. These are MY final offerings.

What must I do to reach you? I died a horrible, painful, humiliating death. There is much you will never know how I suffered. I cried out to MY Father and He would not listen. And I was alone in MY pain and suffering. It was horrendous and it was MY love, MY display of love. I gave all to save you: to give you hope; to give you health; happiness, and life. You make ME suffer again when you reject ME. I suffer over you, your loss. You will reject the Son of Man and be rejected by MY Father and suffer great loss, eternal loss. How can I make you see? What can I do to make you see the time is short? Won't you even consider MY offer? I am a loving God and I give greatly, I gave all as a demonstration of MY undying love for humanity. What more can God do?

These are MY words. These are MY pleadings. I am ready to pull the bride out to safety. Be among her and live. Accept MY offer and live, live well. Why wait? Soon it will be too late. Then you will have eternal regret and suffering at the hand of the enemy. He is ruthless and uncaring, he cares not for mankind. Don't be deceived. He will leave you behind to die a horrible death. There is no way to the Father but through ME.

I am your only hope: turn, repent, surrender, and run with ME in the fields of bliss in heaven. I await to take you with ME. I invite, you reject. Time is short. Your rejection will be your last action soon, if you don't accept MY offer. I am God. I will not be mocked. I gave all. Do not trivialize MY words, MY offer. Soon time will be up and your chance to surrender will be too late. Consider this seriously. I would rather you be hot or cold, as it is, I must spit you out. Come to ME. Come quickly. I am pleading for you to wake up. I cannot wait forever. These are MY final offerings.

I love you, but rejection will be your last action. Choose life, choose now. This is your Lord Jesus speaking. Give ME your life and we shall be together forever.

I wanted to share this wonderful letter of encouragement I received from someone, across the globe from me, I had never met before but it meant so very much to me to receive this and this is for everyone who is out there doing the work of the LORD and trying to warn the people and facing persecution, I couldn't have said this better if I tried.

Hi my Sister,

I am so happy that you answered me, Don't worry, Sabrina knows me already, we are friends already.

For this negativity you guys are receiving, please let me tell you something;

1. We are living in last days, and the Bible said: there will be many mockers, people will like to hear what pleases them, people will reject the TRUTH.

2. As servants of the Lord, you guys are not doing this end times works to please people, but God. Paul said, if I am pleasing people, I am not a servant of God.

3. Don't expect that everybody will agree with you. If people did not agree with Jesus when He was on earth, so do you think all will agree with you, never.

And Jesus said; "If MY wet wood they did like this to me, what about your DRY WOOD?"

4. One of the most important things: people minimize you guys and these messages, is because people LOVE this world and things of this world too much. So these messages are not welcome to them, because they are enjoying this evil world. They are the image of Lot's wife who looked back because she loved SODOM and GOMORAH.

5. Jesus said to the people: "HYPOCRITES, you know to discern the weather, climate, how you cannot discern this time?" Those who send you negative words, simply don't discern what is going in this

evil world, I am very sad for them.

6. The devil knows that through you guys, many souls will be saved and awaken for the soon coming of our Lord Jesus, so he is trying to discourage you. Please don't give up, you guys don't know how many souls are saved and awakened these days through what you guys are doing for the Lord Jesus. The devil is a liar, he will not succeed, resist him. Jesus is Lord forever.

7. Remember, Jesus said: "I know MY sheep and MY sheep know me, and they know MY VOICE." The Lord's sheep knows that all those urgent messages from our Lord are TRUE.

Paul said: We have the same Spirit with our Lord Jesus. It means those who are truly in Christ know that these messages came from our MASTER, because we have the same Spirit.

8. The Holy Spirit is preparing the true believers, the true church for the coming of Christ and the esprit of the antichrist is also preparing the LAODICIAN church to deceive them through the antichrist.

9. Finally, the last book of Revelations said that those who are Justified, let be them more Justified, and those who are wicked, let be them more wicked.

P.S. your CROWNS are waiting you guys in Heaven.

God bless you.

SORRY FOR MY POOR ENGLISH, I AM NOT ENGLISHMAN, BUT A FRENCH SPEAKER!

This is an important message from a very devoted follower of the LORD who is a very good friend of mine—the LORD has led him to put this important message out and I agreed to help get the word out.

Dear, dear sister Susan,

Take this before the Lord and see what He gives you about the attachment. It might just be for me only to use to reach Christians who are in no way ready for His return.

There is so little time and the question that was placed in MY mind – How can a Christian be reached quickly? The attachment with the new challenge at the bottom came to me today.

Jesus said, "And I, if I be lifted up from the earth, will draw all men unto ME." John 12:21

Jesus said, "No man can come to ME, except the Father which hath sent ME draw him: and I will raise him up at the last day." John 6:44

And the Father was drawing that crowd in John 6 by focusing all of them on the true BREAD OF LIFE – His Son!!!

Jesus said of the Holy Spirit, "And when He is come, He will reprove the world of sin, and of righteousness, and of judgment." John 16:8

The attachment begins with Jesus' own words- If you love me you will of obedience.

What would cause us to truly repent – to see the glories of what our Lord has done for us? Then at the end is the WARNING TO REPENT.

In His love and for His praise, Esher,

A weak, little lily of the Valley in the Hands of the Water of Life and a wild rose of Sharon grafted into the Vine by the Husbandman who produces fruit on the little branch.

Isaiah 40:29. He gives power to the weak, And to those who have no might He increases strength.

Zec. 4:6. Then he answered and spake unto me, saying, This is the word of the LORD unto Zerubbabel, saying, Not by might, nor by power, but by MY spirit, saith the LORD of hosts.

Ephesians 6:10. Finally, MY brethren, be strong in the Lord, and in the power of His might.

I surrender the circumstance or issue to Him and then He will use His strength through me. Be strong in the Greek is passive voice. He must do it all through me!

We are to take the first step of repentance and He takes over!

2 Corinthians 6:17. Wherefore come out from among them, and be ye separate, saith the Lord, and touch not the unclean thing; and I will receive you.

Come out – active voice, I must take the first step in true repentance, be ye separate – passive, it will be done by Him in, to and through me!

HE RECEIVES ALL THE GLORY!

WHAT A WONDERFUL LORD WE HAVE!

HERE IS THE MESSAGE:

"Jesus answered and said unto him, If a man love me, HE WILL KEEP MY WORDS: and MY Father will love him, and we will come unto him, and make our abode with him." John 14:23

HOW CAN I NOT LOVE AND OBEY HIM WHEN JESUS:

Looked inside of MY heart and saw what was absolutely abhorrent to His pure soul, MY sin nature which was dead in trespasses and sins, Eph.2:1, – DEAD! DEAD! DEAD? These dead things were spiritually decaying and putrid smelling! Only God could handle that repugnant, eternal stench. Jesus saw all of MY filthy deadness in the cup He was offered by His Father in the Garden of Gethsemane and wept. He willingly took that horrifying cup and drank it up fully.

HOW CAN I NOT LOVE AND OBEY HIM WHEN HE:

Saw MY sin nature and said I will be judged and punished for this cesspool? This polluted ocean was filled with things lurking to be fulfilled even though I had not acted on all of them. He saw all of the following swirling around in MY heart tempting me, waiting for me to say "yes" to: negative thoughts and desires, critical spirit, unforgiveness, disobedience, hypocrisy, gossip, cursing, strife, slander, bitterness, intolerance, unbelief, resentment, sexual impurity, vanity, uncaring, pouting, manipulation, faultfinding, judging, spite, selfishness, addictions, stubbornness, immorality, malice, coldness and so much more, Rom.2:28-32. "BEHOLD WHAT MANNER OF LOVE THE FATHER HAS BESTOWED ON US, THAT WE SHOULD BE CALLED CHILDREN OF GOD!", 1 John 3:1.

HOW CAN I NOT LOVE AND OBEY HIM WHEN HE:

Actually became MY sin and MY curse, Gal.3:13; 2Cor.5:21? Jesus not only took the above cesspool but BECAME IT! He felt inside of Him all that was in that cesspool! Dear God, that overwhelms MY heart that on the cross You were completely flooded by what You hated. Your Word declares that You DESPISED THE SHAME of the cross, Heb.12:2!

The old hymn says it all, THE LOVE OF GOD IS FAR GREATER THAN TONGUE OR PEN CAN EVER TELL. !

HOW CAN I NOT LOVE AND OBEY HIM WHEN HE:

Was blamed for what I was and had done? Jesus, was punished for guilty me in His spirit and soul, as well as His body, as if HE WAS THE GUILTY ONE! He said, "I HAVE LOVED YOU WITH AN EVERLASTING LOVE. ", Jer.31:3.

HOW CAN I NOT LOVE AND OBEY HIM WHEN HE:

Said, "MY God, MY God why have You forsaken ME?" He knew that the judgment for all those who die not desiring or accepting His sacrifice would be separated from Him forever. They would be made to repeat their own words: "I DID IT MY WAY!" "I didn't need You or Your sacrifice." The words came back for Jesus, "IT WAS NOT ENOUGH!" Jesus was totally forsaken so that I would not be forever forsaken in a place where God does not exist. "IN THIS IS LOVE, NOT THAT WE LOVED GOD, BUT THAT HE LOVED US AND

SENT HIS SON [TO BE] THE PROPITIATION FOR OUR SINS.", 1John 4:10.

HOW CAN I NOT LOVE AND OBEY HIM WHEN HE:

Made the offer of His salvation a completely free gift to me so He alone would receive all the glory, Rom. 6:23; Eph.2:8,9? "BUT WHEN THE KINDNESS AND THE LOVE OF GOD OUR SAVIOR TOWARD MAN APPEARED, NOT BY WORKS OF RIGHTEOUSNESS WHICH WE HAVE DONE, BUT ACCORDING TO HIS MERCY HE SAVED US. ", Titus 3:4,5.

HOW CAN I NOT LOVE AND OBEY HIM WHEN HE:

Lives to watch over me, Heb.7:25,? He loves me so much that He came to live inside of me and will never leave me, Gal.2:20; Deut.31:6,8. He actually feels all the pain that I will go through because He lives in me, Isa.63:9. He gives meaning to the troubles I will go through, 2Cor.1:3-5, so that I can help others. He gives His promise to limit the temptations, 1Cor.10:13. "WE LOVE BECAUSE HE FIRST LOVED US.", 1John 4:19.

HOW CAN I NOT LOVE AND OBEY HIM WHEN HE:

Loves me so much that He will discipline me in the right way to live which will give me peace, Phil.4:6,7; Heb.12:6,? He experiences everything I would go through to sympathize and be deeply touched in all MY weaknesses, Heb.4:14,15. "AND WALK IN LOVE, JUST AS CHRIST ALSO LOVED YOU, AND GAVE HIMSELF UP FOR US. ", Eph.5:2.

WARNING: WORLD EVENTS, PROPHETIC WARNINGS, ONE WORLD GOVERNMENT ON THE RISE, RFID CHIPS BEING PLACE INTO PEOPLE AROUND THE WORLD. CHRISTIAN DO YOU SEE THE SIGNS? ARE YOU REALLY READY FOR HIS COMING? AFTER YOU HAVE READ THE ABOVE HOW CAN I NOT LOVE AND OBEY HIM WHEN HE. CAN YOU SAY WITH ALL YOUR HEART, THAT'S ME!

IF NOT, PLEAD FOR HOLY SPIRIT GODLY SORROW AND REPENT! HE'S IS WAITING!!!!

PRAY PSALM 139:23,24!!!!!!!!!!!!!!!!!!!!!!!!!!!! AND THEN TURN!

Esher's website: http://www.songofsolomondevotional.com/
Some info about seeking & finding GOD:
http://sites.advancedministry.com
A very encouraging helpful website for seeking GOD:
http://seekgod.org/
Previous letters from the LORD can be found at this link:
http://end-times-prophecy.com/blog/

PART 7

This was the first letter we received that the LORD really talks about the world to come and where the Bride is going.

October 7th, 2010.

Dear Friends—Once again, I received a letter from the LORD JESUS Tuesday night and I was amazed about the topic HE discusses—about our homes in the world to come—this truly amazes me, because I never know what direction HIS letters will go in until the moment He dictates it to me. This letter is truly inspiring and also has an important dire message as well! God bless, Susan Davis.

Letter 22. Tuesday, October 05, 2010.

Write it down. I am coming soon. The world is not ready, but I am coming anyway. They think I am not coming but I will do as I say.

These words are true. MY words are true. I do as I say I will.

Daughter, write it down. Soon the day will come and it is coming fast when I touch down and pick up MY bride to deliver her home safely. She will fly with ME home safely and I will bring her home to pamper her, to care for her, to love her, to be with her. We will be together and it will be so glorious. All is prepared for her. She will be received by an army of angels in the air and flown to safety. It will be a wonderful sight. I am anxious for this moment to greet her in the air. It will be a glorious sight. Many will be amazed and startled at this sight. She will be so beautiful. Angels will marvel at her beauty.

I am anxious for her to fly with me to heaven. The preparations have been made to receive her. As we fly to heaven together she will arrive to a beautiful Kingdom and she will see beautiful things. There will be much for her to do and see upon her arrival. She will be amazed at the sight. MY people have no idea what wonders await them in their new homes. They will be startled at the sight. It will be a moment of awe and magnitude. I, Jesus will bring her into her new home across the threshold. Together we will explore her new habitation and she will see the wonder awaiting her.

All will be amazed at the sight. MY bride will be made ready by her countenance and her jewels given to her by ME, her King. I will capture her heart into Mine. She will see the wonderful homes prepared for her. The scenery will be dazzling. I will sweep her off her feet. Her mansions will put anything earth has to shame.

The mansions are all ready for her arrival. Everything is ready. We have her home ready. She will be amazed at the beauty. There is so much to say. This heavenly home will be like nothing she has seen before. These homes are spectacular. I have made sure that every detail is in place. There is a life waiting for the bride.

Write it down. The home prepared for MY bride in heaven is so amazing. We have many wonderful things made ready for the bride. She will be astounded. There will be wonderful activities to do. There will be all kinds of family to meet.

MY bride will be in complete bliss. I, Jesus have made her a wonderful home that is destined to amaze. It is hard to describe the indescribable. Earth lacks the experiences to describe such beauty. MY city will be pure and clean. Nothing dirty will enter in, only those pure of heart. I, Jesus am ready to show these homes to the children. I am ready to let them see their homes. All is ready.

MY winged forces are ready to receive the bride and bring her home. It will happen soon. The time is short, brief. All need to get ready. We must depart soon and leave this world behind. She is coming home to the home she belongs to. Keep watching for ME. I am always with you.

These are MY words. Write it down. We have much to discuss.

These homes for the children are ready and waiting. I, Jesus have made sure they lack no good thing. Each home is made with loving hands to match the interests of MY children. I made sure these homes accommodate their unique interests. MY children are all different and have unique likes and interests. They will find these homes greatly to their liking. They will enjoy exploring their homes. All is made ready. I know MY children. I know who they are. I know the homes they are going to, will astound and amaze them.

Write it down.

I am ready to bring MY children home. It will happen soon. MY children will be so happy in their new homes. The days are growing darker on earth. I am ready to depart and receive MY bride. Life in heaven will be beautiful. There will be much to do. It will be a place of wonder and beauty. The children will love their new homes and the spectacular scenery. This is an eternal home unmarred by human hands. This is a home of grace and beauty. These homes will leave MY people breathless in awe. I spare no expense for MY children. All is ready and waiting for their arrival. They will truly be astounded.

The time is closing in. The hour is closing in. Soon, we will fly away to our homes and reside together in bliss. MY loved ones, I want you to see how lovely this world is and how you will be so happy. All is ready. Surrender your lives to ME in this hour so that I might take you with ME to your new homes, heavenly homes, to beauty unimaginable, where there is no mar or imperfection. You can see it.

You can be there too, it is yours if you surrender your life to ME now. I am your Lord. Make no mistake, I will not be mocked. I will not be trifled with by men who do not truly understand God and MY ways. If you knew ME, truly knew ME, you would not mock MY words; MY desire to warn you; MY desire to bring you to Myself in this waning hour. But you mock ME and refuse to listen. I have a wonderful heavenly home prepared for MY children, MY loved ones. But make no mistake, choose against ME, reject MY offer and you will miss all this. You will not see the Son of Man in all His Glory. You will miss the most wonderful experience for eternity.

I am sorry for your loss, but the choice is clearly yours. I cannot choose for you. You must choose. Choose life or death. The choice is yours to make: beauty or ugliness; eternal life or eternal death. The choice is yours to make. Do not underestimate the shortness of this hour. I will not wait forever on you to choose for ME. No choice is a choice. Think this through clearly and decide how you plan to spend eternity. I am GOD, I allow you to choose, but the time is short and your life is in your hands to decide. Choose well. This is your moment to decide.

Sabrina received this message from the LORD on Wednesday Oct. 6, 2010 regarding this letter:

"Write it down. These are MY words. Anyone who does not take MY Words seriously, will suffer greatly for all eternity. Don't make it hard for yourself, choose now. I AM is coming to rapture MY bride, MY beautiful bride. I AM is coming to take her home, her eternal home, where she will be astonished by the beauty of it. All is ready, all is done, come MY children, look towards heaven, I AM is ready. I will always love you with an everlasting love. MY love is so different than yours, MY love is perfect, MY love is beautiful, MY love is perfect. Therefore, take heed of these warnings, written in love for you MY people. I AM is coming and the time is closing in. Those who have ears will listen."

Some info about seeking & finding GOD:
http://sites.advancedministry.com

A very encouraging helpful website for seeking GOD:
http://seekgod.org/

Previous letters from the LORD can be found at this link:
http://end-times-prophecy.com/blog/

Dear Friends in Christ,

We have received many emails about people who are concerned for their lost friends and loved ones. So if you have many around you who are lost and you are concerned for their eternal welfare, we recommend the following: pray for them to be covered with the precious blood of Christ; pray for them to have a hedge of protection around them; pray for the LORD to send angels to guard them; pray for the HOLY SPIRIT to open the eyes of their hearts and to fill them with the truth. And never stop praying or fighting for your loved ones, God hears your prayers, and your prayers count! God is especially tender to the prayers of a mother for her children.

We have received many emails about people who are concerned for their own salvation. We have provided a couple links with details and verses that would be very helpful from the Bible here above. Matthew 7:21-23 says: "Not everyone who says to me, 'Lord, Lord,' will enter the kingdom of heaven, but only he who does the will of MY Father who is in heaven. Many will say to me on that day, 'Lord, Lord, did we not prophesy in your name, and in your name drive out demons and perform many miracles?' Then I will tell them plainly, 'I never knew you. Away from me, you evildoers!'

The key words in this section are the words "I NEVER KNEW YOU", in the Bible the word know means to be intimate with and this is what Jesus is saying here, these people were engaging in works, but Jesus is saying you never actually knew ME intimately. How do we know anyone intimately? Well we get to know them through their likes, dislikes and spending time with them. With Jesus, that means reading your Bible, spending time talking to Jesus and getting to know Christ. So if someone doesn't know Jesus very well, they may be more of a casual acquaintance instead of an intimate friend or follower of Christ. Jesus wants more than a casual acquaintance relationship, HE wants it all: your heart, soul, and mind. Surrender everything to HIM and allow the Holy Spirit to come into your life to change your heart and renew your mind, it can't be accomplished without the Holy Spirit working in a fully surrendered follower. May you find Jesus in a new way today. God bless you.

PART 8

In this letter, JESUS talks about His bride and also talks about the evil of hell. We included the letter from Sally Richter who received a very similar message from the LORD.

October 11th, 2010.

The LORD JESUS dictated this letter to me and I am sending it out because the message is urgent. I have also included below it another letter given to a Sally Richter from the LORD that we received recently. The message and voice are the same, so we are including it with this latest letter, God is trying to warn HIS children about the late hour–God bless you, Susan Davis.

Letter 23. October 10, 2010.

Write it down daughter, this is your Lord Jesus. Susan the hour is waning. Soon I will be coming. Many do not believe. They will be surprised. I cannot help them if they do not believe. They choose not to believe on their own because I have given them plenty of warnings. Why do they wait to find ME when I have given them warnings? I have so much for them in heaven when I take MY bride.

All is ready. I am coming soon. This is the season of MY coming. Many are not aware of how close it is. They will be caught off guard when I come to get MY bride.

Write it down. The time is near, even at hand. The majority will be left to face the worst. I love them, but their hearts are far from ME. I have a wonderful place in heaven waiting for them, but they choose this life over ME. Even this life here would be good if they were with ME.

ME, Susan: Why are the people around me not seeing this?

They are not seeing it because they choose not to. I have given them many signs to see the truth, truth right before them, but they

49

refuse to believe that they are the generation.

The people will know I am God after MY people are taken and they are left. They will know that I can't be trifled with and their hypocrisy is a stench to ME. I desire for them to follow ME and be sold out, but they refuse to listen and so many will be left. The Son of Man is coming in the air. There will be much regret for not following ME.

This is what I have to say: stay close to ME, if you want to surrender. Satan is a roaring lion looking for whomever to devour.

Susan write it down. Thank you for meeting ME here. I am your Divine Lord Jesus, beauty spectacular. Eyes have not seen the beauty of the Lord God. Soon the bride will behold the beauty of her Groom and Maker. I am Jesus, her Love. She is Mine. I love her with a never-ending love. All will see the way I adore her. She is MY love for eternity. The bride is spectacular and I, Jesus hold a special place for her in MY heart. She will rule and reign with me forever. Her tenderness will be known throughout eternity. What love she has for ME and what love I have for her. I am forever hers. Our eyes are one; our hearts are one; our love is one. We are united in love and Spirit. She walks beside ME. MY love knows no bounds toward her. Surrender to ME and become MY love and bride. I will take you with ME when I come to get MY bride. We will rule and reign together forever. All is ready for the bride to flee away skyward.

MY love is awaiting her. I am ready to begin. I am ready for her to come to ME. The time is now and I am ready. There is so much for the bride to do in heaven when she arrives. These closing days bring us nearer to the hour of MY arrival. The hour is urgent. The people do not wake. They sleep. Sad they will be when they are left. What a sad time for them. All I can do is plead if they will not listen, what can be done? They refuse to listen and they will be left to fend for themselves. I cannot save those who turn their backs to ME. They must know their rejection of ME will be fatal and final. Their demise will be dismal. I cannot do more than I am doing. They must choose. The choice is theirs to make: a life of love or of destruction.

Write it down. The world does not know what it is doing by rejecting the Son of Man. It will soon find out how sad it will be to reject ME. I am prepared to save whomever surrenders to ME, but reject ME and all is lost for eternity.

I hold out MY hand and give all, but the world rejects. It chooses second best. It rejects the best, the Son of Man in all His glory, beauty, and love spectacular. What incredible loss, and for what? Worldly compromise, the things of this world are shallow and trite compared to MY unconditional love. I love with so much beauty and grace, the human mind cannot comprehend the incomprehensible love I offer. There is no comparison. Life is empty without MY love; without MY power; without MY Spirit. The world is shallow, empty, lost, and confused. There is no good place to turn for truth without the One who is Truth.

There is no other truth to be found. The beauty of MY truth is all encompassing and life is empty without it. I can only offer MY hand to those who will take it and be saved. If the people will not take MY hand, MY love, and believe MY words that I am coming, then they will awaken very soon and find themselves left without a Savior and rejected to the life that they have chosen instead of MY love and warmth.

I don't want anyone to be left in this last moment, but I cannot save someone who does not turn to ME and repent of sin and follow ME with complete surrender. This world offers nothing and this truth will win out in the end: sad for many and beauty for few.

Write it down.

These words are for those who will listen. I, Jesus, Son of Man have a plan. I will take MY bride away to safety: to bliss, to life everlasting, and love never ending. I am a God of Truth. I wait on you, I warn, I wait and you reject. You see the world and it looks so inviting, but it offers you emptiness. So many step off into eternity: to nothingness and emptiness, suffering, and destruction. I offer more than these things. MY love is a fount, a road, a way. It leads, it

51

guides, and spreads out beauty in front of you, a feast of love, peace, satisfaction, and you will miss this because you do not seek answers and truth. You do not seek God. You love the world and you find emptiness and pathways to hell. Hell that is unending.

I, God am true to MY word. If you turn your back to ME, I will lose you for all eternity and the sadness and horror will never end, the worm that never dies. I cannot retrieve you out of hell once you are there. It will be eternal loss and eternal suffering. Do not go this direction. Think hard and choose life. Choose ME: I am the Life, the Way, the Truth. You will not get to the Father except through ME.

I cannot retrieve you out of hell once you are there. It is an unending choice that cannot be undone. Please see the truth. I do not want to see you in hell. This was not MY intent for your life. But you must choose. If you don't choose for ME, you will die and suffer. I died and suffered so you can avoid this end, but you reject MY gift. I suffered greatly so that you would not have to. What do I, God, need to do to wake you to this truth? Please believe the simple truth. It is a choice. Surrender your life to ME and follow or find yourself on the path to destruction: beauty untold or horrors unending.

This is it. You must choose. I am a patient God, but MY patience is wearing thin on this evil generation who blasphemes her Lord and Savior and rejects truth openly in exchange for gross evil. What can I do to wake you up? Come to ME now. Wait not, you will wait too long and then the door will shut and it won't open again and you will suffer greatly at the hand of MY enemy. He is ruthless and savage. He hates humanity and will kill and destroy without abandon.

Wake up now. This is your Lord and Savior speaking. Run to ME. I am swift. I will take you to safety. You will be covered under MY wings of glory. All will be safe. I am giving you final warnings. Please wake up. Do not slumber. The evil world is forming. All is growing dark. There will be no place to run and hide, let ME free you from the coming nightmare. It will be the darkest hour man has ever known. Let ME free you of this hour, spend this hour with ME in peace and security in a beautiful heavenly home. Choose against

ME and suffer the consequences of your choosing.

I hold out MY hand, latch on. I will never let you go if you reach for it and hold on tight, I will never let you go. These words are true. In your heart you know the lateness of the hour. Don't be deceived by those around you who are blind. I, Jesus am for you. Who can be against you?

We recently received this letter from Sally Richter, I believe she is from Germany, and we were amazed at the similarity of the voice and message to the letters that Sabrina and I have received from the LORD so I wanted to include also this letter received from the LORD by Sally Richter, please note: this letter has been translated to English:

17 September 2010 at 06:00am, German time.

Write MY child. MY glorious Spirit is upon the earth. It will be over soon. Many things would come fast and hard for many people. This is Jesus, Your Lord and Father. I am sounding the trumpets now. Do not harden your heart to MY voice, tell all people. It will come in a split second and those who did not repent will perish and for those who believe and had prepared, a glorious day, banquet and all that I have prepared. The evil is lurking everywhere now strong and powerful at these days. They will devour anyone and many. MY little children will suffer a while but it is only their bodies, their soul I am taking care of.

Unto MY spirit I commend men to be cleansed by MY Holy Blood but many of them do not take heed of MY warning. Many will suffer at the hands of the enemy. Many will cry and wail at the end but I cannot deliver them for I called them hard, but they do not like. The serpents are roaming around now much stronger. They are taking many people, many souls because of their own desires. They are eating fruits of this earth and this fruits bear sins never dirtiest as before. It is rotten and full of sins. It is coming to their deepest and eating their souls.

Sally, MY child, prepare yourself. I am stirring your spirit for you to love ME, you obey and you came from me. I know your sufferings and pains. You cried for many souls, but I cried harder for them and on the cross I bled for them. I gave them mercy, but they do not have mercy on ME, MY Spirit is rejecting them. I knew how they laughed and shunned you and it hurts me deeply for it is I, they reject, not you, and their soul I cannot save.

It will be over soon MY child, the hour of vengeance is at hand. On that day they will cry on ME but I will not listen nor give ear to them like how they do to ME. I love them but they are full of sins, no humbleness in their hearts, no spirit of fear that I AM GOD.

Do not believe the love that you hear in this world, believe only in ME for I have loved you more than ever and more than anyone. Do not contaminate yourself of the sins of men and believe in lies. Seek always the truth and the glow of love in men's hearts will prevail. The bread I gave you will strengthen you. The enemy is after you, but I covered you with MY Holy Blood and Holy Spirit. They cannot harm you. Go on spreading the mark of the beast, fast. that they cannot blame ME and have an excuse on the day of MY judgment. I love you, MY daughter. It will be over soon and you will rest in MY Kingdom together with many of MY beautiful and obedient children around the world.

This I published now, with the Lord's confirmation to me in His words, The third Epistle of John.

Yesterday, September 23, 2010, "Do not harden your heart to MY voice."

Why are so many not wanting to see that the LORD is coming so soon? I believe that 2 Timothy 4:8 is key to why people can't see what is plainly before them:

2 Timothy 4:8. Now there is in store for me the crown of righteousness, which the Lord, the righteous Judge, will award to me on that day, and not only to me, but also to all who have longed for his appearing.

According to the Bible, there is a crown of righteousness awaiting those who long for the appearing of Christ. God awards those who long for Jesus' return with a crown. So this is a key point because I believe if you are not longing for his appearance then something else has displaced that longing.

What could replace the longing for Christ's appearance in a Christian's life? Could it be other worldly interests and pursuits that have filled the place of that longing as top priority? If so, then there is definitely not room for the longing for Christ's appearance.

If you are not longing for Christ's appearance because something else has usurped your time and interest then any mention of the possibility of Christ's return being at hand is not going to be of interest to you. This is because you have no longing for his appearance. If you did, then you would not be resistant, disinterested, or disengaged from the idea that Jesus' return could be so soon.

People who long for anything are not disengaged from the things related to what they long for. Hence, those who long for the return of JESUS, as mentioned in 2 Timothy 4:8, will not be put off, disinterested, or even hostile to the things that suggest that the return of the LORD is near, but rather they would embrace such information.

So if the "longing for His appearing" holds no sway in your life then you might want to ask yourself what does? James 4:4 says: You adulterous people, don't you know that friendship with the world is hatred toward God? Anyone who chooses to be a friend of the world becomes an enemy of God. If your friendship with the world is replacing your longing for the appearance of Christ then you probably don't like the suggestion that Jesus' return could be so soon.

You may say to me as in 2 Peter 3:4 "Where is this 'coming' he promised? Ever since our fathers died, everything goes on as it has since the beginning of creation." But God says for the true Christian you are to long for Christ's appearance and that it can't be less important to you than a friendship with the world. Jesus says to surrender all to Him and the lukewarm church wants to give Him just a portion because they are sharing their longings with the world. If you aren't longing for the appearance of the LORD in your heart than your eyes aren't going to be open to the idea that the LORD's return could be so soon.

The word "longing" also means a persistent and strong or yearning desire. David and Isaiah used the word "longs" to describe their feelings toward the LORD in these terms:

Psalm 63:1. A psalm of David. When he was in the Desert of Judah. O God, you are MY God, earnestly I seek you; MY soul thirsts for you, MY body longs for you, in a dry and weary land where there is no water.

Isaiah 26:9. MY soul yearns for you in the night; in the morning MY spirit longs for you. When your judgments come upon the earth, the people of the world learn righteousness.

I also want to mention that 2 Timothy 4:8 is not a date-sensitive command. God makes no statement in this verse to "long for Christ's appearance" after a certain date or time in history has passed. Isn't that interesting? So who could possibly long for Christ's appearance and simultaneously be disinterested in things related to watching for Christ?

If in MY heart, I think Christ is not coming back for many years into the future despite all of the signs having come to pass, I doubt very much that longing for His appearance will be of any great interest to me. This is something you need to ask yourself as a Christian, are you following the mandate of God to long for the appearing of Christ or are you just totally disinterested? How do you discount the signs He has given that are coming to pass before our very eyes and yet maintain to be a surrendered Christian? Without a longing for HIS appearing and without studying and acknowledging that the signs in the Bible point to the very soon return of Christ—you cannot be a surrendered Christian–the two are disconnected. This leaves you in the category of lukewarm–a very dangerous place to be.

PART 9

Susan just received this letter over a two-day period and it is a very serious letter given to Susan by our Lord JESUS. The Lord addresses the seriousness of the hour and also HIS anger for the lukewarm church. We have also added to it a letter given to Sally Richter from the Lord on 10-13-10 that also speaks volumes about the urgency in His voice. Also with these letters at the bottom we are including a testimony from a friend of ours (Sabrina & Susan) who has been reporting to us about having visions which started the beginning of this past summer 2010 and have been happening right up until the last couple days.

October 18th, 2010.

I just received this letter over a two-day period and it is a very serious letter given to me by our Lord JESUS. The Lord addresses the seriousness of the hour and also HIS anger for the lukewarm church. I am not hesitating in getting this word out to you. I have also added to it a letter given to Sally Richter from the Lord on 10-13-10 that also speaks volumes about the urgency in His voice. Also with these letters at the bottom we are including a testimony from a friend of ours, Sabrina & Susan, Buddy Baker who has been reporting to us about having visions which started the beginning of this past summer 2010 and have been happening right up until the last couple days. The incredible thing about his visions are that they began about a week apart and now they are each coming just a couple days apart. So we encouraged him to write out all of his visions that the LORD has given him and to provide his email address to tell others about what he is experiencing and how this amazing testimony is yet another sign of the nearness of the coming of the LORD. I pray you are blessed, encouraged, and can see the seriousness of these messages we must put out from the LORD. I implore you to seek the LORD while HE can still be found, Susan

Davis.

Letter 24. 10-15-2010. dictated to Susan by the LORD JESUS.

Write it down. The days are coming. I am at the door. It is coming fast. MY words are swift. The hour is near. It is closing in. We will leave soon. Take off. This is all prepared for MY retrieval of the bride into the air. We will go off together. The world will be amazed. They will not know what happened to them. Suddenly it will be worldwide calamity and chaos. The people will not know what hit them. Nothing will be the same again. It will be devastating. The people will not know what hit them. Many will be in shock. MY people who call themselves "Christians" will realize they've been left and they will know then they were lukewarm.

Life is going to change. All is ready. The hour is now. We must leave together. The time is set. I have MY plans. I work MY plans. I bring about these things. You will be loved. The world will see what changes are being made. The hour is nearing.

Susan write it down. 10-16-2010.

The times are closing in. I am coming swiftly with MY mighty angel army. Everyone will see soon as I make MY entry to earth. The hour is waning. Soon I will depart with MY bride. It will be just as the days of Noah: eating, drinking, and making merry. Then I will come and all will go dark. The world will go dark. The hour is closing in.

I am coming before they turn around. The world will be astounded. It will be incredible. They will be in shock, those who are left. The darkness will be immense.

These are MY words. Write them down.

The people must get ready. I have much to do in a short time. The people will see it is I, Jesus, that has come to take MY people home. Many will know they have been left. Great sadness will consume them.

It is not MY way or desire that they be left to face the cruelty they

59

will encounter. But, they have chosen against me if they cling to the world and do not turn to ME in this very hour. This is the deciding hour. I am looking for decisions to be made now. No decision is a decision. Choose ME and be saved. Choose against ME or make no decision and your loss will be great.

I am not looking for those who choose against ME, but for those who want to come with ME to their new homes in heaven. If you turn your back to ME, I cannot help you. These are MY words. I am looking for those who want to be saved ,who are seeking ME with all their hearts, souls, minds, and strength. Those are the ones I am seeking out now. Seek ME and be found. Reject ME and be lost. A simple choice is before you. Time is wasting. Soon it will be too late to be found. The door is shutting soon.

Write it down.

The hour is closing in. The people are asleep. They are not watching. They will be lost. I am sad for them. It is going to happen soon. The world is growing dark. Evil is closing in. There is very little time left. I promise and MY promises are true. I speak truth. These are MY words. I, Jesus, am true to MY words. The people doubt but when I come and they are left, they will know I am true to MY words. They will then learn the sad truth that MY words can be trusted by all.

We are nearing the end of this age. It is coming swiftly. The time is at hand and I am ready to retrieve MY bride: those who are ready; waiting; watching; looking to ME; and surrendered to ME. If they are of the world, they are lost and the world will be theirs. But MY surrendered ones will know ME. It will be utter bliss for them: ecstasy, life never-ending surrounded by love ever-lasting, beauty, splendor. I am true to MY words.

MY people who look to ME now will never be disappointed. I am their Savior and I come to rescue them from the horrors to come, to retrieve them from man's worst hour. Make no mistake, MY word won't be trifled with, I will not tolerate rejection. The result will be devastating, I am sorry for their loss, but they have been warned and I have been true about these warnings. Please believe ME, I am not to be trifled with, I am the Lord who loves, but reject ME and know the consequences of your choices.

These are MY warnings. Soon all will know that I am God. MY word is everlasting. MY power is everlasting. MY might is everlasting. I am God. Men cannot know the gravity of their choice if they choose against ME, their loss will be devastating, absolute. Look to ME: it is life or death, life everlasting, death everlasting. So much is at stake. Don't falter in your choice. It will be your final choice to make.

Turn from your evil ways and turn to ME. I will pull you out of this evil world. I can save you. I am Jesus, the only name that saves. No other name saves, no other name. This is your hour to choose. Come to ME. I will save you. MY love is like a saving balm. I calm, I comfort, I am peace, I am love, I am yours if you turn to ME. You will be relieved from this hour of grief, this great hour of grief and sadness, devastation. I am pleading with you to turn to ME. Now is the hour.

I am waiting a little longer but only for a short time. It will be over soon and then it will be too late. Turn to love. Turn to MY love. I long to bring you home with ME. I long for you to come to MY open arms. Please believe MY words and MY warnings. I love MY children. Don't make it hard on yourselves, heed MY warnings. The hour is short.

The lukewarm church will be lost. It will be left. I have no time for the lukewarm. They have one foot in this world and one foot in MY world. I will spit them out. I will not tolerate a church that has a halfhearted love toward ME. They trifle with MY love. They play games with ME. They want ME and the world both. I do not want their love. They want ME on their terms. They want ME only when it suits them. I have no time for their halfway love and commitment. I want a sold out church. I want a bride who only has eyes for ME. I am a jealous God and I will have no other gods before ME. Their halfhearted interest in ME is abominable. It is wretched.

I do not want their relationship. If they cannot choose for ME with complete abandon to ME, they are not fit for MY Kingdom. I am seeking a church who is only in love with ME. Very few walk this path. Very few will be ready to go. I am sorry for the rest, but these are MY terms. I am clear about what I ask of MY people: all or nothing. I want your all, complete surrender. If you still have time and eyes for this world, I cannot help you. The end is coming. Soon you must choose: all or nothing. Give ME your all. I gave all. I ask nothing less of you. This is your hour to decide. Give ME your heart. Give ME your life. Let ME take you home to safety. You will be safe and unharmed to a happy home of peace everlasting. Please let ME protect you and keep you from this coming trouble.

I am the only door to safety. You will not find help anywhere else. Choose wisely, give ME everything and I will give you freedom, and a life, a beautiful world, an everlasting Kingdom where we will rule and reign together forever. It will be glorious. The choice is yours. I do not force. I am standing in front of you. You have this choice to make, I ask nothing less than complete surrender.

Letter dictated to Sally Richter, Germany, by the LORD:

THERE IS NO TIME!!!

13 October 2010 05:00am, German Time.

I woke up at exactly 05:00 a.m., I am in great pain. Then the voice of the Lord came to me.

Write MY child. The covenant I made for you, is binding until the end.

You will rest in MY kingdom. You will hear the trumpet sound.

BUT, Many will come to me, but it will be too late. I am calling them with deep sounds.

Many are still sleeping, they do not take heed. Many will go to the "GREAT TRIBULATION."

Lay down your life for me or they will perish in time.

Write MY child. THERE IS NO TIME!!! Anymore. Oh YOU!!! FOOLISH PEOPLE. THIS WORLD IS PASSING!!!

I am giving you authority to command men to change. When you speak it is the voice of the Lord speaking unto you. Write MY child. I AM YOUR GOD! THERE IS NO OTHER GOD. OTHER GODS ARE MUTE: THERE IS NO LIFE IN THEM: THEY CANNOT ANSWER THEM. I, JESUS, YOUR LORD IS THE ONLY GOD WHO LIVED AND WILL COME FOR THE WORLD.

I WILL JUDGE THEM according to their works. REPENT Oh! Foolish men. REPENT! FOR MANY OF YOU CANNOT ENDURE WHAT IS TO COME. I AM IN SORROW, MY HEART IS GRIEVING!!!! YOU DONT KNOW WHAT IS COMING. MEN ARE BOUND FOR HELL, SINS ARE EVERYWHERE. COME TO ME AND CLEAN YOURSELF.

I HAVE WARNED YOU, but many of you do not listen. People of perdition, YOU CANNOT ENDURE WHAT IS COMING. I HAVE PREPARED GREAT THINGS FOR YOU IN HEAVEN: EVERYTHING IS THERE. COMPLETE AND BEAUTIFUL BEYOND YOUR IMAGINATION: HOUSES OF GOLD, WATERS ARE CLEAN GIVING LIFE, JOY TO THE FULLEST, DIAMONDS, RUBIES, SILVER LININGS EVERYWHERE. A BEAUTY TO BEHOLD.

Turn your ways to me people of this world. I cannot save you if YOU cannot hear the trumpet sound for your stubbornness.

Cleanse your heart. COME TO ME AND LET ME FILL YOU WITH MY GRACE.

I AM YOUR LORD WHO LOVES YOU! NO ONE CAN SAVE YOU BUT ME.

I GAVE YOU MY LIFE. COME TO ME. I LOVE YOU!

EVERYONE OF YOU!!! I AM IN PAIN FOR YOU. GRIEF AND SORROW IS INTENSE:

YOU WILL CALL TO ME!!! YOU FOOLISH PEOPLE LISTEN TO ME. THERE IS NO TIME!!! YOU CANNOT ENDURE. MANY OF YOU CANNOT ENDURE. IT WILL BE EVIL. BRUTAL.

Children, I WANT YOU TO REST. REST IN MY KINGDOM!

THIS WORLD IS NOTHING. THIS IS PASSING. THERE IS NO TIME!!!!

BY: JESUS, YOUR LORD.

The Lord is waking me up almost everyday now, giving me messages in urgency.

PLEASE !!! Take heed as He said, we do not have time.

14 October 2010 05:45am.

I am publishing it now with our Lords confirmation in 1 Corinthians 14: "Follow after charity and desire spiritual gifts but rather that you may prophesy."

1 Corinthians 14 deals with the prophecy.

PART 10

The LORD warns people in the letter to Susan that a vile nation is forming and the people are not paying attention to what is coming. Through Sabrina's letter the LORD pleads for the people to repent and come to HIM before it is too late.

October 23rd, 2010.

The Lord told me He had more words to share and so I took down this letter as I heard Him speak to me, Susan. These are serious words from our LORD JESUS. I want to share with you that as I heard and wrote His words it was a different experience for me than before. Although I had seen the movie "The Passion" before, MY son and I had just watched it again and we sat stunned knowing that our beloved LORD JESUS had suffered so greatly for our sins. Also knowing that the portrayal of this film was probably not even as harsh as the actual event has made this task of putting out this letter much more sobering for me personally. Please consider the significance of the LORD's words in this letter and please share with your friends and family. Sabrina has also received serious words from the LORD that HE dictated to her in a second letter here below. We are clearly not the only ones in helping the LORD send out warnings in this final hour.

Your sisters in Christ,

Sabrina of Belgium and Susan of the U.S.

Letter 27. October 21, 2010.

Susan, write it down.

I, Jesus am your Lord, I have a letter for you. These are MY words.

This generation is lost. It is not looking to ME. It seeks life through everything but ME. I implore it to seek ME. Why can it not see ME? Why can it not see that I am its Savior, only Hope, only Love, only

Life?

These are MY words. Write it down.

I, Jesus am the One and Only True Savior for all mankind. I am HE. There is no other. Look though they may, they will never find the answer through anyone or anything but ME. I am the one true Shepherd to the flock. I can lead them out. I can save them from the horrors to come in this late hour. No other Savior exists who can rescue the people but ME. Look no further. Don't look to money, people, things, culture, I am the Way, the Truth, the Life. I am the One who saves. Why do they seek after other gods, wooden idols that don't speak?

They are a sad generation lost in their sin, in their devastation. Time is running out and I am ready to bring MY bride out to safety away from this tragic generation of lost people. These people are far from ME, groping in the dark, looking for answers to life through all sorts of vile means and gross activities.

I, God have seen enough. Time is running out. I am about to leave this world to its own devices to linger in its own sin. I cannot stomach this sin much longer. The world has turned its back to ME and gross darkness is setting in all around.

The people die from lack of knowledge. They do not shed a single tear over their evil ways. They look away from goodness as if it is vile to them. They are wretched and lost, a foul stench to ME. Holiness is far from their minds. They completely have lost themselves in evil and have forgotten how to blush.

I, God cannot take their ways anymore. I am about to leave these people to their own devices and give them up to their evil and allow them to be completely consumed by the evil they engage in. How much more do they expect a Holy God to tolerate?

If they turn from their evil, I would receive them. I would take them back and clean them up with MY Word. There is but a little time left to turn, repent, and to come clean and surrender to a Holy, Pure

God.

I love MY children, but I can't allow the world to continue forever in the stench of evil unabated. It must come to its end. I will remove MY people, MY bride and carefully place her in a safe place away from all terror and darkness. Then the world will change and I will lift MY hand of protection away and the darkness will consume the world and all in the world will know the evil that engulfs it. It will be man's worst hour unrivaled by any other time in man's history.

I am sending out MY warnings and pleas to mankind. Please surrender your all to ME and escape this horror to come. I am pleading with you as only a loving Father would do before he sees his children depart into utter darkness. These are MY pleadings. I am Love and I want to rescue you and I will, but you must come to ME and lay down your life before ME and give ME everything, so I can save you this hour.

Oh, you foolish people wake up from your deep sleep and recognize the lateness of the hour. A vile nation is forming under your noses, a dark and evil force is coming together to plan for your destruction and demise. There is no hope in the ways of the world. The world offers you emptiness and hopelessness.

I, God am true to MY Word. I have outlined this in MY Word. You are in the dark because you refuse to see, but it is all there and it is coming to pass as I said it would. There are no deep secrets. It is written and I am true to MY Word. You can choose evil or you can choose ME. I bring goodness, wholeness, peace, comfort, love. The enemy brings death, destruction, lies, and hopelessness, eternal hopelessness, unending loss. This is what you will face if you turn your back to ME.

I, Jesus am extending MY hand a little bit longer and then I will have to pull it away, shut the door, remove MY bride, and scurry to safety while darkness floods the earth. This is truth. I will return, but for a time the world will experience MY wrath. And I want you to believe that MY truth cannot be toyed with and I will do exactly what I say I will do. Love ME and live, reject ME and die, extreme beauty or extreme ugliness.

You must choose. Not choosing is choosing against ME. Choose ME and live, live well in a heavenly home that is indescribable. Let ME take you into MY arms, hold, and comfort you. Let ME save you. I am waiting, but not for long.

This world is growing darker and soon it will be very dark and foul. Step out of harm's way and come away with ME. Put all your trust on ME. I am your Deliverer. I can keep you safe. Now is a deciding moment. The tide is turning. Men will quake at what is forming. Be relieved of this consuming, engulfing coming evil. Turn toward ME, I, Jesus can save you. I love you dearly. I died a horrible death so you can be safe. Let this be.

Please turn to ME your Savior. The hour of change is closing in. Let ME save you.

I love you,

LORD JESUS.

Letter dictated to Sabrina on October 22, 2010.

MY heart is breaking for you, MY people. MY heart is longing for you. MY heart is bursting with love for all of you. I died MY death for all of you. I suffered horrible for all of you.

Heaven has a place for all of you. But many places will not be taken, as hell is becoming larger every day. Don't you see that? Don't you know that? How many warnings do I have to give to all of you? Let it be enough.

MY love is enough to save all of you, but you have been given a free will. Choose MY love, use your will in a wise way. Choose ME and not the lusts of your own heart and your oh so dear fleshly desires! What good are your fleshly desires? Do they satisfy you that much? I don't think so. Not one of you is truly satisfied without ME. I am the only peacemaker. I am the only One Who saves. I am the only way to satisfy your hearts.

I understand your grief and pain in this life. For some it is a hard life. But I am the door to come in. Come, the door is still open now, but only for a very short time. The door is about to close and many of you will realize then what a treasure you have missed. I will be away with MY bride. I will celebrate her victory in ME. She will be amazed by her beauty in ME. I will be in her and she will be in ME. But, oh how sad for the ones who didn't see this truth in the first place.

Please, I am begging you one more time. come to ME NOW! NOW is the time. Time is about to end. This age of grace is about to end. Now it is easy to come to ME. So come NOW. If you only knew the treasures laid away for you in heaven. If you only knew the bright future laid away for you in heaven. Would you come then?

I want you to come now. I proved MY love for you. For all of you. I didn't need to do it, still I chose to. Therefore, I am asking you: come to ME, MY people and make MY heart happy for you. I am happy when you come to ME.

Why do you choose the world before your God, your Creator, by the way? You have no life without ME. You cannot even breathe for one second without ME. Do you realize that? I gave you life and I offer you eternal life with ME in Mine and MY Father's Kingdom. Why throw it away?

Hell is a real place. Many of you do not realize that. You will soon find out if you die without ME. So don't be a foolish one. Be wise. I have given you enough intelligence to be able to choose wisely. The choice is yours. The door is about to be closed. Turn from your sins and repent while you still can. The devil will overtake you if you don't. He is waiting and wanting to destroy you and for many of you, he is about this close.

Repent MY people. I died for you. I rose out of the grave for you, so you can have everlasting life with ME: a life that is truly unseen here on earth. a life that is unheard of here on earth. Please, one more time, choose wisely, choose life, choose ME. MY Name is I AM. I

AM has always been and I AM will always be. End of MY words.

Ecclesiastes 12:13-14. Let us hear the conclusion of the whole matter: Fear God, and keep his commandments: for this is the whole duty of man. For God shall bring every work into judgment, with every secret thing, whether it be good, or whether it be evil.

Awhile back, Sabrina had inquired of the LORD for me about who the bride is and I decided that it might be a good thing to share those words with you too because so many are seeing these messages. These were the words the LORD gave to Sabrina for MY question about how Jesus describes His bride:

MY bride is the one without stain, nor spot, nor wrinkle.

MY bride is the one who is worth it to sit together with ME at MY wedding table.

MY bride is the one who loves ME with her whole heart, soul, and mind.

MY bride is the one who does not live for herself anymore, but for ME and for others.

MY bride is the one who gives up everything and follows ME.

MY bride is the one whose hearts are 100 percent well pleasing to ME.

Ephesians 5:25-27. Husbands, love your wives, just as Christ loved the church and gave himself up for her to make her holy, cleansing her by the washing with water through the word, and to present her to himself as a radiant church, without stain or wrinkle or any other blemish, but holy and blameless.

Mark 12:30. Love the Lord your God with all your heart and with all your soul and with all your mind and with all your strength.

Exodus 20:3. You shall have no other gods before me.

PART 11

In this letter JESUS talks about the lukewarm condition of the church, the darkness coming over the earth and the cruel master the enemy will be. Charlotte Hill's letter is included from the LORD with very similar words for the people.

October 29th, 2010.

Dear Followers of Christ:

Each letter we receive from the LORD seems to be more intense than the previous one, as the letter HE dictated to me Oct. 27 here below. So many people are dismissing the idea that the LORD could be coming soon because I think we have become so accustomed to the world around us that we have lost sight of the standard of God's holiness and of how we could be over stepping our limits of rejecting a holy God.

With this first letter from the LORD, we are also including a letter posted by Charlotte Virginia Hill with yet another important message from the LORD with the identical message both Sabrina and I have received from HIM most recently. All of it is very serious. We would gladly talk with anyone about our testimony and regarding the importance of knowing the LORD JESUS as the center focus of your life.

God bless, stay strong, Maranatha!

Sabrina and Susan.

Letter 29. October 27, 2010.

Susan Write it down.

This is your Lord speaking.

I am the great I AM.

I always will be and I always have been. No man knows ME and I am the great I AM who will be forever.

This letter is important. Time is short. Time is of the essence. We are nearing the end of this age swiftly. There is precious little time left before all becomes dark. There is a shift in the forces. The world grows darker each day. Evil crowds in around the earth.

Men are oblivious to what is happening, but MY bride sees it. She is not in the dark. MY bride's eyes are open to truth. We are one, she and I. Soon she will join with ME for eternity. Evil man has joined forces with dark rulers of the air to create a new kingdom which is forming to rule over mankind. It is a dark hour for mankind. Men cannot truly see how dark this hour will be.

Soon men will plummet into darkness and sorrow. It is coming swiftly. I am greatly saddened by the hour at hand. I cannot keep this from happening. The people have chosen the master they wish to serve.

Time is short. If MY people wish to come with ME when I rescue the bride, they may come. Total surrender is what I want. Anything less and I will not be pleased. I do not want their lukewarm efforts.

All or nothing, the hour is at hand to decide. What will it be: ME, the Savior of the world or the enemy of mankind? He is a cruel master, he kills and destroys. He knows no limits. He lusts after death. His hatred is complete. He has no limitations on evil. He reigns in darkness and rules in death. He is the prince of the air and his evil is uncontrollable. He hates mankind and deceives at every turn. The people follow blindly his deception. Their way is cruel when they fall for his trickery. He is the ruler of deception and lies, the father of lies.

Sadness will overtake those who wake up to what they have given themselves over to, when people realize that they have given themselves to the wrong ruler, to the ruler of the air and darkness. Their agony will be unquenched. It will be the worm that never dies and MY people will have to die to escape the madness. They will have to die for truth. Then they will see the value of MY Word, MY truth, MY beauty. Then they will know that I, Jesus am the one true Savior that they rejected and they will be forlorn, lost, and there will be unquenchable sadness, overwhelming sadness.

Face the truth now and avoid the horrors to come. This world is closing down. It will not be the same, soon it will not be the same again. MY church sleeps, blinded, and cannot see around it what is forming. The enemy has them captivated by worldly pursuits and they are lulled into a daze. They think all is well. They think everything is fine and that life will proceed as normal but it will soon change and the complexion of everything will be dark. Truth, love, hope, beauty, peace, and MY Word will fall to the wayside as evil schemes will grow and pick up steam. The people will not know how the complexion of life could have changed overnight. One day life is normal, the next day life is consumed in darkness. It will be.

MY wrath will come upon the earth. I cannot tolerate man's rejection of GOD. Man chooses to reject its GOD. It chooses to reject ME and I will let the earth have its choice. Choose against ME and find out just what life is like without a just and long suffering GOD. I bring the rain down on evil and good alike. I love all, but reject ME and know the wrath of MY anger. I will not tolerate rejection from this evil generation that believes I am not worth following, not worth knowing.

I died for all a gross, heinous death. I was attacked and mutilated by evil men like sport and I did it to rescue mankind. This is what a HOLY GOD did for His creation who He loves. Do you not see O' earth, I am worth knowing? I am worth choosing? For have I not shown you the level of MY affections and love? Can you not see that I, Jesus came down from MY beautiful Kingdom and died a gross death to save you? Am I, Jesus not worth any of your time?

I took time for men. I wait for MY creation and patiently I watch to see who turns to ME. I ask so little: even a mustard seed of faith. A tiny effort and I meet you where you are in all your sins and sadness and I come and pick you up and hold you as only a Father can do.

No other god, no other love, knows you the way I do. But, I will not tolerate rejection or competition for MY affections. I am a jealous GOD.

I will have a bride who is single-minded and who is fully committed to ME. These are MY demands. But, I will not force MY love on anyone, so you must choose. Love ME and come with ME to a beautiful Kingdom where love never ends or reject your Creator and leave behind the only One who really knows and truly loves you. Everything else is empty. MY Words are true, I am giving final pleas.

Very soon easy choices will be hard and difficult. Many will choose me, but it will be hard and painful. I do not want this for you. I want you to come to ME now while the choice is easier to make.

How much do you love ME? If your love is lukewarm, I cannot use you in MY Kingdom. You are not fit for it. There is no regret in MY Kingdom. The rewards are great for those who choose well in this life. Choose ME now. Surrender all and experience everlasting love and beauty that you will never see anywhere else.

You think you have all the time in the world. You do not. I am coming soon. I will receive those who are watching for ME. Those who are waiting on ME. Those who recognize the lateness of the hour. Those who are troubled by the evil in the world. MY bride waits, watches, sees what is going on. She is not in the dark. She is ready. She is fit for MY Kingdom. MY bride knows ME and I know her. We are one and we will fly away together to our glorious nest in the sky. It will be beauty, sheer beauty and I am ready for this moment, this great and grand moment.

I, Jesus stand at the precipice and I am about to take MY flight to retrieve MY loved ones. I love you. I will not disappoint you.

Think this through carefully. This is your deciding moment.

Ecclesiastes 8:16-17. When I applied MY mind to know wisdom and to observe man's labor on earth, his eyes not seeing sleep day or night- then I saw all that God has done. No one can comprehend what goes on under the sun. Despite all his efforts to search it out, man cannot discover its meaning. Even if a wise man claims he knows, he cannot really comprehend it.

Ephesians 2:1-2. As for you, you were dead in your transgressions and sins, in which you used to live when you followed the ways of this world and of the ruler of the kingdom of the air, the spirit who is now at work in those who are disobedient.

HALLOWEEN.

by Charlotte Virginia Hill on Monday, October 25, 2010 at 2:21pm.

Dearly Beloved,

I was praying to the Lord today to see if He had any words to give to His children, so that I will share His heart to them in this hour.

I prayed first and asked God to speak through ME and this is what I received.

MY people, listen to ME. I will NOT tolerate this sin any longer. What you are doing is an abomination to ME.

Either choose ME and have life, OR choose satan and lose your life. If you continue to live in darkness, I will have no choice but to spit you out of MY mouth.

Can't you see that is I who gave you life? Can't you see that satan wants to destroy you? He HATES your life. REPENT and turn away from these lies. Run to ME while you still have time. The door is about to close.

MY children seek ME while you still can. What you are doing is not for fun. Satan has a firm grip on your souls. REPENT, REPENT, REPENT. Come to ME and I WILL save you. If you refuse, then I will have no choice but to let satan have his way with you. It is NOT MY intention for you to be destroyed. I love you. That is why I am giving you this final warning!

The world is growing darker because of sin. If you believe in ME, if you love ME, then turn away from these evil practices. It is I who can help you. It is ONLY I who can forgive you. REPENT and turn to ME for forgiveness MY children. If you Love ME as I love you, you will know that what I say is for your own good.

WRITE THIS MY CHILD:

I am using this vessel to speak MY words. MY words are holy. I will no longer tolerate this lukewarmness from MY children.

Soon I will come for MY Bride. Only those who are ready, only those who have extra oil with them. I will NOT tolerate lukewarm unrepentive Christians any longer. RETURN to ME, for I AM your holy God.

No sin will enter MY sight. No sin will I allow into MY heavenly Kingdom. So many of you are so deceived. You are choosing destruction over life.

Your life has worth. I made you because I love you. You are important to ME. Come out of your lukewarmness, when you still have time. Soon I will come. If anyone does not heed MY words I will have no choice but to leave you behind.

This is MY FINAL warning. MY trumpets are ready to be blown by MY angels.

Get ready. REPENT and return to ME with ALL your hearts and souls. Don't give into temptation. It is I who have called you. It is I who have set you apart. Please choose life, NOT death MY children. Go and shine MY light into this dark and lost world.

ALL IS READY! I am coming, remain in ME and I SHALL remain in you.

This is MY warning!!

This is only a few times I have done this, so bare with ME.

Please pray over this, as it is best to see that this is a direct word from our Lord. Especially when I am learning to journal. When two or more are gathered Jesus is in our midst.

I love you MY brothers and sisters. God loves ALL of you and so do I.

Love your sister in Christ Jesus, Charlotte Virginia Hill.

PART 12

In this letter the LORD talks about the darkness coming over the earth and how little the people are paying attention to what's happening to them around them. The LORD tells how HE will see His plans through no matter whether the people are ready or not.

November 2nd, 2010.

Dear Friends in Christ,

2 Timothy 4:8 says: Now there is in store for me the crown of righteousness, which the Lord, the righteous Judge, will award to me on that day, and not only to me, but also to all who have longed for his appearing.

Do you long for Jesus' appearing? Well if you do, you have a crown of righteousness in store for you. People everywhere all the time think it is weird to talk about the LORD's coming as being so soon. Well God says it is so important to "long" for Christ's appearing that HE awards a crown of righteousness to those who do just that. How much more should we be "longing for His appearing" then, when the signs given in the Bible are for right now? We are living in the last days and this verse should be for us more than any other generation. What does this verse mean to you?

This letter dictated by the Lord Jesus to me is very, very serious. I encourage you to read this and pass it along.

Your friends in Christ, Susan & Sabrina.

Letter 30. October 31, 2010.

Susan write this down. I am your Lord Jesus. Susan I have a letter to give you. Please write as I speak. Listen to what I say and write it down.

Susan I have much to tell. This letter will give you new information.

So listen closely as I explain.

The world is going to see a great shift in darkness now. The end is growing closer. I am about to proceed with MY plans. The darkness is closing in. The times are drawing to a close swiftly. All is growing dark.

People don't see it because they refuse to look. The hour is closing in of MY promised delivery of truth, I am true to MY word. I will do as I say. All will see soon.

The world thinks there is no retribution for their behavior. The world thinks there is no consequence for turning their backs to God, a Holy God. They are wrong. There will be a price to pay for openly rejecting a Holy God. I am God. I will not be mocked. They mock ME at every turn. They humiliate ME at every turn. I suffered and died for them. I laid MY life down for them. I am a Holy God. I cannot look upon evil. I cannot see this evil and allow it to continue. I know the people think I do not exist and that they can carry on however they want, but this I cannot continue to tolerate.

Everywhere you turn there is evil. The evil has taken over the land. It runs unchecked. It has no limits. It runs unabated. It flees and it takes control so that the people have completely lost themselves in it. They are overtaken by it. I, God, I, Jesus have seen enough. I cannot allow this to carry on.

The people are in the dark. The evil does not seem bad enough to them. They die from lack of knowledge and so they cannot see for themselves the wretchedness of their ways and those around them.

They are so consumed by evil and overtaken by it they dismiss it and say to themselves: "Things aren't so bad, surely God will not come so soon. Life will go on. I can do as I please." This world will soon find out what it means to toy with a Holy God unchecked. I did it before during Noah's time and I will do it again. MY people had better find themselves and prepare. They can come with ME to safety or be left to face the consequences of their choices.

The people think I am playing. They think MY Book is good for nothing. They think MY Words are empty. I, God am not to be tried. I am not to be tempted. I am God and what I say, I will do. When I say I will do something, I, God will do it.

Even MY people who call themselves Christians mock ME with their disregardful attitudes toward MY Word, MY Holy Words. I have laid out MY plans in advance to this generation so that there can be no doubt about what I will do, so that no one will be in the dark when it is time for ME to make MY move. I am not untruthful like the enemy of mankind. I have been up front, open, truthful about MY plans. The truth is plain for those who seek ME for those who read and study MY Words. I am Truth and when I say I am doing something, I will do it. I am a God of truth. No one rivals ME in truth. I give MY Word and I see it through to completion.

There will never be a Truth like mine. No one carries out truth like I do. I am a force to be reckoned with. I am a God of complete and total follow through. When I say I will do it, I will do it. I will carry out MY plans, make no mistake. Only a fool says there is no God.

There is precious little time left. MY people need to prepare. I am ready to take MY flight very soon. It is coming. I am a God of utter, impeccable, unquestionable truth. I cannot be questioned. When I speak, I speak absolute truth. MY Word is clear for all who bother to read it. I have laid out MY terms of what I plan to do and what I expect from MY people. It is all set out and absolutely clear. There is no question that now is the hour. Yet you choose to disbelieve ME. I am your God. I would not deceive you. I gave you signs of MY coming and you know that I have made them clear.

The people don't believe because they choose not to. They are enthralled with this world. They knew that there would be a time that I would come again. They knew that I had told them that a day would come when I would pull MY people out to safety. They refuse to believe that it is now because they do not want to see it. "It is as it has always been," they say to themselves. Yet the signs I told them to watch for are happening right before them and they refuse to see.

They refuse to believe. They are a sad, doubting, lost generation and evil has overtaken them. They find comfort in their possessions, in their pursuits, in their love of money, everywhere but with ME, their Lord and Maker. Do they think they can be so utterly satisfied with these temporal things that they can't even hear the one calling them to safety, to prepare for the plan I have laid out before them. Even the Christians are woefully unprepared and they will be shocked when they find themselves left. I am sorry for their loss, but I have warned them and I have outlined MY plans and MY terms for them to be saved.

They must turn to ME and surrender everything; give ME their lives; repent of their evil and sins, and turn toward ME and I will heal them of their infirmities, and their illnesses, and their sin sickness. I am the only answer for mankind. There are no other answers although they try to find them in so many ways. Their wholeness will never be found in anyone or anything but ME, the one true God.

MY people need to lay down their lives before ME and repent. Let go of the world. The hour is late. Release your grip from a world that is crumbling, falling apart, and doomed to destruction. I, God can save you for just a bit longer, then you will face the worst, a world that is coming undone. This world will soon never be the same again. I am crying out to you. Please listen, the time is short. I am telling you because I love you. You have precious little time left to prepare, to repent, to surrender. Please hear MY pleadings. I am trying to warn you to wake up and see what is coming. I cannot allow the dark forces to go unchecked. The world will soon know MY wrath, MY wrath against evil gone amuck: evil that has consumed every area of life. It is pervasive and it has consumed every part of human existence. How can I allow this to go on? I cannot.

You think I will continue to look away and man can carry on in his hopelessness. It cannot be. Soon the world will know that I, God, I, Jesus will whisk MY people away to safety, who is MY loyal bride and I will turn away to allow the world to experience MY wrath. What happens when a Holy God releases protection over the world? This world is harsh, but nothing like it will be without MY bride and with

MY hand of protection pulled away.

You have but a little time left. Don't live in denial any longer. Face the truth. Humble yourselves before a Holy God and I will open your eyes. I will show you truth. I will show you the way to safety. I will give you relief from the madness to come. I will bring you to a beautiful home in the sky prepared for those who call ME their God. This is MY truth. There is no other truth. Do not dismiss or gloss over these words lightly. Soon you will long to hear these words and soon the door will be shut. You will have to do the hard things to come to ME.

I cannot change this hour. It is set. You think you have all the time in the world. This is man's thinking. If you humble yourself, truly humble yourself before ME, I will lead you to God's truth, MY truth. Now you are in a cloud believing every fuzzy doctrine under the sun. The enemy is wreaking havoc over the people. The people are in cloud of delusion and cannot see that the Words in MY Book match up with the signs of the time and MY coming is so near, even at the door.

Wake up O' earth. The hour is late. The hour is at hand. I am waiting, but not for long. You have precious little time left. Take MY hand. It is extended out to you. But soon, I will take MY bride and we will fly away. Join with us. It is not too late. Don't wait too long though, many will be left as described in Revelations. Do not be so sure of yourself. Turn to ME now before it is too late. I, Jesus speak truth. Come now before it is too late.

PART 13

This letter primarily the LORD talks about the world's descent into darkness and the people's refusal to pay attention to what's coming. In Sabrina's letter the LORD implores the people to follow HIS commandments and the importance of following them.

November 7th, 2010.

Dear Friends of Christ:

I, Susan, received a new letter from JESUS on November 5 and we are getting it out right away. Sabrina also received a letter on November 6 from the LORD right after I received the letter below so that they would be both included here in this message. Both these letters contain very, very serious messages for you from the LORD.

I am including the verses from Ezekiel 3:16 through 21 because I want to stress to you the seriousness of the task in front of us. When you read this passage you will see that Ezekiel is told to take the LORD's Words and give the people HIS warnings. More specifically this section shows that if Ezekiel refuses to warn the people he has blood on his hands because the people are not warned. So if we want to stay in the close relationship that we enjoy with the LORD, we must put out these words. If we want to see people saved before it is too late, we must put out these words. So when Sabrina and I surrendered our lives to the LORD we agreed to the terms to obey our LORD and this is what HE has asked us to do and we have no choice but to make these letters available to you.

We continue to appreciate the kind notes and letters we receive, they bless us immensely.

Your friends in Christ, Susan & Sabrina.

Ezekiel 3:16-21. And it came to pass at the end of seven days, that the word of the LORD came unto me, saying, Son of man, I have made thee a watchman unto the house of Israel: therefore hear the word at MY mouth, and give them warning from me. When I say unto the wicked, Thou shalt surely die; and thou givest him not warning, nor speakest to warn the wicked from his wicked way, to save his life; the same wicked man shall die in his iniquity; but his blood will I require at thine hand. Yet if thou warn the wicked, and he turn not from his wickedness, nor from his wicked way, he shall die in his iniquity; but thou hast delivered thy soul. Again, When a righteous man doth turn from his righteousness, and commit iniquity, and I lay a stumbling-block before him, he shall die: because thou hast not given him warning, he shall die in his sin, and his righteousness which he hath done shall not be remembered; but his blood will I require at thine hand. Nevertheless if thou warn the righteous man, that the righteous sin not, and he doth not sin, he shall surely live, because he is warned; also thou hast delivered thy soul.

Letter 31. Friday, November 05, 2010.

Dear Susan, write these words down.

This is your Lord and Master JESUS.

I come to you today with new words. There is much to say. These words are for all who will hear them.

I am GOD. I am JESUS. Make no mistake these are MY words.

The hour is closing in. I am coming soon.

Susan, write it down.

Soon the world will know MY fury: the fury of an angry GOD; the fury of a rejected GOD. These words are to this lost generation. These words are for whoever had ears to listen. I watch the world. I know all. Nothing gets by ME. I am GOD, all-knowing GOD. I am JESUS, Savior of all.

This world is about to descend into evil, unstoppable, untamable evil, evil unleashed, unbridled, evil that can't be conquered by men. Only GOD will be able to stop it. But until that day, men will endure the worst. I will take MY people to safety and the evil world will come into the open. No one will ever have seen or will see again this much evil.

The time is drawing near. The hour is closing in and I am about to make this happen. I, GOD have seen enough. Men are helpless to stop what is about to happen. The world is about to see what happens when I, God step aside and allow the people to have the kingdom they have chosen. They have chosen a kingdom without a just and righteous GOD. without a Holy, merciful, loving GOD.

This world has never known the likes of living without MY ever-present hand of protection hovering over the lands. But this is what the world wants. It has chosen a world without a Holy GOD. The world wants to remove holiness from its midst to do as it pleases and so it shall have its way. I shall step aside, excuse Myself, depart with MY chosen bride and leave for a heavenly home prepared for MY beautiful bride, the one who loves ME and who I love as well.

We shall sing songs and join together in the sky. We shall love, laugh, and sing it will be sheer beauty. It will be so beautiful. Earth cannot comprehend such beauty.

The people on earth shall have their wish. They shall see life without GOD looking on and keeping them from unbridled evil. It will be a dark hour.

The people laugh at MY warnings. They jeer at the idea that this will happen to them. In their hearts, they think MY Words are stories that will never come true. They believe each other, but not their GOD who made them. They console each other and say GOD will never come back. These are fables: they pat each other on the back and laugh at MY Words as if it is all make believe. Soon the stories will come to life and MY Words will come to pass and those who mock MY Words will learn that I am a GOD of great reliability and when I say I am going to do something, I, GOD will see it through.

This world thinks GOD is not real or greatly underestimates who they think I am. I am God of truth and this hour is coming and the people need to prepare themselves. They can surrender, repent, and come with ME, their GOD to safety and beauty or be left to face the consequences of their choices.

MY message is here for a short time. This world is coming to a stop. It is changing rapidly. Soon the people will find out about life without GOD. I am ready to do this thing to pull MY people out, to see this through. I want you to seek your GOD, humble yourself before ME, and be sorrowful over your sinfulness. Weep over your wrongs and iniquities.

You think you are not that bad, but you are wicked to the core. You blaspheme ME with every other word spoken. You take MY Name in vain. You use MY Holy Name in casual conversation in crass ways as if I am not looking on, as if I don't exist and see all this. Who do you think you are? I created you. I brought you into this world. I set you into this place. I give you breath. You come, you go, and I know everything about you. I can no longer tolerate your evil perpetrated against ME and all the little innocent ones. Oh, you think I don't see what you do behind closed doors. What you whisper in your heart. How you plot. how you scheme against each other. against ME, a Holy GOD who is omnipotent and omnipresent.

Do you actually think I am not aware of your comings and goings in the dark? I GOD see all. I know it all. I hear it all. Nothing slips by ME. Without MY salvation, the sins you commit will find you out. No evil thing committed will be hidden from the light without MY forgiveness, without MY precious blood covering your sin.

You have a short time to come clean. Wash yourself in MY blood. Accept MY salvation as the one true Savior of the world. Surrender your life to ME completely. Repent to ME of your evil and find peace with GOD, for no one can come to the Father except through ME, JESUS. I am the only way. You must lay your life down before ME. Follow ME without question and find peace, everlasting love, and beauty eternal.

This is your hour of decision. I am making MY pleadings and

stretching forth MY hand for all to grasp, cling to, and receive MY love and then I must shut the door. Then you will wait too long and the door will be closed. Death will be the answer to your escape from a world gone mad. This evil is taking over the world, evil without bounds, without compassion, without remorse. It will be shocking and horrifying for those left. Few will survive the rigors of such evil. MY protection will be removed and MY wrath will be poured out.

I am not a fable. I am not a tale. I live among you. I live in MY bride. MY Spirit dwells within MY bride, but soon MY bride will be removed and the protection I have provided her will be lifted from the earth. I protect MY bride and keep her safe, but soon she will not be among you. She will have left you to go to safety. Life will change without the bride among you and MY Spirit that lives within her. The change will be obvious and painful for all those left behind.

Why do you cling to this life so? Your hope is false. You put your faith in a world that has grown cold, unfeeling, and cares only for greed and evil ambitions. Good works done apart from MY blessing are empty ramblings of a world trying to make a case of living without a Holy, loving GOD. Men's good works are shallow and empty without GOD. They strategize and plan without seeking MY face and their end will be empty. Don't they see that without GOD, all their planning is empty and temporal?

Men's empty plans will lead to their destruction without ME, their Holy God. Soon men will be lost without ME in a world gone mad. a world given over to evil. a world without the protection of a Holy GOD.

O' MY people, I am trying to reach you. You resist ME. You resist MY pleading. One day soon, you will find out it is too late and that you have been left to face the worst and it will be the worst time in mankind's history unrivaled by any other time in the history of the earth. It will be a sad, lost, dark world left to its won evil devices. Truth will be hard to find. Love, peace, kindness, the things you have rejected in your hearts, you will long for and not find.

The descent into madness is already happening. Relief through peace, love, kindness, will not be found. It will be a dark period for all of mankind. Repent, surrender now and I will receive you into MY peaceful, safe, and beautiful Kingdom where I am a GOD of kindness and protection. You must choose.

Scoff not at MY Words. I am sad for scoffers and naysayers. They will have great regret at their doubt and be disappointed over their losses. It will be a sad day on earth when the world realizes the truth that everyone is left to face the coming dark hour.

Turn to ME, your beautiful Savior now. Look upon MY nail pierced hands. See MY outstretched arms toward you. I am calling you to come to MY safety and security. There is no other way. Soon I must leave. Decide now. Choose now. These are the final moments.

I love you. MY love is pure and tender. Call ME your God and I will call you mine before MY Father and His Holy angels. I will give you a new home. I will bring you to a new beautiful home. All this will be yours.

I, JESUS love you.

Sabrina writes this: This is a very serious letter again, regarding the letter I received from the LORD above. Wow. While reading it, the Lord told me He had a letter to add and I knew it would be serious too, so I first prayed, read MY Bible and now here I am to listen what He has to say. The Lord also led me to the Bible verses below after this word, Please note the letter was originally given by the LORD to Sabrina in her language Dutch and she translated to English here below:

Letter dictated to Sabrina in Dutch by the LORD and later translated to English here, Saturday, November 06, 2010.

"MY dear daughter, write it down. Hear what I have to say to you. I speak to you to warn MY children. Many still live in sin and do not live after MY word. They think I am an all-encompassing God that overlooks everything through the fingers. MY word however says that I do after MY word. This includes the blessings, the prophecies, but also MY wrath. I am a God that is not amenable to even be consumed by something.

I am a God of love; a greater God of love will not exist in eternity. Therefore, I cannot bear sin. I am a God of purity and cleanliness and a blazing fire. Live after MY Word MY children! Don't think it doesn't matter. Every action has a consequence for eternity. Everything is seen, everything is marked, everything will be revealed. Many of MY children think it is okay to not take MY Word so very precisely. I am telling you that it certainly matters! MY Word stands firm. MY Word is written. MY Word will not change. I God do not change. Therefore, MY people listen to ME. Live after MY Word. Every commandment is important.

I have given MY commandments to MY servant Moses, so it would go well with you. Why are you living then under your own commandments? You are making yourself a god by these 'commandments.' I do not tolerate this. I am an all-consuming God. And also the violation of MY Word I will not tolerate. I love you MY children, MY love is infinite. But sin is sin.

Study MY Word and live after MY commandments. Or do you think I am a God that lies and does not honor His word? I tell you, I, God, do honor MY Word and I am loyal to MY Word. I don't lie. MY Word stands firm. Keep the commandments so it will go well with you. Oh sure, I died for your righteousness and I am risen so you would have eternal life with ME, but I did not die so MY Law, MY Word would be ignored. MY commandments reflects MY all, I AM. And I AM changes not.

Wake up Christians! MY commandments are etched on stone with MY own Hand. Why do you throw these in the water! I know what is good for you and if you live within the boundaries of MY Word, it will go well with you. Study MY Word and act by it, so your blessings cannot be counted any more. This is MY Word."

2 Corinthians 12:19-21. Again, think ye that we excuse ourselves

unto you? We speak before God in Christ: but we do all things, dearly beloved, for your edifying. For I fear, lest, when I come, I shall not find you such as I would, and that I shall be found unto you such as ye would not: lest there be debates, envyings, wraths, strifes, backbitings, whisperings, swellings, tumults: And lest, when I come again, MY God will humble me among you, and that I shall bewail many which have sinned already, and have not repented of the uncleanness and fornication and lasciviousness which they have committed.

Ezekiel 1:27-28. And I saw as the colour of amber, as the appearance of fire round about within it, from the appearance of his loins even upward, and from the appearance of his loins even downward, I saw as it were the appearance of fire, and it had brightness round about. As the appearance of the bow that is in the cloud in the day of rain, so was the appearance of the brightness round about. This was the appearance of the likeness of the glory of the LORD. And when I saw it, I fell upon MY face, and I heard a voice of one that spake.

1 John 5:2-3. By this we know that we love the children of God, when we love God, and keep his commandments. For this is the love of God, that we keep his commandments: and his commandments are not grievous.

PART 14

JESUS pleads with the people to come to HIM now. Only HE can save them. Repent and to turn to Him. Also for the people to stop clinging to the world.

November 11th, 2010.

Dear Friends of Christ:

I have received yet another very urgent letter from our LORD & SAVIOR JESUS CHRIST. This is very urgent as the LORD told Sabrina to put the letter out right away.

Your friends in Christ, Sabrina & Susan.

Letter 35. November 10, 2010.

Susan I will give you words. Susan, write it down.

I am your LORD JESUS. Here are MY Words:

Susan, I am coming.

The world stands in disbelief that I am coming. They trifle with ME. Their disbelief is incredible. I AM true to MY Words. If ever there was someone true to their words, it would be ME, I AM GOD!

Do they think they can toy with ME? The people carry on in their sin as always. They look up from their sinful activities, notice something different, they notice different tribulation in the earth. It doesn't trouble them a bit. They explain it away. There is always an explanation. They call it all sorts of things, but to admit there is a GOD Who is angry with their sin is too much truth for them to grasp. That would hit home too much. Then they would be guilty of the lifestyles they lead in front of a HOLY GOD, too much for them to admit to. Then there would be a need to repent and surrender to ME, a HOLY GOD. They can't have it. They want to carry on in their sinfulness too much.

MY lukewarm church lives in denial as well. They are also blind to truth. They need to wake up before it is too late, shake off the earth they have grown too comfortable with. They want to cling to it and its evil ways. It is their great pacifier. It sickens ME the way they cling and grasp the world and all its iniquities. They hold on with both hands tightly. Soon the earth will crumble and fall apart between their tight grasp and they will be standing there holding nothing and they will reach out for ME in their nothingness and find that I have already left them with MY bride in MY arms away to safety. They will have clung too tightly to the world and only to discover the world can't save them and the only One who can has stepped over the threshold with HIS bride and closed the door permanently behind HIM.

They will then turn and face the horrors of what they are left to live with. The only escape will be death. Many think MY message is too harsh. Many think I am too frightening with MY harsh warnings. Soon the reality will set in and the warnings that should have been heeded will do no good. The harshness of MY warning will only be a memory as reality sets in as to what the world has become.

Sin will flow. Evil will run like a rushing river over everyone in its path consuming and terrorizing everyone. Life will be so harsh, answers won't be easy. Peace and serenity will be gone. Life will be difficult. No one will be unaffected. It will encompass everything and everyone. The earth will be demonized and the enemy will blanket the earth. I am telling you the truth.

MY little flock, come to ME. Come to safety. I cannot tolerate this earth anymore. All are affected by evil. You cannot escape it. If you are MY follower, you see sin and evil at every turn, everywhere you go.

Come to ME now. The hour is closing. Evil man wants to control the earth and whoever stands in their way. Dark clouds are rolling in. The world is crumbling. Even those who call themselves Christians believe MY Words in MY Book are empty phrases. empty promises. They enjoy MY Book as if it is lovely fables to teach with and forget that MY Word stands the test of time. MY Word will outlast any who blaspheme against it. MY Word stands. MY Word is the standard. Turn back to it. Don't revile it. Embrace it. Soon MY Word will be hidden from men and truth will be a precious, hard-to-find commodity in a world gone mad over evil and lies.

I am warning you now. Get your life in order. Clean yourself up in MY blood, MY precious blood. Repent, surrender all to ME. I will save you from utter despair. This is MY desperate plea. Quit following men. Turn to GOD. Turn to ME, JESUS. I am the Way, the Truth, the Life. You must turn now. Please turn to ME now. I can't wait much longer. I love you so much, but I must leave with MY bride very, very soon.

Don't be left to face the worst because you think all is well and everything is fine. You know in your heart that things are not fine. You feel in your spirit that evil runs around you unchecked. You know that the world is hanging by a thread to stay together and that the world is teetering on a thin line and that destruction is at the door. You see prophecies given in MY Book long ago coming to pass.

Please pull the covers back from over your head, and pull your head out of the sand, and see truth. I AM TRUTH. There is no other truth. All the evil delusions that you spend your time on that keeps you from seeing things the way they truly are will not save you in this late hour. It is not yet too late. Wake up now.

Men cannot save you. Money cannot save you. Your possessions cannot save you. False teachings cannot save you. Pagan religions cannot save you. I, JESUS can save you. I am the only way. I am the narrow path. Get to the narrow path, come to ME!

Come away with ME to safety, beauty, love, peace, salvation, truth, holiness, life everlasting. Do not delay. These are MY warnings. Do not trivialize MY warnings. Put down your idols and turn to ME. Your wooden idols will not save you. I am alive. I can save you. I am desperately pleading with you. Let MY love consume you. Find

93

safety and peace. These are MY offerings O' lost men. Come to your senses. These words are true.

Your only LORD and SAVIOR,

JESUS.

The LORD said to add this Scripture with the letter above:

Psalm 28.

1Unto thee will I cry, O LORD MY rock; be not silent to me: lest, if thou be silent to me, I become like them that go down into the pit.

2Hear the voice of MY supplications, when I cry unto thee, when I lift up MY hands toward thy holy oracle.

3Draw me not away with the wicked, and with the workers of iniquity, which speak peace to their neighbours, but mischief is in their hearts.

4Give them according to their deeds, and according to the wickedness of their endeavours: give them after the work of their hands; render to them their desert.

5Because they regard not the works of the LORD, nor the operation of his hands, he shall destroy them, and not build them up.

6Blessed be the LORD, because he hath heard the voice of MY supplications.

7The LORD is MY strength and MY shield; MY heart trusted in him, and I am helped: therefore MY heart greatly rejoiceth; and with MY song will I praise him.

8The LORD is their strength, and he is the saving strength of his anointed.

9Save thy people, and bless thine inheritance: feed them also, and lift them up for ever.

PART 15

In Sabrina's letter from the LORD He speaks about hell and how the bride needs to be free of spots and wrinkles. In Susan's letter JESUS talks about the Bible as the standard against all other schools of thoughts. It also speaks of the evil nation forming and darkness coming over the earth.

November 14th, 2010.

Letter dictated to Sabrina, of Belgium, and translated from Dutch into English:

November 13, 2010.

"Write it down MY daughter. It looks like nothing is going to happen. People are not ready for MY coming. I am very sad for this fact. I have done everything to warn MY people. Yet they choose to harden their hearts. Good. With freewill I have created you, with a freewill you shall also go. The destination you choose yourself. The gospel is clearly written in MY Word. If you choose to obey this Word, you have eternal life, if not, eternal death in the scorching heat of hell.

Hell is a real place. From this also I have written in MY gospel. Yet some of you live as if this is a fable. Oh really? Come to your senses MY people. NOW is the time of conversion. Share these words with everybody you know. Share MY gospel. Share the reality of heaven and hell. Make people alert they have to choose NOW.

Oh, MY people, MY heart bleeds for you. I am coming soon for MY bride and then it is every man for himself. These words will resound bitterly for some, for others disappear forever. The taste will not be sweet, but pure horror. The reality of hell that is coming is indescribable. Are these words too hard? Too frightening? I tell you, they are more realistic then the chair you sit on now.

I God am an almighty God and I do after MY Word. I am a merciful God. I am a loving God. But I am also a holy God. I alone can save you from what is coming. I am willing. MY grace is still here. But the horror of hell is coming. She will not be long in coming any more. So how long MY people before you give attention to these words? Not many are willing to enter the narrow road. Not many are willing to live holy. Not many of MY children are willing.

I am coming for a bride without stain, spot, and wrinkle. This means no compromises with the world or MY Word! No compromises! Oh, MY Word is holy. Live after MY Word MY people! Do you still think it does not really matter? I have told you before it certainly does matter. Fine, you live after your own rules then. I have MY rules set forth in MY Word. Take it all or lose it all. No compromises. If only you were willing to set your heart on this. I work out everything in someone's heart.

The heart is unreliable. Therefore I have told in MY Word to give your whole heart, soul, and mind to ME. All these things are unreliable. Live in MY Spirit! Live in MY Spirit and it will go well with you. Live in MY Spirit, MY people. I have sent Him to this earth to inhabit MY people. Shall you not give attention to Him? He is the most precious possession that you can have in this life. Do not throw Him away, do not grieve MY Spirit! I beg you, do not grieve MY Spirit! This is the worst that you can do. Yet many of you are doing it. Live after MY Word and be led by MY Spirit every day. Only this way you can serve a Holy God. I am holy. You also be holy. The time is up."

Letter given to Susan, of the U.S.

Letter 36. November 12, 2010.

Susan I have words for you. Susan these are MY words. I speak with care. Write it down. MY words are different than your words. I am GOD. Susan the hour is closing in. There is precious little time left. The hour is short: little time left.

I am your LORD and SAVIOR. These days are the final days. There are only a few days more and then many things are going to change. The world is about to change dramatically. Why do you question MY Words? Why do you doubt I am GOD? These are MY Words.

Nothing I am saying here has not been said in MY Book, if you care to read it. I gave it to you as a guide book, a book to understand the things of GOD: the expectations I have for living righteously; for bringing up children; for getting along with neighbors; for managing money; for understanding GOD; for living the way I want you to live; for being intimate with ME. I have provided these guidelines, yet you do not follow them. You follow every other book written by men about living, but the one given to you by your CREATOR. Why is this?

You are sidetracked into all types of thinking of men and you go in all directions, but to the ONE Who has all your answers. You are reviled by the Word of GOD, the Sacred Words of GOD. You are disgusted with righteousness. You make fun of it like it is a disgusting, foul way of life. Anyone who remotely engages in righteousness is freakish in your minds. You have departed from the right path so far, that right, clean living seems strange to you. People who embrace holiness make no sense to you.

Have it your way. You disdain holiness so much, than you may drown in your evil. You may have a large dose of it. You will drink a cup of evil very soon and reject the ways of GOD. I cannot stop what is set in place. The evil has begun. It will not stop until I come back to end the madness. It will be so bad for those left, they will want to die to escape it.

I want you to know that I love you, but I cannot tolerate your complete and total disregard of MY Word, MY instructions to you. MY Word is sacred, holy, pure, with practical instruction and you follow after every other man-made school of thought under the sun seeking answers. I have ALL the answers you are seeking, but you won't look. You are an ill-advised, sad people. You are dying from lack of knowledge. You are wasting away from lack of truth. You are disintegrating from a lack of holiness. You lack ME. I am the center of all things right and holy.

Words given to me 11/13/2010.

Susan Write it down.

The world is coming to an hour of change. Change is upon it. The change will be big. An evil nation is forming. Evil that will be unstoppable. This is the defining moment. Will you stay because you reject MY truth and MY offer to come away to safety or will you leave with ME when I come to retrieve MY bride, MY beautiful bride?

Here is what you need to do if you choose to come. You need to surrender all, repent and wash your robes in MY blood, yes MY precious blood. I alone can make this change in your life. There is no other way, search though you may for answers to your life. You may find answers, but they will not lead you to life. They will only lead you to your demise, to your eternal death, torment in hell.

MY Words are harsh but they are loving, truthful Words. If I did not warn you, MY Words would not be loving. I am trying to reach you in this late hour. I, JESUS am trying to get through to you. I am extending MY hand out to you. I want you to know how much I love you. How much I care for you. Do not separate yourself from ME for eternity. It will be a fatal, everlasting choice that cannot be undone once it is final. Separation from GOD for eternity is hell unending. This is not what I want for MY children, for MY creation. Please choose wisely.

I have given you this choice to make. You must choose. The world is tantalizing. Everything seems so attractive to you. You want to touch and experience it all. It is death and it masquerades as life. But reach for it and die. Embrace it and fall into its deadly trap. Follow the path of the world you long after and you will never escape it. Then you will know you have chased after the wrong answers.

Come with ME your LORD JESUS and I will bring you down the right path to truth, righteousness, purity, holiness, love, and life everlasting. These words are true. The world is rejecting ME and soon I must step back and allow the worst to happen. I must let the world embrace the lord it chooses, the evil lord it chooses to reign over it. Then the world will understand the way of evil it has embraced. It will find the true meaning of the choices it has made. Soon the world will see what it means to embrace the wrong god and reject the one true GOD.

Evil will reign and rule the earth. Truth will be forgotten and the prince of the air will be the one true god of their choice and it will be a one-way ticket to death. MY people can come to ME then, but it will be through fire, they will have to walk through fire to get to ME. And I am sorry that it must be this way, but I am being clear about MY warnings and very few will heed them in time.

I God, I JESUS, am telling you truth. The days are growing darker now. The evil is increasing. The people have become too accustom to evil. They cannot see what is coming. They lack understanding. They lack discernment about holiness and they are being entrapped into the hands of the enemy.

I am sad for them but they must choose who they want to serve. Do they want to serve an evil, ruthless master or a loving, truthful Master, the ONE, Who created them? The people need to decide whether they want to serve the CREATOR or the creation. They will serve someone. Who will it be: the one who kills and destroys or the ONE, Who loves and saves? Wake up O' earth. Your SAVIOR is calling out to you. Turn to your SAVIOR. Let ME save you. Make peace with GOD and live in eternal bliss. Come as you are now. I do not expect you to be perfect before you surrender to ME. I am the only ONE Who can clean you up. I can clean you in MY blood. I can set you right before MY FATHER.

There is no other way. Do not be deceived. All other ways lead to death. I am the Way, the Truth, the Life. Come to ME now. I am waiting for just a little longer. Don't wait too long. Your regrets will be great if you wait too long.

I love you, but you must make ME your LORD and MASTER and surrender all to ME. Repent of your sins in front of a HOLY GOD. Accept MY terms, and I will rescue you at this late hour. The time is disappearing. Wait no longer. Soon it will be too late.

I, JESUS have spoken.

The LORD said to add this verse:

Psalm 82:1-8. God standeth in the congregation of the mighty; he judgeth among the gods. How long will ye judge unjustly, and accept the persons of the wicked? Selah. Defend the poor and fatherless: do justice to the afflicted and needy. Deliver the poor and needy: rid them out of the hand of the wicked. They know not, neither will they understand; they walk on in darkness: all the foundations of the earth are out of course. I have said, Ye are gods; and all of you are children of the most High. But ye shall die like men, and fall like one of the princes. Arise, O God, judge the earth: for thou shalt inherit all nations.

PART 16

The letter to Susan from JESUS speaks strongly of the trouble the lukewarm church is in. In Sabrina's letter the LORD warns to listen to His prophets, He speaks of standing before Him one day and keeping HIS commandments.

November 18th, 2010.

We submit these letters to you which we each received.

Letter 39. November 17, 2010. dictated to Susan from the LORD JESUS.

Susan, these are the last days.

Time is winding down, closing in. The world is in trouble. If the people don't see it, they are not looking. They have their eyes closed. They need to wake up. Their lack of discernment is deeply troubling to ME. I love them, but they are lost and far from ME.

I give them MY heart, but they trample on it at every turn. They want nothing to do with ME. They choose sin. It is more tantalizing, more appealing. SO BE IT. This is what they choose. Then sin is what they may have. I GOD will give them a big dose of the medicine they prescribe for themselves.

I am a loving GOD, but turn your back to ME and learn the consequences. This generation has turned away completely and loves ME not. It does not love MY ways, MY Holiness. I am a pure, perfect, loving GOD to be feared. I love deeply, but I punish deeply. Turn from ME and learn the seriousness of your decision. Decide against ME and I decide against you. Reject ME and I must reject you. I cannot help you if you walk away from MY salvation and go it alone.

These are MY terms: surrender, repent, and turn back to ME. Confess your commitment to ME, JESUS, to others and it will go well for you. I am looking for sold-out, 100-percent solid commitment. I do not want your half-way commitments. This is not what I want. Your non-commitment and half-commitment will be rejected. I will not receive it. I do not want it. It is an abomination to ME. I gave you all of ME. I laid down MY life. I, GOD, I JESUS did this for you and your weak commitment means nothing to ME.

You come to church once a week and then I don't hear from you again all week. This is not a relationship with ME. I don't want your half-hearted attempts to reach ME. I would rather you be hot or cold, but as it is I must spit you out. Don't insult ME with your lukewarm affection. I won't have it. It makes ME sick. You love everything else more than ME. You spend hours with your other wooden idols and with ME you spend almost no time. This is no relationship. Don't think you will stand before ME and be saved. I will say, "I never knew you" and I never lie. I am GOD and I am a force to be reckoned with. It would be better for you to have never been born then to reject ME, the ONE WHO created you.

I am giving out final warnings. Quit embracing these wooden idols. They can't return your affection. They are cold, lifeless. They are cruel mistresses. They will lead you to paths of destruction. You know of the idols I speak of. you know what I am talking about. It is your first love. I was your first love, but you have walked away and now you spend your time with other gods.

I will have no other god before ME. Choose these gods and die. They offer you pleasure for a time, for a moment. then it will be hell eternal. a very long moment. a very big price to pay for a brief love affair with a wooden idol. Embrace your idols and see how it goes for you. You know what idols I speak of, it is anything you find more worthy to devote your precious time to than ME. Even your families you put above ME. Do this and you will lose ME and your families you cherish so deeply over ME. I am a jealous GOD. I will not share MY love with other idols, other lesser gods.

Be warned. I am coming soon for a devoted wife. One who puts ME above all other gods and idols. She will have ME and I love her. I cherish MY bride and will love and protect her forever. It is not too late for you. But don't waste valuable time on your lesser gods or you will find yourself in the soon-coming darkness. Then you will not find relief from your idols you so cherish. They will look back at you with a blank stare and you will weep over your loss. I am warning you now. Scoff if you like, but the day will come and your sadness will be great because you have rejected life and love, purity, wholeness, and all that a Holy GOD offers.

You decide. I cannot make this decision for you. You have this choice to make: life or death. I put it before you. Time is at hand. The hour is at hand. Please think carefully. I, JESUS am here waiting, but soon the door will close. Get your lamp full of MY refining oil. I cannot help you once the door closes. You will have to go through the fire of the enemy.

Please make this choice. Choose well. Save yourself. Warn others. I will wait only a little longer, than I must leave with MY faithful wife.

These are MY Words. I, JESUS have spoken.

Letter Sabrina received from the LORD JESUS. November 17, 2010.

"Why do you believe prophets do not matter anymore? If they do not matter now, they didn't matter in the past, because I always have been sending MY prophets to speak to MY people. I am talking seriously through MY servants here. Anybody who has ears LISTEN! Listen to MY prophets MY people. They are MY chosen ones. They do not seek honor for themselves. They only choose to serve and obey ME.

If you neglect their warnings through MY Voice, you are very misled. Listen to MY prophets and open your ears to MY words, not to your own reasoning. There is a good reason I am sending out all these warning words. The reason is I want to save you from final destruction. Hell is the final destiny forever. You do not want to be there. Many pastors and their followers are spending eternity there. Why? Because, they did not attend to MY words, they did not listen to MY prophets. They choose to rely and depend on their own wisdom.

All human reasoning is no wisdom of Mine. I am the source of all wisdom. Come to ME NOW. Now is the time. I told you before, time is up. Why then do you read these letters and then just continue and go on with your lives as if nothing has to change? Something serious has to change in your way of thinking.

Now listen to ME. Keep MY Word. Keep MY commandments. Listen to MY prophets. Read MY Gospel and read what I said to the unbelievers at that time. Read the whole Bible and see why MY principles and commandments are so important. They always have been. They always will be. MY Word will never fade away. So come to your senses. Which you think they are so good and beautiful. Come to ME NOW. Now is the time. Time is up MY people.

If I would not love you, I would not give you these warning letters. If the Father's grace would not be so big, you would not even receive these end-time warnings. I love MY daughter Susan, as I have seen she is a willing and very obedient vessel in these last days. She knows what it is to surrender everything to ME. Watch for these letters and take them very seriously. As I have spoken through MY servants Moses, David, and Elijah, I am speaking now through MY chosen vessels.

MY love is so deep for all of you. Don't you see that? Don't you understand that? Why then, MY people do you reject them? Why do you reject MY end-time prophets? Be careful and repent for this. These are MY words. Everybody who is rejecting MY Words, are rejecting ME. If you reject ME, I will have no choice but to reject you in the end. Choosing ME means TOTAL surrender. Many of you still do not choose to do this. Your own flesh is in the way. Crucify it! Crucify it! Crucify it! Live HOLY before your Lord God Almighty.

Who do you think you are? I died a horrible death at Golgotha for you, for all of you, MY loved ones. Please do not deny MY Words. Do not treat them like some cheap toy. I am not a God to be toyed with. This you will all discover in the end. Everybody has to stand before MY Throne of Judgment, everybody. Will you be ashamed and put your head down or will you be able to look ME in the eyes with the knowledge you've surrendered everything with an open and honest heart towards your God? If this is the case, you will enter into the beauty of MY Kingdom. Oh, so much beauty I have prepared for you, for all of you. It is waiting for all of you. But there is a price. Give ME your life, heart, soul, and mind COMPLETELY. No compromises with the world or with MY Word. not at all. You take MY word and surrender to it wholly. There is no other way. Listen to MY prophets. They are everywhere. I appointed them to help you in these dark days. Do not think 'small' things do not matter before your God. They do matter.

Read MY word, from Genesis to Revelation and get to know ME. Get to know your God and stop listening and reasoning for yourself. Your reasonings will get you nowhere. Salvation comes only through ME. I died for all of you at that cross. Nobody can ever understand MY suffering for you. Oh you will, when you enter before MY throne. Please, don't spent eternity in hell for disobeying MY Word. Don't think it doesn't matter. Your eternity depends on it. You are thinking about grace now? Where is the grace, I hear you say? This very word IS MY grace. Ask me for understanding and revelation and I will show it to you. I will show you the condition of your heart. Ask ME to search your hearts and to reveal the truth to you all.

Oh yes, I have many servants. They are hidden in the secret places, waiting for their time to be sent out. Now, come to ME NOW people. I am returning soon and I cannot take you with spots or wrinkles. Wash and clean yourselves with MY blood. It's the only way. I provided the way and the source. You apply it. That's something I cannot do for you. That's your job and your freewill. Oh, MY Father is about to give the sign. I ask Him for one more moment of grace, MY children. But soon it will be over. Listen to these words of warning and love and grace."

Your JESUS.

The LORD wanted this Scripture added to these letters:

Psalm 22.

1My God, MY God, why hast thou forsaken me? why art thou so far from helping me, and from the words of MY roaring? 2O MY God, I cry in the day time, but thou hearest not; and in the night season, and am not silent. 3But thou art holy, O thou that inhabitest the praises of Israel. 4Our fathers trusted in thee: they trusted, and thou didst deliver them. 5They cried unto thee, and were delivered: they trusted in thee, and were not confounded. 6But I am a worm, and no man; a reproach of men, and despised of the people. 7All they that see me laugh me to scorn: they shoot out the lip, they shake the head, saying, 8He trusted on the LORD that he would deliver him: let him deliver him, seeing he delighted in him. 9But thou art he that took me out of the womb: thou didst make me hope when I was upon MY mother's breasts. 10I was cast upon thee from the womb: thou art MY God from MY mother's belly. 11Be not far from me; for trouble is near; for there is none to help. 12Many bulls have compassed me: strong bulls of Bashan have beset me round. 13They gaped upon me with their mouths, as a ravening and a roaring lion. 14I am poured out like water, and all MY bones are out of joint: MY heart is like wax; it is melted in the midst of MY bowels. 15My strength is dried up like a potsherd; and MY tongue cleaveth to MY jaws; and thou hast brought me into the dust of death. 16For dogs have compassed me: the assembly of the wicked have enclosed me: they pierced MY hands and MY feet. 17I may tell all MY bones: they look and stare upon me. 18They part MY garments among them, and cast lots upon MY vesture. 19But be not thou far from me, O LORD: O MY strength, haste thee to help me. 20Deliver MY soul from the sword; MY darling from the power of the dog. 21Save me from the lion's mouth: for thou hast heard me from the horns of the unicorns. 22I will declare thy name unto MY brethren: in the midst of the congregation will I praise thee. 23Ye that fear the LORD, praise him; all ye the seed of Jacob, glorify him; and fear him, all ye the seed of Israel. 24For he hath not despised nor abhorred the affliction of the afflicted; neither hath he hid his face from him; but when he cried unto him, he heard. 25My praise shall be of thee in the great congregation: I will pay MY vows before them that fear him. 26The meek shall eat and be satisfied: they shall praise the LORD that seek him: your heart shall live for ever. 27All the ends of the world shall remember and turn unto the LORD: and all the kindreds of the nations shall worship before thee. 28For the kingdom is the LORD's: and he is the governor among the nations. 29All they that be fat upon earth shall eat and worship: all they that go down to the dust shall bow before him: and none can keep alive his own soul. 30A seed shall serve him; it shall be accounted to the Lord for a generation. 31They shall come, and shall declare his righteousness unto a people that shall be born, that he hath done this.

PART 17

This is a letter from JESUS to Susan telling the people to listen to HIS warnings and that the people are not paying attention at all or listening to His warnings. The world is blind and not seeing what is coming. Also includes a letter from Mary of Texas who received a similar word from the LORD.

November 20th, 2010.

I received a very serious letter from the LORD and was told by HIM to get it out right away. With this letter is another letter from Mary of Texas, U.S. She had approached me about the letters that she too had been receiving from the LORD herself. We were told by the LORD to add her letter to ours and send it out too. I pray you seek the LORD JESUS for salvation and to be the MOST important part of your life.

Letter 40. November 19, 2010, dictated to Susan from the LORD JESUS.

Susan these are MY words. I am ready to give you words.

I am in front of you MY people pleading. Listen to ME. The hour is short. The evil is forming. You must hear ME. I speak truth. Soon you will not hear any truth. Soon the world will become completely black with darkness. It will grow dark and cold uninhabitable, unreliable people at every turn. Truth will disappear.

MY people who preserve truth will be gone up into the heavens with ME to their glorious homes, homes I have prepared for them to be taken to for safety away from the maddening rush on earth. Evil will ensue, strongholds of evil unrivaled to any other time in history. People will cry out for justice, but it will be replaced with treachery and the divine will be replaced with gross evil.

Where are your heads, MY people? Where do you hide your heads, in the sand? Can you not see what is right before you? You are afraid to look up and see because you think all is well. MY life is untouched. Things are fine. The world goes on as it always does. MY church does not tell me any different. All is well.

Susan, write it down.

The people are mesmerized and taken over by their own maligned beliefs. They see not because they choose not to look. It is there. Those who bother to look see it and they warn others to save them from the coming storm and are met with opposition at every turn. MY people wake up. The truth is there before you. The hour is closing in. Listen to reason.

You think these words are empty. You think I, GOD am not speaking. You think I, GOD do not exist. Let me tell you, I am a force to be reckoned with. I will avenge MY enemies: those who choose to reject ME; those who choose to harm MY children; those who choose to hate GOD. Will you choose to be against ME or will you choose to receive MY salvation, MY blood-bought salvation.

Get on your knees before ME. Repent! Turn your hearts back to ME before it is too late. Show regret for your adoration of the world in front of a HOLY GOD who hates evil and protects the widows and orphans. Show ME your repentance. Show ME your sorrow over your lust for the things of this world and I will heal your hearts and bring you back to MYSELF. You will be found worthy to fly away with ME to safe hiding to MY Kingdom far away. I will hold you and love you. I will protect and keep you. You will be MY possession and I will love you forever.

Reject ME in this hour and I must leave without you. I am sorry, but I cannot take you if you do not surrender all to ME. Half-hearted commitments cannot be accepted. I love completely. Love ME completely and be saved, be spared from gross disaster.

You are listening to men if you do not see this coming. You have folded in with the wayward sheep who have left MY pasture. You are following blindly the sheep headed away from their lovely

Shepherd into the darkness. The wolves are waiting in the wings to capture you when I take MY faithful flock to safety. You will be devoured. This is not a parable or story. It is truth. You are blind if you cannot see it.

I am before you pleading. Open your Bibles. Read the truth. Stop listening to men. Seek ME, your LORD JESUS. Pray to ME. Read about ME. Ask MY Spirit for truth. Ask ME to open your eyes to truth and I will help you see. I have the answers, not men. You are blind leading blind. Take off your blindfolds. The hour is short. Seek ME. I will give you truth. There is no other truth. I am the AUTHOR of truth.

Oh, listen to ME, MY people. These are not empty words. Get on your hands and knees before ME and pray for your very souls to be saved. I will do it. I will see your humble hearts and I will lead you out. Give ME your all and I will save you from gross, endless evil that only I, GOD will stop. MEN will not be able to stop the evil forming, try though they might.

They are not fighting flesh and blood, they are fighting principalities of the air. Only I have the armor to fight this enemy. Come to ME and I give it freely. Be wise. Be discerning. Know the times. Read MY Book. Seek MY Face. Do not waste what little time is left on worldly pursuits. Seek MY Face. Humble yourself before ME. Show ME your adoration for the GOD who breathes life into you everyday. Without ME you would not be here.

You cannot accept a GOD who rejects HIS children, you say. MY Word explains this clearly. Salvation is through a relationship with ME and MY blood covers you. There is no other way to the FATHER but through ME. I AM THE ONLY WAY.

Count the minutes ticking away: like mist through your fingers. You are wasting precious time on pursuits that don't matter. Your idol worship will not save you. Release your grip from death. Continue in this way and you will surely die without ME and I am mankind's only hope despite what the enemy may whisper in your ear. If you cohabitate with the enemy in your thinking and schemes, you will lie down with death and I cannot help you.

You say, "HE rambles on with these empty warnings, I do not see it." Open your eyes, you lost generation. You are caught up in the world and cannot recognize truth. The world calls, invites, appears so normal. It deals in death. It is a snare; a trap awaiting to take you under. So many have already fallen in her eternal trap: never to be seen again. So many more will fall into the eternal trap of outer darkness and hell. There are many paths to lies and only one narrow way to truth. I AM THE WAY.

MY name is JESUS. SON OF GOD. LIVING TRUTH EVERLASTING. PRINCE OF PEACE. GLORY UNENDING. POWER FOREVER. KING OF KINGS. LORD OF LORDS. EXCELLENCE. MAJESTY. LION OF JUDAH. BEAUTY UNTOLD. I AM.

You are about to miss glory everlasting traded in for a fallen world. Wake up O' earth! Grab for MY hand. See the piercing. This is what GOD did. I stepped down from MY Kingdom and died a horrible death because I did not want to lose you for eternity. Why do you refuse ME? If you are not watching, you will miss it. MY faithful who watch will be taken. This is your LORD speaking. Consider these words carefully.

I, JESUS have spoken.

Letter dictated to "Mary of Texas" by JESUS. November 16, 2010.

The enemy is blaspheming MY Name. This is why you have heard, "You have been tried and found guilty of treason by the Most High God." There is no time to delay. Take up your cross and Follow ME, Yeshua. All your sins are forgiven you. When a thought comes to mind, evaluate it, discern it, check it with your soul. Take out the trash – remember it no more. I know you are deeply hurting about these thoughts and it's MY purpose that you experience this. I am making you a soldier and teaching you MY armor. You are in the army of the Most High God. All of MY people are in MY army. Now

111

you must fight.

The evil one is strong and wants to destroy MY Kingdom. MY soldiers are ready for battle. Wait for the battle cry. I will send you out. You will know what to do. No harm will come to you. Shout for MY people. Get their attention. Offer MY Word as your sword. MY breastplate of righteousness will keep you standing. Your shield of faith is strong. Your belt of truth takes pleasure in exposing other's wrong doing. Stop doing that. That is not what it's for. Stand yourself for truth. Work on your own words, kindness. These are MY words. Your helmet is lop-sided and confused. I AM straightening it. This will gird your mind and ease your soul of unwanted despair. Guard your eyes and ears in this dark world. Take "cover" in MY Word.

MY hope is yours. MY salvation is yours. Take cover. Take out the trash and take cover. I AM trying to tell you once and for all that you are Mine, that you are to be a soldier. This is a battle we are in. I AM your commander. You listen well or you would not be writing this down. Your boots are worn out. I will restore them. You have been in battle without full protection. This is why you suffer. You are awake now in this battle. Your eyes and ears now tell you the truth. Feelings are without reproach. Take them. Use them lightly. don't disregard them, but don't use them all.

Now walk in MY spirit. This armor is not heavy as metal is heavy. This armor is light – like MY yoke is light and not a heavy burden. I AM working. I AM the One giving the orders while you are ready for battle in MY spirit – or you are not going to hear MY orders because the dark world is very LOUD. All MY people line up now! Hold your shields tightly. Make your swords ready. Hold on. Gird your thoughts and stand firm. Tighten your belt. Be in your breastplate at all times. MY shout is at the door. I AM waiting for MY Father's hand. I keep His commands. The retrieval time is here. Gird up! Stand and wait with ME. You have nothing to fear. All is well.

MY Kingdom is ready for you now. All the rooms are complete. I have made beautiful rooms for MY beautiful Bride. She is worth it. Joy comes in the morning. In MY Kingdom – joy IS – and IS forever.

Oh how I love MY Bride!

Get ready to depart. I need you to be ready now. Don't delay. Detach from the sights and sounds of the dark world and be ready at all times. Stand and be ready. Yes, look up. I see you. I see MY Bride waiting, yearning, even despairing. I am ready to take you into MY arms, into MY Kingdom. We will live together forever. All of MY words are true. I love you. MY love is deep. MY love is everlasting. MY love wants you. MY love sees you and nurtures you. MY love is everlasting. It does not waiver. It cannot waiver. It doesn't know how. MY love IS, and is forever.

Overwhelmed children follow me. I have rest for you. Let me nourish you. Don't turn from ME in your tears. I am holding you and you will make it. I know all of your tears. I know all of your turns while you search. But, I am with you. Just turn to ME. I am here. Gird up. Breathe deep. Gird up and stand. Now compose yourself in MY Spirit, MY direction. We will all be together soon. The world is Mine. The Universe is Mine. Everything that IS – is Mine.

You have made the right choice to follow ME. The world will burn and bleed and cry and scream. It will be strong horror. Many will suffer. Many will fall.

Keep writing. All MY territories you see will be destroyed, looking at maps inside MY Bible. All of that is Mine and will be restored, looking at Israel. It will be beautiful – no longer desolate – no longer barren. All will be taken and restored. All will know MY Name. The battle is Mine. I know who is in it. Some of MY people will suffer. I know this full well as I wait for MY Father's hand.

There is little time left before it all becomes dark. Woe is this time. I am serious about MY instructions to MY people – who aren't listening. They will be caught by surprise – as by a thief. The roof's of your houses won't save you. Many will perish in fear. This is a time of woe, intense woe. All MY words are true and absolute. These people who will not turn but remain in the stubbornness of their hearts will melt like wax as they burn. MY warning is strong.

You must share this. Even if it only saves and warns a few, it would be better than if no one hears it and is not warned. Woe is this time! The manner in which they refer to ME, is detestable and it must stop and it will. Their houses are covered with hyssop and barley and will burn with a mighty burn.

I am the Most High God. Even their children are detestable to ME. I AM angry about this. They have no reason to live any longer and I want them out of MY sight! These are harsh, but true words. Their rejection of ME runs deep for many generations. I will cause them great fear and they will still reject ME. Because I know this, I will blow MY fire on them as a torch as they are an abomination to ME.

I am a jealous God. I know whom I have created. Man's armor will do them NO good. They are like toy soldiers – these unbelievers, these apostates that pretend, on purpose, to know ME and are using ME as a device for the enemy. I will not stand for such trickery. This battle is not finished. I call all MY soldiers to battle. Stay girded. I will pull you out of the trenches before the great explosion. You will be with ME long before the earth and the ones left behind start total destruction and annihilating themselves. This is the final war. Gird yourself and be ever ready. When you hear MY command – look up- then leave ALL behind.

End of His words. November 16, 2010.

I had to look up the word reproach, referring to feelings, to see why they would be "without" reproach. I've always been told not to trust feelings, however, He tells me they are without disappointment. "now" being the operative word in this case,

I looked up hyssop and barley. I'm not an herb person really, but it said barley was used in beer and hyssop was referred to as a "holy" herb and used to brush the blood of the lamb on doorposts during Passover. MY impression is that these people have offensive items as well as holy items, mixed up or lukewarm, not serious about Him, in their households.

Overall, MY impression while writing was that He wants us ready as an army would be ready to obey any command while we wait for His return, and is about to happen – that many are getting weak and becoming vulnerable to attack, which is the need for our "armor."

PART 18

This message has three parts. First a letter Susan received from the LORD JESUS, then second a letter Sabrina received from the LORD JESUS, and finally a word from a young 10-year-old girl who had communicated with Sabrina. The messages from the LORD are stressing the importance of following the commandments of GOD. The commandments are not obsolete as so many seem to think by their disregard of them. It is clear in this verse Revelation 12:17, a New Testament verse, that GOD's commandments are not obsolete for this generation. JESUS speaks in His letter about the many roles He can play in a person's life. Also in this letter to Sabrina, JESUS warns about not keeping His commandments including keeping the Sabbath holy.

November 23rd, 2010.

These messages from the LORD JESUS are stressing the importance of following the commandments of GOD. The commandments are not obsolete for this era. It is even clear in this verse found in Revelation 12:17, a New Testament verse, that GOD's commandments are not obsolete for this generation:

Revelation 12:17. Then the dragon was enraged at the woman and went off to wage war against the rest of her offspring, those who keep God's commands and hold fast their testimony about Jesus.

Letter 41. November 21, 2010. letter dictated by Jesus Christ to Susan.

Susan, write it down. These are MY words your LORD JESUS.

Today is a new day. Tomorrow will be another day. Day after day, the days go by. People think nothing new is going on. "Same today as yesterday, each day folds into the next," they say. But, let ME tell you the time is running out. The hour is waning, precious moments disappearing. Time is dwindling away. The hour is closing in. Each moment is precious is now. These moments are precious.

Please consider what I am about to say. Your life here is in the balance, hanging in the balance. Your hour is dwindling away. You are running out of time to decide whether you are going to choose ME your LORD JESUS or to go with the enemy. He is waiting to see what you will do. The hour is closing in. There is a battle ensuing for your soul, your very soul. You have no idea what is going on around you. The enemy is a raging force, a raging lion waiting to devour you.

It is true, the hour is at hand. Men are asleep. They cannot see the condition of their hearts. They are far from their CREATOR. They are miserably far. They are far from reason. They have lost their minds. They are losing their souls.

MY pleas are desperate. The hour is waning. closing in. Time is short and you think you have all the time in the world, but sadly you do not. The clock is ticking away. What choices will you make? Are you ready to walk away from this world into MY wide outstretched arms and to leave with ME? I will be leaving with the church soon. She is ready. I am ready. I, LORD JESUS am ready. We are ready. Will you join us?

Evil is closing in. You are blind if you can't see it. You have left the path of light if you can't see the darkness closing in. Where is your head? Have you lost your senses? The time is short and you are enamored with the world and all its iniquities. It is a disease, a plague. You cannot have ME and love the world.

MY children back away. Look at what lies ahead. Come to your senses. See the evil brewing. All segments of life are touched by evil. It is pervasive, controlling, relentless, futile. Life is over as you have known it. The end as you have known it is here. You may escape with ME or stay and experience a new way of life. It will be most unpleasant for anyone who craves peace, love, happiness, purity, wholeness, GOD's peace. These moments you crave, will be a thing of the past, a distant memory.

You think all is well now. The hour is short. Normal will be no more very soon. Nothing will be normal soon. Sin will be exponentially greater. Evil will abound. The love of many will grow cold, stone cold. Harsh sounding? Honesty. I am giving you truth. The winds are changing.

I am leaving with MY people soon, MY beloved people. Be among them and you will escape all this to come. Why stay and be subjected to torture and death? Why? I offer you a beautiful home in heaven. The difference between the two is stark. You have two choices. Choose ME and live in beauty, eternal peace, and bliss. Reject MY offer and die in squalor. Die a sad death.

I AM GOD. I know the future. I see what's coming. I am trying to warn you. Be with ME and you will never regret your choice. Stay and regret will be your constant thought. Let ME be your FATHER, PROTECTOR, COMFORTER, SAVIOR, LOVER. I AM ALL. When people put themselves in outer darkness apart from their all-knowing, all-loving CREATOR for eternity, they abandon all hope. There is endless hopelessness. It is the worm that doesn't die. The loss is far greater than the human mind can comprehend. Walk through that door and be lost forever more.

I am the source of goodness, all things good, sweet, pure, beautiful. This is who I am. Shut yourself off from ME, reject MY proposal and never-ending emptiness, darkness, torment, hopelessness: hell is real. Many, many are going there. The regret is eternal. Your mind has trouble grasping eternity.

Choose against ME and discover that you have made a move that has eternal consequences. You will never see ME again. You will never hear MY voice. You will never experience MY ways: I am LOVE. I am HOPE. I am KINDNESS. I am PEACE. I am WISDOM. I am KNOWLEDGE. I am STRENGTH. I am SAFETY. I am BLISS. I am JOY. I am TRUTH. I am GREATNESS. I am LIFE. I am ADORATION. I am all the good things you enjoy in this world. Hell does not have these things. It will be never-ending sad futility.

MY children who are in hell have no hope. They will not find hope or love again. They are experiencing the worst things. Some of MY children have witnessed hell and speak of it. Many have been there for short times and experienced its anguish. But there is nothing worse than an eternity apart from ME, your MAKER. I am sorry for their loss, but MY Word is clear and the people are without excuse if they choose against ME and find themselves in hell.

Now I am putting forth MY final pleas and I am warning you about the horror to come. This world wants horror instead of GOD. This world cherishes horror over GOD, so this world will have its horror and I shall not bother it. MY people left will have to go through the worst imaginable things. I want them to know that the choice they are making now has severe consequences if they choose against ME. Come with ME and be saved, stay and suffer.

Let ME tell you something. Your choice now will have long term ramifications. It will be very hard for those who want to turn back to ME. The choice now is easy. Later it will be very difficult. Choosing for ME will be very hard after I take MY people home. Come with ME now. Follow ME now. Save yourself. Time is running out. Don't waste precious moments. Turn, turn, turn NOW. Repent! Lay your life down before ME. Give ME everything. I will save you. Now is the deciding hour. Time is running out.

I, GOD, I, JESUS am waiting for your answer.

Letter dictated to Sabrina by the LORD JESUS November 22, 2010.

"MY dear daughter, write it down. Where are the people seeking ME earnestly because of all this? I have sent out many warning letters by now through a lot of MY sons and daughters. They read it like some secular magazine.

I am asking you: Where are the people searching ME earnestly? How many faces do I see on the ground? Many of you think this is just for the ones outside, but everybody should search their hearts constantly in order to be saved. I came to die for you, but you must work out your salvation daily. Live HOLY before MY Face. Lay down before MY Face. Cry out before MY Face. Long for ME with all that is in you. I am your GOD. Do as I tell you in MY Word. No compromises with MY Word. Read the commandments and ask ME how to live them. Not how you think you should live them.

Keep MY Sabbath Holy. I see many of you walking around on Sunday from one place to another. This can never happen! MY Day is a Holy Day, set apart for ME. Why do you run to worldly places then? You cannot be out of church soon enough to go and do your own things. I am telling you MY people, and this should not come as a surprise, as I have given warnings. Keep MY Day as a Holy Day! Go to church, honor ME, worship ME, listen to MY Words. This day is not a day to go out and shop. Woe to them. They are in great danger! Listen to MY prophets.

Read the testimony's of why good Christians end up in hell. Why, because they ignored MY Commandments. I cannot tolerate this. Haven't you read that I GOD never change? Haven't your read that I GOD have given you these guidelines so it would go well with you? Read MY Word from Genesis until Revelation and you shall find it.

Ask ME to open your eyes and you shall see it. Listen to ME MY people, I beg you. Take MY Word seriously. Do not go by your own reasonings. This is a great deception and you are in great danger when you do this. Your own reasonings cannot be trusted. Oh the ones who search ME earnestly, shall found ME! They shall see the truth, because they long for only ME, pleasing and loving ME, not their own flesh.

Crucify your flesh daily MY children! Everybody who reads this, take this very seriously, because I do not see a lot of changes yet in MY people. I do not want to condemn you. I only want to save you. I provided the tools: MY death and resurrection. You do the rest. I cannot choose in your place. I created you with freewill. Now choose and search ME earnestly. If you would only have a glimpse of heaven and hell, you would know what to choose. Still, I send many and they are not believed. Listen to MY prophets! These are the last warnings."

Nehemiah 13:15-18. In those days saw I in Judah some treading wine presses on the sabbath, and bringing in sheaves, and lading asses; as also wine, grapes, and figs, and all manner of burdens, which they brought into Jerusalem on the sabbath day: and I testified against them in the day wherein they sold victuals. There dwelt men of Tyre also therein, which brought fish, and all manner of ware, and sold on the sabbath unto the children of Judah, and in Jerusalem. Then I contended with the nobles of Judah, and said unto them, What evil thing is this that ye do, and profane the sabbath day? Did not your fathers thus, and did not our God bring all this evil upon us, and upon this city? yet ye bring more wrath upon Israel by profaning the sabbath.

Isaiah 56:1-5. Thus saith the LORD, Keep ye judgment, and do justice: for MY salvation is near to come, and MY righteousness to be revealed. Blessed is the man that doeth this, and the son of man that layeth hold on it; that keepeth the sabbath from polluting it, and keepeth his hand from doing any evil. Neither let the son of the stranger, that hath joined himself to the LORD, speak, saying, The LORD hath utterly separated me from his people: neither let the eunuch say, Behold, I am a dry tree. For thus saith the LORD unto the eunuchs that keep MY sabbaths, and choose the things that please me, and take hold of MY covenant; Even unto them will I give in mine house and within MY walls a place and a name better than of sons and of daughters: I will give them an everlasting name, that shall not be cut off.

Isaiah 58:13-14. If thou turn away thy foot from the sabbath, from doing thy pleasure on MY holy day; and call the sabbath a delight, the holy of the LORD, honourable; and shalt honour him, not doing thine own ways, nor finding thine own pleasure, nor speaking thine own words: Then shalt thou delight thyself in the LORD; and I will cause thee to ride upon the high places of the earth, and feed thee with the heritage of Jacob thy father: for the mouth of the LORD hath spoken it.

Proverbs 28:9. He that turneth away his ear from hearing the law, even his prayer shall be abomination.

FRESH REVELATIONS TO A 10-YEAR-OLD GIRL:

A few days ago, November 19, a young girl contacted me, Sabrina, through email. Her name is Philipa and she is 10-year-old and though she is still young, she is very smart and loves Jesus so much. Philipa said she was open for any advice/words. I wrote her back that same day and to MY surprise the Lord had a beautiful word for her. I will share the last sentence: "I long to hear your voice MY beautiful child, so come, come! I will surprise you with MY presence and you will hear MY Voice. I love you deeply, Your Father and friend forever, Jesus."

November 21. I, Sabrina, received this mail from Philipa:

LAST NIGHT, I HEARD THE LORD TELLING ME THAT HE WOULD USE ME FOR HIS WORK. SO WHEN I WENT TO CHURCH GOD SHOWED ME A CLOCK AND TOLD ME THAT IT IS LEFT WITH ONE MINUTE MORE FOR HIM TO COME. AND HE SAID THAT MY CHILDREN REPENT, REPENT. AND HE SAID THAT DARKNESS WOULD SOON TAKE OVER THE WORLD AND THAT HE CAN NOT BARE THE SIN OF MAN ANY LONGER. SO I SHOULD SPREAD AND TELL THIS WORD TO PEOPLE. AND THIS AFTERNOON, HE TOLD ME, "MY CHILDREN CHANGE. FOR ONE MINUTE IS NOT ANY LONG TIME. HELL IS BEYOND ANY HUMAN KNOWLEDGE. HUMAN KNOWLEDGE IS NOT ANY GOOD KNOWLEDGE. HELL IS NOT ANY GOOD PLACE. MY CHILDREN CHANGE, CHANGE! MY CHILDREN WHY HAVE FORSAKEN ME? GET OUT OF THE DARKNESS."

I, Sabrina, wrote Philipa back that same day and the Lord had another personal word for her to encourage her to share these words with her parents, church, friends, and family. I had communicated with her mother before and she shared that they are preparing for the rapture and are missionaries in the French-speaking country Guinea with 92% muslims.

Philipa has asked me to pray for her, so that God will use her for His work as He has started. May I ask all of you to pray for this little girl and her family, who is so open and willing for the Lord and truly an example for me.

November 22: Another vision given to Philipa:

I HAD ANOTHER VISION ALSO TODAY. I SAW A MAN ON A HILL HOLDING A STAFF,WITH HIS HANDS AND THE STAFF UP WHILE THE PEOPLE WERE DOWN THE HILL. AND THE MAN WAS SAYING, "REPENT FOR THE KINGDOM OF GOD IS NEAR." BUT, THE PEOPLE STARTED LAUGHING. -PHILIPA

Acts 2:17: And it shall come to pass in the last days, saith God, I will pour out of MY Spirit upon all flesh: and your sons and your daughters shall prophesy, and your young men shall see visions, and your old men shall dream dreams:

PART 19

In the letter to Susan the LORD talks about the people being far away from HIM. HE also talks about the way the people profane HIS Holy name in this letter. Primarily this letter addresses the trivial way the people use GOD's name and HE will avenge the use of His name.

November 25th, 2010.

These messages were dictated to us and other people as well. If you take a minute to read this message, you will see the urgency in the tone and the great sadness of the times we live in and the incredible way the world has turned its back to its LORD and MAKER, JESUS.

If each person who reads this message felt so compelled to forward it to just one person then the warning would go out to alert the people everywhere. I hope the Christians will start paying attention to the lateness of the hour and seek the LORD. If they do not, they are putting out the wrong message to those around them that all is well and therefore putting people into a dangerous condition of unpreparedness. GOD bless and love to you all.

Letter 43. November 24, 2010. Dictated by the LORD JESUS to Susan.

Yes, Susan, I am ready to give you words.

The season is changing. Swiftly comes the change. The people sleep. Soon they will wake, but not in time to be taken. Many, many will be left behind. What a sorrowful moment. I truly regret that so many do not seek ME. I am sorry for their loss. I cannot change their minds if they refuse to pay attention to MY warnings in MY Book and the warnings of the times. Everything coordinates. Just as I said it would.

I foretold these events as they are coming to pass, yet the people refuse to pay attention. They are not looking, watching. Their eyes are captivated by the things of the world and not on ME. I have warned them to keep their eyes fixed on ME and to be watching for ME. But things are as they have always been just as their fathers before them they say and they care not to pursue ME, their LORD and MAKER, MASTER, LOVER. I am not even in the forefront of their minds. They have given heed to the wanderings of their human minds and the teachings of demons. This is the direction they move in. GOD is not even on their radar. I do not hold a place in their hearts. I am far away from their minds, their thoughts. Anything but GOD they make time for, anything but ME their CREATOR.

Why is there such a large gap between us? I did not do this. MY Arms are opened wide. The people have chosen to separate themselves from ME. They put space between us. They choose to be far away. I am not on their minds. So be it. These people want ME away. They create all sorts of excuses for themselves to stand apart from ME. They embrace all forms of evil and I am not included in their daily lives. Not a thought comes to mind as they traverse through their days. I don't enter their minds at all. GOD is a distant memory to most. The people think I am a fable, a great made up tale.

Soon, the world will know MY Name. Soon the world will remember I exist. I have a place in the world. I made the world. I am Divine. I am GOD. Who are these people fooling? MY Name enters their mouths as a curse word. This is how I am remembered. I give them life and I am nothing more to them than merely a word to use in vain to curse someone. Well I, GOD, am sickened by their hostility toward ME.

Stand before ME and repent for your foul treatment of MY HOLY NAME. I did not create you to take MY Name in vain, to trample on it with your ugly, disrespectful use of it.

This generation is lost. It is profane, abusive, foul, a stench under MY HOLY Nostrils. I cannot take it any longer. I bless and bless the people with life, with wholeness. I died. I suffered. I gave all. I bled out. I gave MY back to scourging. Oh the torture I endured. Oh the suffering. The beatings. The foul language. The spitting. The horror of it all. This was MY gift to mankind, to save a peoples lost in sin and degradation. I did this from MY heart. MY love poured out on the ground and now the people turn their backs and put ME to shame all over again. They have no respect, no awe, no adoration for who I am, for what I have done, for the sacrifice I made. MY Name is down-trodden in the mud, foul language. MY Name is used in crass ways, for crass purposes.

I am an angry, powerful GOD and I will stand for this no more. You have trampled on MY good Name too much and MY patience is about to end. Your disrespect sickens ME. You are a foul people run amok in your sin and degradation, your evil, and MY Name has been defiled and defamed enough. Do you really believe I will allow this to carry on much longer? I cannot. It is a full-scale attack on MY HOLINESS, MY BEAUTY. Disrespect has risen to MY throne, MY very throne. And, I, GOD cannot tolerate this ill treatment of MY HOLY, PRECIOUS, ILLUSTRIOUS NAME any longer.

I am a humble, loving GOD Who stepped down from beauty to ugliness at its height and gave all there was to give. MY sacrifice was complete. I had nothing else to give that day on the cross. But MY patience is ending with this generation of foul-mouthed evil and sinful, disregardful people. I have seen and heard enough and if you think other wise, if you think this can continue on, then you too have lost sight of what a HOLY GOD represents and what I have already endured.

Your love of this world sickens ME. You don't watch for MY coming because your eyes are too tightly glued to your wooden idols. You can't move away long enough to grope in the dark to look for your CREATOR to find ME. You need ME, you need ME desperately. But you are so lost in your lust for this life and this ugly, evil world that you cling to it and it is obscene to ME.

I know how you feel toward ME. I know how little I enter your mind. When things go awry you cry out to ME, but then when things are normal again, you forget quickly who I am. Your lackluster commitment to ME is noted and when you stand before ME unless you repent of your lukewarm commitment now, I will not recognize you and your loss will be great. If you knew how great, you would stand up now and pay attention.

Why do you think you were created? Do you think I created you to worship wooden idols? Is that what you think? You were created to worship ME. You were created to get to know ME. I gave you MY Book and I gave you a brain to seek ME and to find ME. I wanted relationship with MY creation. You scatter in all directions to all kinds of lesser gods, but to your one true LOVE.

I am waiting only briefly for you to come to your senses. Lay down your life in front of ME. Repent for your evil. Seek MY FACE, MY GLORIOUS FACE. Do this and I will save you in this evil hour that is at hand. Reject MY offer and I will allow you to face the world you so embrace. It will not be pleasant. The enemy has all sorts of torment and torture planned for those who reject ME, their GOD. He will not play fair. He will not be nice. He will destroy, rape, pillage, plunder. No one will escape it. If you take his mark, you will be tortured and tormented forever.

Think this through carefully. Escape this madness, avoid hell on earth. I will be holding out MY Arms a little longer, but make no mistake, the evil world is about to take hold and I will allow it.

I am sad about the people, but MY patience has been pushed too far and your disregard of ME, your GOD, is about to end. Why do these people, even MY people believe I can tolerate this much longer? MY Name is Holy and I will avenge MY Name. I will punish those who trifle with MY Name, these who use it so commonly as if it is any other word in the language. What a sad, disrespectful generation that has completely abandoned holiness and GOD's beauty embracing every foul thing the enemy puts out. The people have abandoned themselves to the gross and profane. Humanity has lost itself. Soon the world will find out what happens when you get what you want and it is hell and horror. Horror glamorized will soon be horror reality. It won't be pretend horror. It will be real life horror. GOD will be tending to HIS beautiful bride as the world engages in its brand of evil.

These are MY warnings. Those who have ears hear and those who have eyes see. All looks well on the surface. But underneath dwells an enemy that is so ruthless and blood-thirsty, if I, GOD did not come back to end the madness no one would be left standing.

You lack discernment MY people. You look around and see what your neighbors do and you make no changes. Quit running with the crowd. I told you the path is narrow and few find it. Broad is the road to hell. Heed MY Holy Words. I spoke them. I change not. The road is narrow. I am the only ONE Who can get you to that road. Seek MY SPIRIT. Seek MY FACE. Start by getting down on your hands and knees and repenting for your evil mouth. I will have a pure bride. I cannot take you if you are spotted and wrinkled. These are MY terms.

Time is running out. Walk away from the crowd. Step out. Step away. I am seeking a bride set apart. Come away from the things of the world. Put down the unclean things. Stand back from the unholy. Be different. Be unique. Stand out from the people. Be set apart. Come and receive MY refining fire. I will create you new. I will make you ready. Only I can do this for you. I alone can purify your heart and bring you to this holiness. Get ready. I am taking with ME a bride who is made ready. Time is short. The way is made clear. Walk in it, but a short time then the door closes.

I, JESUS of Nazareth have spoken.

Last night, November 25, 2010, I, Sabrina, had a terrible dream. GOD however told me that this dream was from HIM. I understood that it was about the coming tribulation. Here is a brief description of the dream:

I was with a lot of people in a small place in a home. A woman used the toilet, and I was afraid that something scary would happen. When someone opened the door, the woman had just drowned herself in the cesspool of the toilet. It was a horrible sight and when

I woke up I was still disgusted. After prayer and Bible reading, GOD gave me the following explanation:

"The darkness will strike in this world so hard after MY bride is removed and many will take their life. Just like you disgusted by this picture, I loathe the sin and the aversion that many have for me. Their end will be terrible and despair and suffering will be their eternal part in the lake of fire."

GOD told me also that He was very sad.

Revelation 3:16. So then because thou art lukewarm, and neither cold nor hot, I will spue thee out of MY mouth.

Ezekiel 20:43. And there shall ye remember your ways, and all your doings, wherein ye have been defiled; and ye shall lothe yourselves in your own sight for all your evils that ye have committed.

Ezekiel 36:31. Then shall ye remember your own evil ways, and your doings that were not good, and shall lothe yourselves in your own sight for your iniquities and for your abominations.

PART 20

This is a very serious word. First is a letter with words as told by the LORD JESUS to Susan. Second is a letter from the LORD JESUS as told to Sabrina. Third we have included the story about Philipa, a young girl who is the daughter of Guinea missionaries, and the messages she has received from the LORD JESUS since contacting Sabrina. We have included the story about how Philipa came to hear the voice of the LORD and three very serious additional messages she has since received from the LORD. In this letter to Susan the LORD speaks quite a bit about the world as a cheating mistress lusting after the world. Sabrina's letter from the LORD speaks of the importance of listening to HIS warning messages.

November 28th, 2010.

This is a very serious word. First is a letter with words as told by the LORD JESUS to Susan. Second is a letter from the LORD JESUS as told to Sabrina. Third we have included the story about Philipa, a young girl who is the daughter of Guinea missionaries, and the messages she has received from the LORD JESUS since contacting Sabrina. We have included the story about how Philipa came to hear the voice of the LORD and three very serious additional messages she has since received from the LORD.

It is quite interesting to note that Matthew 7:21 and Matthew 25:11-12 share the same theme although they are from two different parables. But the message in both sections speak of those who come expecting to be let into the Kingdom of heaven yet the LORD tells the people HE does not know them. The clear message is how the importance of knowing the LORD is directly related to being received by HIM. What constitutes knowing the LORD? Well not the "works" of these people in the parable. The word, "KNOW" in the Bible often also means "to be intimate with." So the question you might want to ask yourself is: just how intimate are you with JESUS or is HE just a very casual or even distant acquaintance? This is an important question you may want to ask yourself in this late hour.

Matthew 7:21. Not every one that saith unto me, Lord, Lord, shall enter into the kingdom of heaven; but he that doeth the will of MY Father which is in heaven. Many will say to me in that day, Lord, Lord, have we not prophesied in thy name? and in thy name have cast out devils? and in thy name done many wonderful works? And then will I profess unto them, I never knew you: depart from me, ye that work iniquity.

Matthew 25:11-12. Afterward came also the other virgins, saying, Lord, Lord, open to us. But he answered and said, Verily I say unto you, I know you not.

Letter dictated by the LORD JESUS to Susan, November 26, 2010.

These are MY words for you Susan.

These are the last days. All is coming to a conclusion, a close. Soon the world will implode on itself. The evil will infiltrate and men will go amok toward evil. Nothing will be sacred anymore. Truth will be hard to find. The world will be caught up in the worst possible sin and unimaginable evil. The people will be shocked by what is about to happen. There will be horror from all angles. Peace will not be available.

The evil days are coming. Pleasant living will be over. Clean, peaceable living will be over. The world will know no peace. It will be each man for himself survival. Those who come to me after I remove MY bride will know the worst kind of persecution. It will be unrelenting. The evil will have an unquenchable appetite. It will be an all-out war on the true Christians. If you know ME and want to be saved by ME death will be the way to ME. The enemy will hunt you down and kill you. This has happened before in history, but never on the scale it will be, soon. It will be worldwide assault on anyone who claims to be a Christian and rejects the mark of the beast.

I am standing here waiting for MY children to turn to ME now and to avoid the terror to come. Avoid it. Turn to ME NOW. I will save you. I, JESUS, will take you with ME to safety. Back away from the world. Stand apart from the world. Turn to ME now. Grab MY hand. Surrender your all to ME. The hour is now. Cling to ME with everything you have. There is nothing that can save you now. Your money cannot save you. Your friends and family cannot save you. Your government cannot save you. You have one way to salvation. There is only one way. I am the Way.

I cannot hold back what is coming much longer. I will allow it to take place because this generation refuses to accept ME, its one and only true SAVIOR and GOD.

I love MY people but I cannot tolerate this rejection any longer. I have given all and MY people run to the world panting after it like a deer in heat. MY people make excuses to reject ME, their GOD, to be like the world at every turn. The world will not satisfy them. Seek it though they may, it will leave them empty every time. Many are in hell because they chose the world over MY love. But hell is nothing like the world. It is torture, torment, and it is unending. There is no relief from the torment.

The people in hell are tormented night and day. There is no rest. There never will be. They will never experience rest again. It is unstoppable and they will never see the light of day ever again. No hope. Harsh you say? Hell is the opposite of the presence of GOD. Live in MY presence and know eternal beauty. Leave MY presence and understand eternal damnation, unrelenting horror. That is what you receive when you choose against ME. You put yourself outside MY world and without ME there is hell, horror, torment, torture, and there is zero opportunity for relief. Come to MY world with ME and discover endless peace, love, beauty, hope, paradise, splendor, joy. It is so much more wonderful than the human mind can comprehend. Delight yourself in ME now and your delight will be eternal.

If you abhor ME now than you will receive the wages of your decisions. I do not take well to those who reject ME. I created all.

When MY creation chooses to reject and deny ME as their creator, I will put them in a place where they will receive their desire. Then they will understand the desires of their heart and what it means to deny ME. I am an honest truthful GOD and I make MYSELF very clear. You either choose ME or you choose against ME. If you only have a partial interest in ME, I will give you the lukewarm destination you so desire.

You want to play games with ME. You play ME like a cheating mistress. You have one eye on ME and one eye on the world. You go back and forth, what suits your purpose at the time. I am not good enough for you to surrender and devote all to. You must run into the arms of your other lover, the world. So be it. I am leaving with MY devoted wife, who only has eyes for ME. You may have your other mistress, the world. I don't want any part in your half-hearted love toward ME, your tepid affections, your lackluster performance as MY follower.

You wear MY Name on your shoulder like you belong to ME. You use ME when it suits your purposes then when you are done using ME, you go back to your mistress, the world, and indulge yourself in its evil. You worship idols and spend time with your lover. You pull ME out of the closet for show or when you think you need GOD. Then when you are done, I go back in the closet until you pull ME out again. I can't take you. You will have no place in MY beautiful home prepared for MY lovely bride. You think ME cruel? I am GOD. I created you. I died for you and I am willing to save you and care for you for eternity. But you want no part with ME.

You may have your way. I give you this choice, but I want to be clear about what this choice is so you can understand what your decision is about. Reject ME and your loss is eternal and there will be no looking back. Your decision will be final. You take the mark of MY enemy and your torment will be unending. These words are true.

I am trying to give you final warnings, before the world takes its plunge into darkness. Reach for ME NOW. Don't be fooled by the appearances of the world now. All looks well. Everything looks normal, but soon all is changing. Very soon everything will not be the same.

Susan, write it down.

We are at a great turning point. Life is changing swiftly and the world will soon not look the same. You sense it. Others see it clearly. The blind are leading the blind. You only have a little time left to take your blinders off and see what is coming. I cannot help you if you refuse to see. Soon your refusal to see the obvious will leave you in a state of disaster, because you would not take the safe route, the safe exit I offer.

Turn to ME now. I love you. Can't you see that I am trying to reach you? I want the best for you as any loving parent wants for their child. I want MY children to run into MY safe, open Arms to receive MY affection and to be saved from the madness to come. I will bring you to a place that your mind cannot fathom.

You have no idea how wonderful your home in heaven is and what awaits you. But first, you must surrender. Repent! Turn your life over to ME completely. I want it all, not a partial commitment. I want a full surrender. Let ME wash you in MY blood and clean you up. This is something that only I can do. Come to ME with sorrow and remorse for this sin in your life and I will receive you and bring you to MY beautiful everlasting Kingdom. We will eat together at the marriage supper. This life is empty. Come quickly. Turn to ME NOW. Your days are numbered. Time is swiftly running out. Choose what direction you will take. Come to your FATHER. Let ME save you.

I, JESUS long to save you and bring you home.

Letter from the LORD JESUS CHRIST as given to Sabrina of Belgium on November 28, 2010,

November 28, 2010.

"Everybody, listen to MY Voice! These are MY last pleas. Everybody who does not listen to MY Words are in danger for hell. If I did not warn you, I would not be a loving God. So listen to MY Words through MY prophets that I have assigned for this task, in this hour.

Many will be left behind. Will you be one of them? I have given you all many words by now, I suggest you re-read them all and take them seriously and ask ME to examine your heart and motives in everything you do. Your own heart can be very deceptive. I am a HOLY God and without holiness, no one can enter MY Kingdom.

I have prepared the wedding feast. All is done. I hope you are also entering. I cannot and will not tolerate sin. Don't think it doesn't matter because you think I am a God of love and grace. I explained to you before. Everybody who searches ME earnestly has to go through the purifying fire. Have you been there? If not, you are not ready to enter MY Kingdom.

Many of MY people think they know a lot, because they have been around for a long time. Don't be deceived! Read MY Words and take them seriously. I am getting tired of this. I am getting tired of your reasonings and self-made answers. All the answers are in MY Word, MY Holy Word. Study it and you will find the right answers. Ask MY Spirit for wisdom when you go through MY Word. He will reveal the truth to you. Time is running out. Don't be late!"

1 Corinthians 2:13-14. Which things also we speak, not in the words which man's wisdom teacheth, but which the Holy Ghost teacheth; comparing spiritual things with spiritual. But the natural man receiveth not the things of the Spirit of God: for they are foolishness unto him: neither can he know them, because they are spiritually discerned.

FRESH REVELATIONS TO A 10-YEAR-OLD GIRL:

A few days ago, November 19, a young girl contacted me, Sabrina, through email. Her name is Philipa and she is 10-years-old and though she is still young, she is very smart and loves JESUS so much. Philipa said she was open for any advice/words. I wrote her back that same day and to MY surprise the Lord had a beautiful word for her. I will share the last sentence: "I long to hear your voice MY beautiful child, so come, come! I will surprise you with MY presence and you will hear MY Voice. I love you deeply, Your Father and friend forever, Jesus."

November 21. I, Sabrina, received this mail from Philipa, translated to English:

LAST NIGHT, I HEARD THE LORD TELLING ME THAT HE WOULD USE ME FOR HIS WORK. SO WHEN I WENT TO CHURCH GOD SHOWED ME A CLOCK AND TOLD ME THAT IT IS LEFT WITH ONE MINUTE MORE FOR HIM TO COME. AND HE SAID THAT MY CHILDREN REPENT, REPENT. AND HE SAID THAT DARKNESS WOULD SOON TAKE OVER THE WORLD AND THAT HE CAN NOT BARE THE SIN OF MAN ANY LONGER. SO I SHOULD SPREAD AND TELL THIS WORD TO PEOPLE. AND THIS AFTERNOON, HE TOLD ME, "MY CHILDREN CHANGE. FOR ONE MINUTE IS NOT ANY LONG TIME. HELL IS BEYOND ANY HUMAN KNOWLEDGE. HUMAN KNOWLEDGE IS NOT ANY GOOD KNOWLEDGE. HELL IS NOT A GOOD PLACE. MY CHILDREN CHANGE, CHANGE! MY CHILDREN WHY HAVE FORSAKEN ME? GET OUT OF THE DARKNESS."

I, Sabrina, wrote Philipa back that same day and the Lord had another personal word for her to encourage her to share these words with her parents, church, friends, and family. I had communicated with her mother before and she shared that they are preparing for the rapture and are missionaries in the French-speaking country Guinea with 92% muslims.

Philipa has asked me to pray for her, so that God will use her for His work as He has started. May I ask all of you to pray for this little girl and her family, who is so open and willing for the Lord and truly an example for me?

November 22: Another vision given to Philipa:

I HAD ANOTHER VISION ALSO TODAY. I SAW A MAN ON A HILL HOLDING A STAFF WITH HIS HANDS AND THE STAFF UP

WHILE THE PEOPLE WERE DOWN THE HILL. AND THE MAN WAS SAYING, "REPENT FOR THE KINGDOM OF GOD IS NEAR." BUT, THE PEOPLE STARTED LAUGHING. –PHILIPA

New messages received by Philipa from the LORD JESUS:

HI SIS, SABRINA,, November 25, 2010,

PLEASE, TODAY AS I WAS AT SCHOOL THE LORD TOLD ME:

"I AM COMING SOON MY CHILDREN. LEAVE ME AND YOU WILL FACE ETERNAL DEATH FOR LIFE. I TELL YOU HELL IS GREATER THAN ANY HUMAN KNOWLEDGE. I TELL YOU, I WOULD LOVE AND CHERISH THOSE WHO LOVE ME. I AM EVERY THING THAT MAN WOULD EVER LIKE. HELL IS ETERNAL. LEAVE ME AND I WILL PUNISH YOU SEVERLY. YOU DO NOT KNOW WHAT IT IS LIKE AND WOULD BE LIKE. I KNOW THE SIN OF MAN AND I SAY: COME TO ME LIKE THAT! COME! COME! AND YOU WOUL FIND ETERNAL PEACE. THIS IS MY WARNING. COME! COME! I LOVE YOU SO DEEPLY. I AM EVER READY TO LISTEN TO YOU. NO ONE SHALL FIND ETERNAL PEACE WITHOUT ME. REPENT FOR THE KINGDOM OF GOD IS NEAR. I LOVE YOU. DO NOT BLAME ME WHEN I PUNISH YOU. THESE ARE MY WORDS. JESUS."

DEAR SIS, SABRINA,, November 26, 2010,

PLEASE, I ALWAYS GO WITH MY BOOK, JOURNAL, EVERYWHERE SO IMMEDIATELY, WHEN I HEAR GOD'S VOVICE, I WOULD WRITE IT. PLEASE, TODAY I HEARD THE LORD TELLING ME:

"MY CHILDREN THE TIME IS UP. COME! COME! DO NOT LISTEN TO FALSE TEACHINGS, FOR TIME IS UP! I AM COMING SOON. NO ONE CAN TELL WHEN. FOR THIS TIME, I AM COMING SOON. TAKE MY WORD OR LEAVE IT, FOR MY WORD IS PERMANENT. MY BRIDE, CONTINUE WITH YOUR WORK, BUT IT WILL NOT BE FOR LONG BEFORE I COME. JUST WORSHIP ME FOR IT IS JUST A LITTLE TIME LEFT. WAIT JUST

FOR A LITTLE TIME MORE, FOR I AM COMING SOON!

TAKE MY WORD OR LEAVE IT, FOR MY BRIDE IS READY AND THOSE WHO WILL LEAVE ME, WILL FACE ETERNAL DEATH, ETERNAL TORTURE.

THESE ARE MY WORDS TAKE IT OR LEAVE IT. THERE ARE TWO OPTIONS: GO TO HEAVEN OR GO TO HELL. IF YOU DISRESPECT ME AND GO TO HELL, YOU WILL HAVE NO OTHER OPTION THAN TO FACE TORTURE.

WHY HAVE YOU TAKEN THE PATH OF STAIN MY CHILDREN? WHY? WHY? WHY? WHY HAVE YOU FORSAKEN ME? ISN'T MY WORD ENOUGH FOR YOU? HOW MANY TIMES SHOULD I WARN YOU! GO ON AND MAKE THE devil your new god. IF MY WORD IS NOT ENOUGH FOR YOU, CONTINUE TO DEPART FROM MY WORD. THEN YOU WILL HAVE NO OTHER OPTION THAN TO PERISH FOR GOOD, FOR ETERNITY. FORGET ME, AND DIE AND SUFFER. THESE ARE MY WORDS. JESUS."

DEAR SIS, SABRINA,, November 28, 2010,

PLEASE, TODAY BEFORE I WENT TO CHURCH THE LORD GAVE ME HIS WORDS ENTITLED "THE GREAT STORM"

HE TOLD ME: "BEFORE I COME, THERE WILL BE A GREAT STORM. NOBODY KNOWS WHAT KIND OF STORM. I AM A MIGHTY GOD. I CAN DO ANYTHING. JUST TAKE THESE WORDS. LET THEM BE YOUR ADVISOR. LEAVE YOUR ADVISOR OR TAKE IT, OR ELSE YOU WILL FACE YOUR OWN STORM. I REPEAT: NO ONE KNOWS WHEN THE STORM IS COMING AND HOW IT WILL BE. I TELL YOU I WILL NOT SHOW ANYONE HOW IT WILL BE, FOR MY WORD IS PERMANENT."

I ASKED JESUS HOW AND HE TOLD ME: "THERE WILL BE STORM ALL OVER THE WORLD. I WILL NOT EXPLAIN HOW."

AFTERWARD HE TOLD ME: "MY CHILDREN ARE DISOBEDIENT TO MY WORD. THEY HAVE FORSAKEN ME. I WILL NOT TALK,

BUT JUST PUNISH. I JUST GIVE MY WORDS, WHETHER THEY TAKE IT OR NOT, I AM COMING SOON. TIME IS UP. I TELL YOU, TIME IS UP. TIME IS REALLY UP. YOU HEARD I WAS COMING LONG AGO, BUT NOW I SAY, TIME IS REALLY UP. I AM COMING SOON. I TELL YOU NO ONE CAN TELL WHEN. MY SONS AND DAUGHTERS, I AM COMING SOONER. TIME IS UP. I LOVE YOU, BUT YOU HAVE FORSAKEN ME. WHY? WHY? MY CHILDREN HAVE YOU DONE SO? TIME IS UP."

Acts 2:17: And it shall come to pass in the last days, saith God, I will pour out of MY Spirit upon all flesh: and your sons and your daughters shall prophesy, and your young men shall see visions, and your old men shall dream dreams.

PART 21

This message contains two letters from the LORD. The first was given to Susan about the lateness of the hour and the second letter contains a message specifically for the bride of CHRIST as told to Sabrina by JESUS. In the letter to Susan, the LORD tells the people and churches to stop building for a distant future that isn't coming and instead to get the people ready to be raptured. The letter to Sabrina is more for the Bride about what awaits her in heaven.

December 2nd, 2010.

This message contains two letters from the LORD. The first was given to Susan about the lateness of the hour and the second letter contains a message specifically for the bride of CHRIST as told to Sabrina by JESUS.

A letter dictated by the LORD JESUS CHRIST to Susan.

Letter 46. November 30, 2010.

Yes MY daughter I have words for you.

Susan these are MY final offerings. I am a patient GOD. I am a humble, patient GOD. I wait on MY children to come to ME. Many are coming, not enough, so many will be left behind. MY sorrow is great for them because of their stiff-necked behavior. I must leave them. This is truly not MY way. I do not want this for them. I have made MY offerings. I have put forth MY Words. I have focused MY attention on the people through MY SPIRIT, the HOLY SPIRIT. I have given everything to bring MY children to the end of themselves so that they may be prepared to return homeward with ME in their heavenly home. This is a home of safety and beauty, shear beauty.

Tell them I will not wait long. They underestimate ME and MY plans. The people act as if they know all about ME and MY plans, as if they know when I am coming and in their minds it is not now. Well they are wrong. They are misguided and they are blinded by their own thinking which is clouded by the world around them.

They think they know exactly what I will do and they all have it worked out in their minds, in their small minds they know what GOD will do. They believe they have all the time in the world and that the future looks bright. They see themselves going to and fro, here and there, off to make a profit in a far-away land and back again. This is evil. Doesn't MY book describe this as evil? They do not even know what the next minute of their life holds, yet they plan the future out in their minds, a future that GOD is not part of, a future that their minds have conceived. I am not consulted. These are the ramblings of men. No regard for the ALMIGHTY. This couldn't be more further from the truth. Even MY own people make their plans oblivious of ME.

I am coming sooner than most people think and their plans will be for naught because they were not watching for ME. They were not recognizing the lateness of the hour. MY Book has been clear. Many of MY faithful ones recognize the lateness of the hour and will be prepared. But if you are not watching and ready, MY coming will catch you off guard and your loss will be great.

Stop planning into the distant future. Your world is about to come to a screeching halt. You are either going to prepare yourself for ME and be MY humble repentant bride washed in MY precious blood or you will be caught off guard and left to live in a new world order: a world of no order that will be the world left to those who reject ME now. I cannot account for your poor decision making. If you are not watching as MY Word outlines, than you will miss it and your regret will be great.

I want MY people to stop building, stop planning, get MY Word out and read and study. See the lateness of the hour. Put down your building tools, pick up MY Book and go warn the people. Tell them now to get their house in order. Turn, repent, and humble yourself before ME. Surrender your all to ME. But stop the madness. Stop planning for a future that only exists in your mind. Your disregards for MY Words are a stench to ME. You go about your business as if I am not here, as if MY Words are lame, as if you are deaf and dumb. Wake up MY people. The hour is nigh. The signs are all around you. Turn off your wooden idols and pay attention to MY Words. Seek MY Face, MY Glorious Face. Prepare the way. Follow ME. Tell your neighbors, your friends, your family. Tell them YAHWEH is coming to retrieve HIS beautiful bride and I will take all who want to go: all who are considered worthy to go; all who have made themselves ready to go.

MY people who shepherd MY flocks and who ignore MY warnings and who are not preparing their flocks will be left and their loss will be great. What a sad day when whole churches are left because they did not heed MY Words of warning. Regret and sorrow will be immense. Once I come and collect MY bride the door will be shut. And if you remain the door will be shut to you and you must turn to face your enemy. He will be a raging bull. He will destroy all he comes in contact with. There will be few left standing after the enemy takes over. It will be many sad days: the saddest days of all.

Don't do this. Don't make this choice for yourself. I have so much better for you in heaven. I have a beautiful home for you, I long to bring you to. Come and let ME gather you under MY wings. Come under MY wing of safety. I will rescue you. I have planned this from the start to bring MY people out to see them to safety. MY plans do not change. I am the LORD GOD ALMIGHTY.

I do not falter in MY ways and MY plans. Men do not see it because they choose not to. Other words, other things entice people from GOD's Truth. MY Truth stands. MY Truth is more important than anyone or anything.

Be at peace with GOD. Make your peace with ME. I hold out MY hand. Reach for it. I am repeating MY Words for you. Surrender, repent, turn to ME NOW. Let ME save you. Please, let ME save you. I love you. I created you. Don't let an eternity of hell come between us. I don't want to lose you, but MY Word stands and if you choose against ME, MY Word cannot be altered for you. You will have to depart from MY presence and than woe to you. Please choose wisely. I cannot wait much longer. The dark world is rising. Let ME bring you into the light.

I, GOD, I, JESUS have spoken.

James 4:13-16. Go to now, ye that say, To day or to morrow we will go into such a city, and continue there a year, and buy and sell, and get gain: Whereas ye know not what shall be on the morrow. For what is your life? It is even a vapour, that appeareth for a little time, and then vanisheth away. For that ye ought to say, If the Lord will, we shall live, and do this, or that. But now ye rejoice in your boastings: all such rejoicing is evil.

A letter for the bride from her BRIDEGROOM, JESUS as told to Sabrina. December 1, 2010.

Write it down MY daughter.

I have given so many warnings by now and still people do not know the hour. They plan and act as if these Words of Mine are just a fable, a simple cheap fable, just another story. I tell you many will be left behind. Only MY pure bride who stands with ME in this last hour will be saved and enter MY Kingdom.

I see many planning now for the next year: their future, their career. What future is there if they don't consult ME first in their planning? The end of the year is coming for all of you, I know. And many have been waiting and longing for MY return, I know. MY precious bride is ready. Please hear these words MY bride: the time is near. Your longing to see ME will soon be satisfied. All is ready for you in heaven. You will be astonished.

Let ME tell you a bit about the beauty of heaven. Your mansions are pure gold. There is nothing in heaven that is not woven with MY purity. Everything breathes MY purity. So will you. Even the gardens speak. The animals speak. They all proclaim MY Glory. They are all filled with MY Glory. Nothing is holding back in heaven to speak MY

Glory. You will be astonished, MY bride. You will be amazed. There is no word on earth to describe the purity and holiness in heaven. It is all "beauty on beauty" and you will never be finished with your search for ME. You will think this is 'heaven' and then I will surprise you with something new. You will never stop being amazed by what you will find in heaven. It will be one big journey for eternity. It will never stop. The longing for ME will never stop. You will all be so satisfied. if you could only see a glimpse of it.

I am longing to take you there MY bride. MY longing is so strong. So please hold on and wait for ME. I AM coming. Rejoice yourself in this. In the meanwhile, keep showing your glory here on earth to those who don't know ME. Give them a taste of what is coming. Let them feel MY Love through you. This is why you are still here, MY bride, to shine from MY Glory around you. Don't be afraid and never be ashamed. I will present you before MY Father in heaven when it is all done for you here on earth. I long for you MY precious bride . Watch and be awake, for near is the day.

Your Bridegroom, JESUS.

1 Corinthians 2:9. But as it is written, Eye hath not seen, nor ear heard, neither have entered into the heart of man, the things which God hath prepared for them that love him.

PART 22

In this letter the LORD speaks on those embarrassed by HIM and how He was not embarrassed when He died for them up on the cross. The next part of the letter talks about the people being in a trance over their idols. And how their idols won't ultimately rescue them.

December 4th, 2010.

The letter below was told by the LORD JESUS to Susan.

We are putting out these letters, out of absolute obedience to the LORD, to whoever will receive them. HE dictates the letters to us and we see to it that they go out to warn the people. Many people wonder why there are so many letters and how many more will there be? We do not know. We are just being obedient to our LORD, well quite honestly because we simply love and adore HIM and want to be in HIS will for our lives. This is what HE has asked of us. As a parent, myself, Susan, I have to imagine that you would want to do everything in your power to warn your children of impending disaster and you would do anything to keep them from being separated from you for eternity. This is what I hear in the LORD's voice, LOVE and a longing to save HIS children before it is too late. I hear HIS great disappointment in the way the people have rejected HIM outright. This should make us all sad and give us a desire to share HIS heart with our lost friends and family all around us. We are not the only ones receiving the messages from the LORD that the hour is short and who also see the Bible coming to life before our very eyes. It is most encouraging to hear that people's lives are being changed by the LORD's amazing Words. Praise the LORD!

Letter 47. December 2, 2010. Letter dictated by LORD JESUS to Susan.

Yes Susan, I have these Words for you.

Yes the hour is waning. I am coming soon. The people would be amazed if they knew how close it all is. I, the LORD have spoken. MY servants take down MY Words.

Soon the world will know I am GOD. I am saddened by the world's disregard for ME, their CREATOR. It is incredible the way the people look the other way when something about ME is presented. This hurts ME to the core. They cannot imagine the pain I experience from their rejection. I took special care to create each person. I select their hair color and eye color. I know each person individually in detail. I know their characteristics. I know all about them. I know what makes them laugh or cry. I know their goals, dreams, sadness', and frustrations.

I am such a remote far off GOD to them. All other things take precedence in their lives. The people have put objects and each other before their CREATOR. They do not even care to get to know ME, to read MY Words. I am such a willing CREATOR to engage in the lives of MY creation.

I wanted fellowship and to get to know MY people. I want to share in their lives, their daily comings and goings, but they will have no part of ME. They put ME away, out of their minds. I am nothing more to them than a foul word. I do not exist.

Even those who call themselves Christians are distant to ME. I am not an object of their affections. They hope MY name will not come up in their conversations because I embarrass them. Do they know I was not too embarrassed to hang on a cross for them? I was in front of a maddening crowd and was disfigured before their taunting to save MY lost people. I was not embarrassed, I was determined to save them. This I did for MY own lost creation. I assumed the role of the creation and I bared MY soul to MY people. They did not even realize who I really was when they beat ME and crucified ME. I was their GOD and their CREATOR and yet I suffered immeasurably that day. It was humiliating and humbling, but MY Love is so great for MY lost people. I would have done it again, but MY sacrifice is complete and now you can come to ME and MY FATHER and be part of our Kingdom when I come to retrieve MY bride.

I have all these wonderful things for you in store. There is a world of beauty awaiting you, one that makes this world pale by comparison. Soon I must leave and take MY children. You know it is close if you are watching. You know. I cannot be swayed in this deciding hour. MY FATHER will give the word and I will come to collect the bride. She is ready also. I can keep her at arm's length no longer. I am ready for this hour.

The world has you under its spell. You think all is well. You think MY coming is far off in the future. Who told you this? It was not ME, your GOD. I have made MY signs clear for all to see and study. But most don't care to learn about such things. It is a child's story they think: I am greater than these old stories. I do not need this GOD. I have a life to lead. I can run MY own show. But MY bride is ready and she will see ME in all MY GLORY and we will rise up, join together, and leave. The world will never be the same again as the bride will have left the planet. This will be a sad, but true reality for those who are left.

I am waiting on you MY people. It will be soon. I cannot placate you any further. The event will take place and the world will know the truth in MY Book. Many will seek to read then. Read NOW! See what I have for you now. All the information is there. Why must you put yourself through this? MY Words are stronger than a two-edged blade and these Words will stand. These are MY Words. MY people heed them.

Susan, write it down.

The time is drawing near. I am providing MY people with an opportunity to think through very carefully the choice they need to make. I want them to have every opportunity to make the right choice. The world knows who the SAVIOR is but they run still to every made up religion that mankind can conjure up. They believe every strange fire that blows smoke their way. They are duped by every crazy thought that can be conceived by men and demons. It is repugnant to ME, a foul repugnant smell. I can't take it. MY people worship every strange god and belief under the sun. They worship all sorts of nonsense and throw themselves at all kinds of hair-brained beliefs. But they refuse to pick up the one true Book that has all the answers they could or would ever need. The creature follows the creature about looking for answers to their lives that I have outlined with great care if they would take time to study and read. MY Book would prevent the people from so much hardship and sadness. But now the hour is closing in and the time is running out and the people need to seek ME and seek answers to make their final escape. I offer one solution and one escape route and now is the deciding moment. Soon the time will be up and the people will all know that they have to face the worst and the answers then won't be easy. To be sure, they can pray and seek ME, but I will have to leave them to the decisions they made in this final hour. The fire is what the people will have to endure if they want to come to MY Kingdom. The enemy will be a tyrant and the people will be in shock when they discover the evil they are forced to face.

Their lives of luxury and worry-free living will fade away. All their wooden idols will stare back blankly and offer them no relief. If they plan to refuse the enemy's plan and mark, they will die. Hiding will not be an option. There will be no where to hide. Come to ME NOW and you can be saved from the coming madness. I had hoped you would find ME by now, but you grope in the dark and your loss will be devastating. I am GOD. I do not take pleasure in your rejection of ME. I have saved you with MY blood before and I plan to save you again by taking you out to safety. But you don't think you need to be saved. You can't see the lateness of the hour. The clock is winding down. I cannot replace the time you are losing.

Friends and dear ones, there are many in hell who would pay any amount of money or do anything to undo the disaster they are facing of eternal hell. Oh the regret, oh the loss, oh the shear sadness. Nothing can pull them out of unending torment. There is nothing that can be done. It is final. Their loss is final and eternal. What they wouldn't do to turn back the clock and rethink their choices. Many have regrets about their unforgiveness and anger toward others. Now is the time to think carefully how the very choices and decisions you make now will decide the outcomes of where you will be next. Will you be enjoying wedded bliss with ME in MY Glorious Kingdom or will you be facing the worst the enemy has to offer?

I know this seems highly unlikely to you, but if you read MY Book, you would come to see that I am telling you the truth. And one way or the other, your future is going to change: bright light or horrible darkness. Please warn your families to read and to believe these words. Soon your lack of choice will lead you to sad circumstances I know you do not want to be in.

I am coming swiftly to retrieve MY bride. You may come. Get right with ME NOW. I am waiting only for a short time more.

Your Messiah, JESUS.

Proverbs 29:1. He, that being often reproved hardeneth his neck, shall suddenly be destroyed, and that without remedy.

Jeremiah 5:3. O LORD, are not thine eyes upon the truth? thou hast stricken them, but they have not grieved; thou hast consumed them, but they have refused to receive correction: they have made their faces harder than a rock; they have refused to return.

PART 23

Now, I (Susan) want to share a testimony about the 2nd letter here below that I received from the LORD on Dec. 5. In this LETTER, our LORD JESUS makes mention of the "leaders over HIS flocks" and of the "false prophets of old" in the same section. After the LORD had finished reciting the letter to me, I asked HIM for a Scripture verse. He told me right away, "Jeremiah 23" which I immediately looked up and to MY amazement this section of Scripture is all about the very same topic HE mentions in the letter regarding the "leaders over HIS flocks" and the "false prophets of old." It was an amazing confirmation because although I knew this was mentioned in the Old Testament, I sure did not know the location was Jeremiah 23 as the LORD gave me. The first part talks about not making your own plans but following JESUS' plans. He warns the lukewarm and those who lead their flocks astray.

December 7th, 2010.

The first letter below was told by the LORD JESUS to Sabrina and the second letter likewise to Susan.

Now, I, Susan, want to share a testimony about the 2nd letter here below that I received from the LORD on Dec. 5. In this LETTER, our LORD JESUS makes mention of the "leaders over HIS flocks" and of the "false prophets of old" in the same section. After the LORD had finished reciting the letter to me, I asked HIM for a Scripture verse. He told me right away, "Jeremiah 23" which I immediately looked up and to MY amazement this section of Scripture is all about the very same topic HE mentions in the letter regarding the "leaders over HIS flocks" and the "false prophets of old." It was an amazing confirmation because although I knew this was mentioned in the Old Testament, I sure did not know the location was Jeremiah 23 as the LORD gave me. I hope this blesses you the way it does me. Also, please pray for us.

John 3:36, He that believeth on the Son hath everlasting life: and he that believeth not the Son shall not see life; but the wrath of God abideth on him.

Letter as told to Sabrina, of Belgium, by the LORD JESUS. December 6, 2010.

"MY dear children,

This is your GOD from heaven speaking. I have created you before the foundations of the world. I knew all about you. I have created you with every detail, so I would enjoy all of MY children. Still, many do not want to acknowledge there is a GOD in heaven. I am telling you, there is. HIS Name is JESUS, GOD THE FATHER, and the mighty HOLY SPIRIT. Do you have a relationship with HIM? Do you know HIM? Do you know THE FATHER, SON, and HOLY SPIRIT? If you don't, get to your bibles and get to know HIM. Now is the time.

Isn't it a pity, I have to beg MY children to come to their CREATOR? I have created you all in MY perfect will. Yet many of you turn ME down. I have come to the earth to live among you, yet most of MY people throw ME away like filth, like a stench. MY love for you will never diminish, no matter how much you reject ME.

However, time will not exist forever. And I tell you, time is running out. I have given you many, many warnings through many of MY children. They are faithful to ME and are giving you MY words. They are MY Mouth. Why do you not listen to them? This is not a funny game. This is not just another word. This is the very heartbeat of YOUR CREATOR calling out for His children. Please do not ignore ME.

I know your every heart, motive, and desire. I know all of your plans. Many do not fit with MY plans for you. Many are not walking according to MY perfect will in your life. You would rather make your own plans and then see where I can still fit in with all of that. This is not MY will and if you are walking out of MY will, you cannot enter

151

the beauty I have in store for you.

If you listen to MY Voice, you will walk in MY perfect will. If you search ME earnestly day after day, you will get to know MY will for your life. If you absorb yourself with MY Word, MY Holy Word, you will walk in wisdom and in MY joy for your life. Many disasters can be prevented if you would only do that.

Where is the passion? Where is the fire? Where are the praises? They don't reach MY Throne as they are hindered by worldly interventions. Don't let satan blind you any longer MY people! I came to defeat him, and I did forever. All you do is give him the room to enter and rule your lives. Stop doing that and prepare to meet your GOD in heaven. The time is over. It's almost past midnight. So prepare to meet your GOD.

I, JESUS have spoken.

Exodus 32:33. And the LORD said unto Moses, Whosoever hath sinned against me, him will I blot out of MY book.

Letter 48. December 5, 2010. Letter dictated by LORD JESUS to Susan.

Yes, Susan I can give you words. I, JESUS, am willing to give you words, copy down these words.

I am running out of patience for this world. I have tolerated enough. The time is coming to a close. And I am ready to bring MY bride home as she is ready to receive ME. I am her KING. She is MY bride. We are about to embark on our nuptial celebration. There will be much celebration as we come together, unite in love, and I bring her to MY Glorious Kingdom. MY bride will be so amazed by the beauty, pure beauty and electrified by the love she will feel.

I am ready to make MY descent to earth to retrieve the bride. All is ready. The Kingdom is prepared. The hour is at hand. The beauty is about to begin for the bride, unimaginable beauty. Life will never be the same for her. It will be a wonderful moment as I gaze into each of the eyes of MY lovely children and show them all MY heart toward them. They will never be the same.

Soon the earth will change. I have mixed emotions as I enter this phase with MY creation. I am most excited for MY bride and I am also most saddened for those who choose against ME as they will face the worst in their rejection of ME. Many will be lost for eternity because of their wrong choices. I cannot choose for them. They each must choose for themselves the outcome of their eternal existence.

So what will you choose? Come with ME to eternal beauty or stay to face horrible adversity? I have outlined MY plans now in several letters as given to MY chosen vessels. What do you plan to do with this information? Are you going to act on it and make your life changing decision to follow ME or are you going to reject MY offer because you either don't believe it or you don't want to believe it?

Deep down in your inner being you know I exist. You know there is a CREATOR. You know you came from a higher intelligence because MY creation is too complex to have just come out of nowhere. But to admit there is a GOD, a higher power, would put you in trouble. Then you have to own up to MY Book and MY Rules for your life and you just don't want to do that. It is easier to abolish the notion that there is a GOD than to admit I exist and seek after ME and MY Ways. I know how you dodge and avoid MY Ways because you don't want to follow after right living and get right with GOD, your MAKER.

Susan, write it down.

I have laid MY plans in front of you. Your hour of decision is here. What will you choose? What direction will you move in? Come with ME to eternal bliss or stay behind and go it alone? These are the choices, only two choices. There are no third alternatives. You think this is a dream. You think this is not reality. Life will go on like usual. You make your plans as always. This year will be different. The times are changing rapidly.

The world is entering into a new phase. The world is rejecting GOD on a grand scale. GOD will not exist in the plans man is making. GOD will not even enter into the thinking of mankind as they devise their evil plans. These plans include a world that runs exclusively by the creature with no regard for the HIGHER POWER, its CREATOR. The world will embark on a new phase that includes everything but GOD. GOD will be deleted off the pages, out of the writings, out of the books, out of the minds. GOD will not exist to this new world order. Men will make themselves god and the creature will exalt itself as god. This evil will happen and the worst evil will take hold of the minds of humans that have no rules, no thoughts of GOD. Men will run the world with no regard for their CREATOR. MY Rules, MY Book will be non-existent. MY ways will not enter their minds. It will be a world of complete disorder and evil. It will be a disgusting, foul stench and humans will dive to the depths of depravity as they unleash the evil world they embrace, a world without a HOLY GOD. This is something humans have never really witnessed before on the level it will about to be. It will be unimaginable and shocking. This is the world you are about to inherit if you stay behind.

MY heart breaks over MY lukewarm Christians who are slumbering in their lukewarm churches as the world drifts toward evil that will never be the same again. The lukewarm church is about to receive the outcome of its lackluster desire for its GOD. I cannot rescue those who have such little regard for ME and MY HOLY Ways as long as the lukewarm church plays GOD one day a week and then engages with the world all week. This is the way they have chosen. I do not want this half-hearted church. It can depart from ME into this crumbling world. I will not save it. I will turn MY back as it falls prey to MY enemy. This is the choice of the lukewarm to face the enemy and to consider the error of its lukewarm ways. The half-hearted church will struggle in the new phase of the world.

The world is changing into a dark evil place. Many changes are coming about. It is sad to ME that MY children, who call themselves Christians, cannot see the lateness of the hour and cannot recognize the evil that is already running amok. Do they believe that I, a HOLY GOD, can stand for this much longer? I gave out MY warnings in the Bible, MY Book and I clearly outlined the signs and events to watch for, but the people have met them with absolute disregard. They refuse to see it. They refuse to even look, watch, and study MY Word. What more can a HOLY GOD do?

I must follow through on MY Plan. MY Words stand the test of time. These plans were made before the foundation of the earth. I will see them through despite the disbelief of the creature, MY creation. I am GOD, MY Word stands.

Leaders of MY flocks who do not study, watch, and prepare MY people: woe to you. You have been warned. Stop preaching "good news" like the false prophets of old, as if everything is fine and the future looks bright. There is only one way to brightness and that is not through the door marked, "world." I am the WAY, the TRUTH, the LIFE. There is only one way to the FATHER and that is by ME, JESUS, SON of GOD who died a humbling death by hanging on a cross for your sins against a HOLY PURE GOD.

Surrender, Repent, Turn to ME NOW. Accept MY offer. The door is marked, "SAVIOR, JESUS, MESSIAH, LORD of LORDS, KING of KINGS," I am HE.

Humble yourself before ME and I will save you. All knees will bow before ME. Do it now and avoid eternal damnation, never-ending hell, and a world gone mad, a world rejecting its CREATOR.

I have spoken.

MY NAME IS JESUS.

The LORD also gave me these Scriptures to go with HIS letter:

Jeremiah 23:1-4.

1Woe be unto the pastors that destroy and scatter the sheep of MY pasture! saith the LORD.

2Therefore thus saith the LORD God of Israel against the pastors that feed MY people; Ye have scattered MY flock, and driven them away, and have not visited them: behold, I will visit upon you the evil of your doings, saith the LORD.

3And I will gather the remnant of MY flock out of all countries whither I have driven them, and will bring them again to their folds; and they shall be fruitful and increase.

4And I will set up shepherds over them which shall feed them: and they shall fear no more, nor be dismayed, neither shall they be lacking, saith the LORD.

Jeremiah 23:16-32.

16Thus saith the LORD of hosts, Hearken not unto the words of the prophets that prophesy unto you: they make you vain: they speak a vision of their own heart, and not out of the mouth of the LORD.

17They say still unto them that despise me, The LORD hath said, Ye shall have peace; and they say unto every one that walketh after the imagination of his own heart, No evil shall come upon you.

18For who hath stood in the counsel of the LORD, and hath perceived and heard his word? who hath marked his word, and heard it?

19Behold, a whirlwind of the LORD is gone forth in fury, even a grievous whirlwind: it shall fall grievously upon the head of the wicked.

20The anger of the LORD shall not return, until he have executed, and till he have performed the thoughts of his heart: in the latter days ye shall consider it perfectly.

21I have not sent these prophets, yet they ran: I have not spoken to them, yet they prophesied.

22But if they had stood in MY counsel, and had caused MY people to hear MY words, then they should have turned them from their evil way, and from the evil of their doings.

23Am I a God at hand, saith the LORD, and not a God afar off?

24Can any hide himself in secret places that I shall not see him? saith the LORD. Do not I fill heaven and earth? saith the LORD.

25I have heard what the prophets said, that prophesy lies in MY name, saying, I have dreamed, I have dreamed.

26How long shall this be in the heart of the prophets that prophesy lies? yea, they are prophets of the deceit of their own heart;

27Which think to cause MY people to forget MY name by their dreams which they tell every man to his neighbour, as their fathers have forgotten MY name for Baal.

28The prophet that hath a dream, let him tell a dream; and he that hath MY word, let him speak MY word faithfully. What is the chaff to the wheat? saith the LORD.

29Is not MY word like as a fire? saith the LORD; and like a hammer that breaketh the rock in pieces?

30Therefore, behold, I am against the prophets, saith the LORD, that steal MY words every one from his neighbour.

31Behold, I am against the prophets, saith the LORD, that use their tongues, and say, He saith.

32Behold, I am against them that prophesy false dreams, saith the LORD, and do tell them, and cause MY people to err by their lies, and by their lightness; yet I sent them not, nor commanded them: therefore they shall not profit this people at all, saith the LORD.

Acts 2:17. And it shall come to pass in the last days, saith God, I will pour out of MY Spirit upon all flesh: and your sons and your daughters shall prophesy, and your young men shall see visions, and your old men shall dream dreams:

We have included in this message our friend Buddy Baker's rapture dream and vision given to him just this past week, see past messages for Buddy Baker's recent previous dreams & visions:

Here's the rapture dream this week and the vision I had last Sunday.

I had an amazing Rapture dream this past week. Although it's been a while since I had a rapture dream, the Lord did say He would give me more visions and dreams before He comes and I give Him all the praise, honor, and glory. Halleijuah! Well here's what happened:

In MY dream, MY wife and I were at this huge cafeteria, like you would see in a shopping mall, and we were in a buffet line getting food and then we sat down at a table to eat. I looked to MY left to see a huge opening in a wall, like the wall was missing. Next, I see streaks of light in the sky, like you would see when you see a shooting star streaking across the sky, and how it vanishes within a second. It was day light outside and while I was seeing this, I would hear what sounded like a popping sound that reminded me of what you hear when popcorn is popping, but the popping sound was like a very soft pop. While I was seeing and hearing this, I knew somehow that it was the rapture!

So then, there were a lot of people with their children there and the people were wondering what was going on. At first they just kind of ignored it, but they became more curious and casually got up to look out the opening in the wall and they were wondering what they were seeing and hearing. MY wife got curious also and got up. Then all of a sudden, the children started to disappear, and the instant they vanished it would make that soft popping sound. Then the people and even MY wife started to panic. While all this was happening, I believe the Lord showed this to me to see what people that are left behind will experience the moment the rapture happens. Then I woke up, thanked, and praised the Lord Hallelujah, we're going home!!! Thank you Jesus!!!

I had a vision this past Sunday. I asked the Lord if I could see Heaven and when I closed MY eyes I was standing on Jesus' left side. He had His left arm over MY shoulder and He waved His right hand to show me countless beautiful white mansions. Many of the mansions I saw had round domes on them and they were so shiny and beautiful. I opened MY eyes and thanked the Lord.

Write to Buddy Baker at <u>Buddy_baker23@zoomtown.com</u>

PART 24

In this letter JESUS says He will not accept a partial commitment and to let go of future planning. He speaks of what He endured on the cross and how a lukewarm commitment will not be acceptable.

December 9th, 2010.

This time we are including an urgent letter dictated by JESUS to Susan.

This morning, I, Susan, was thinking about the concept of "two witnesses" in the Bible. Then amazingly, and randomly, during the same morning, I came across references in the Bible and also another book I was reading of how GOD often uses "two witnesses" to confirm a testimony or message. This is why I believe that Sabrina and I were brought together by the LORD for this work, to be "two witnesses" in putting out the LORD's letters. Here are some verses from the Bible that speak of the importance of using "two witnesses" for confirming a message or a testimony:

Deuteronomy 17:6: At the mouth of two witnesses, or three witnesses, shall he that is worthy of death be put to death; but at the mouth of one witness he shall not be put to death.

Deuteronomy 19:15: One witness shall not rise up against a man for any iniquity, or for any sin, in any sin that he sinneth: at the mouth of two witnesses, or at the mouth of three witnesses, shall the matter be established.

John 8:16-17: And yet if I judge, MY judgment is true: for I am not alone, but I and the Father that sent me. It is also written in your law, that the testimony of two men is true.

Luke 10:1-2: After this the Lord appointed seventy-two others and sent them two by two ahead of him to every town and place where he was about to go. He told them, "The harvest is plentiful, but the workers are few.

Letter 49. Dictated by JESUS to Susan on December 7, 2010.

Susan, I do have words for you. Yes, I am ready for you to take down words:

Susan this is your LORD speaking.

I have many words today. This will be a long letter. Susan, write it down.

MY coming is so soon, so near. MY people had better get ready. I know what you are thinking. MY people, I know about your disregard of ME. I know what your plans are. I know you do not plan to turn to ME. I could not be further from your mind right now. I know what you think. I am GOD. I know everything.

I am not to be misunderstood. I am telling you the truth. The world will be changing very soon. The world is taking a dramatic shift toward evil, toward the elimination of all that is good, all that I, GOD stand for. It is coming to a close, the former things of GOD: purity, humility, peace, love, kindness, longsuffering, hope. The world is shifting to the dark side.

MY people need to realize what is taking place behind the scenes. Since your lives go on as usual, it doesn't seem possible what I am telling you. But I am GOD. I know these things. I am warning you. The world is going dark. Evil is creeping in all around you. Why do you say you cannot see it? You can. You refuse to admit it is there. You are clinging to the past with everything you've got. But you can't keep living in the past. You must wake up. You are trying to plan your future with your past and MY children, the past is past.

The future is coming on this earth and it is dark, very dark. Soon the light will be pushed out and the darkness will consume everything. You can see it coming. But you are afraid to admit to it. You want to hold on to life as it has been, but it cannot be. If you continue to fool yourself with this thinking, you will miss the one escape that I, GOD am offering you. You are caught up in the world and the things of the world and I am telling you to take your eyes off the world and put them on ME, JESUS. If you don't make this vital correction, you will be lost. You will be left to face the worst. I am sending out MY warnings, MY pleas.

Please come to ME in this late hour. I do not know what more I can do. Evil man is moving on the earth to vanquish all remembrance of GOD. Yes, there are many coming to ME, but so many more are lost in sin. They are following after pagan religions and pagan doctrines. The world is following after all kinds of greed and idol worship. You can see it everywhere.

MY bride is ready. I am ready to retrieve her and move her to safety away from the darkness that is about burst on the scene. She will not be touched by the evil that is coming. I have spoken about this in MY Word yet you have taken MY Word and changed it to suit your own warped thinking. There are so many schools of thought floating around. Don't you know that MY thought is the only thought that counts? How can you know MY thought if you don't have MY HOLY SPIRIT? The only way you can possess MY SPIRIT is if you come to ME and surrender everything to ME. Humble yourself before ME, repent to ME of your sins, and give ME everything. I want it all. I want your life, your heart, your mind, and your spirit. I want your future. I want your worship. If you think I will settle for less, than you don't know ME.

I gave you everything on the cross, I bled, I died, and you will never know the abuse, horror, and terror I experienced. I was surrounded by callous hungry dogs who wanted to tear me from limb to limb. I endured such torment and heart break from MY own people and MY own creation. But I paid the price required by MY FATHER for the sin committed by the creation toward a HOLY GOD. This was the penalty and I, JESUS paid it in full.

Now if you come to ME in full surrender, MY SPIRIT will take control and MY words will have true meaning to you and you will read and understand the thoughts of GOD behind the Words with the guidance of the HOLY SPIRIT. I, JESUS will give you this knowledge, this renewing of the mind MY Book speaks of so you can understand fully the lateness of the hour and the darkness that is coming around you. The veil over your eyes will come off and you can step into the light, MY Light.

I can bring you to this understanding. But if you continue in your lukewarm worldly ways and your lackluster tepid commitment toward ME, you will not see what MY bride sees. You will not believe MY Book and MY warnings. You will continue in your ways as if nothing is wrong, nothing is going on. Everything is fine, as it has always been. And soon you will experience shock as the dark world will grip you and the release you desire will not come because you disregarded it when it was available.

I, JESUS want to save you. I want to love you, hold you, and keep you safe from the coming hour but you refuse to see it. Soon I will have to leave without you. You will leave ME no choice. I am coming for a pure bride, one who loves ME exclusively with all her heart. This is total surrender. Your heart toward ME cannot be pure without the help of the HOLY SPIRIT who comes to you through total surrender.

Your game playing relationship of on again, off again lukewarm will not get the job done. I will be forced to leave you behind. MY bride sees the lateness of the hour. She recognizes the times and the change in the air. The lukewarm have blinders on and refuse to see. It does not suit their own selfish purposes to see. They regard their plans for the future higher than GOD's truth. I have outlined the warnings in MY Book that are coming to pass now. You are idolizing your future plans. You put them in front of you and worship them before your GOD. Humble yourself before ME and repent of this evil.

You say: "I know what the future holds and it cannot be what the Bible is showing me. I want MY way. I will disregard what GOD has outlined in HIS Book and worship MY way, MY plans, MY beliefs." So be it. Have the god of your desire. Make your plans. Worship your ways or surrender to ME, JESUS. Repent, and turn, so that I can show you the lateness of the hour.

MY HOLY SPIRIT can show you this truth. Don't be caught off guard. Don't be blindsided by the enemy. Come to safety. Yes the path is narrow. But humble yourself before ME, JESUS, and I can get you to that road.

I will not leave or forsake you if you are completely mine. If your commitment to ME is partial, I cannot save you. You must release things to make this commitment. You must be willing to let go of your future planning. You must let go of your lust for this world and the things of this world. They are an enmity to ME. You cannot have both ME and the world. I am a jealous GOD. I do not change. I am jealous for MY creation.

You have seconds left on the clock to choose ME your SAVIOR. If you humble yourself before ME, I will save you. I will allow you to come into MY Kingdom and live with ME for eternity.

Search MY Words, MY Words and Truth. Soon truth will not exist and if you stay behind because you refuse to get right with ME, your CREATOR, you will long to find truth and there will be none. Do not let the creature and the enemy lead you astray in this final hour. Do not allow lies to comfort you. Hard decisions must be made, but the end result if you choose for ME will be eternal victory and you will win big. And the rewards in heaven will be great if you choose for ME NOW.

Surrender, repent, and turn to ME NOW.

Your LORD, SAVIOR, JESUS CHRIST is waiting only for a brief moment.

Make your decision quickly.

After receiving this letter from the LORD, the LORD also led me to read Psalm 22 where I discovered this verse I am including here:

Psalm 22:16. For dogs have compassed me: the assembly of the wicked have enclosed me: they pierced MY hands and MY feet.

1 Corinthians 2:10-14. But God hath revealed them unto us by his

Spirit: for the Spirit searcheth all things, yea, the deep things of God. For what man knoweth the things of a man, save the spirit of man which is in him? even so the things of God knoweth no man, but the Spirit of God. Now we have received, not the spirit of the world, but the spirit which is of God; that we might know the things that are freely given to us of God. Which things also we speak, not in the words which man's wisdom teacheth, but which the Holy Ghost teacheth; comparing spiritual things with spiritual. But the natural man receiveth not the things of the Spirit of God: for they are foolishness unto him: neither can he know them, because they are spiritually discerned.

PART 25

First a letter from the LORD JESUS told to and written down by Sabrina and a second letter dictated to Susan. In Sabrina's letter the LORD makes reference to the occult and I have included a link to an article about GOD's views on the occult. In this letter the LORD says that any plans apart from HIS are not His. He tells how only the humble can hear His voice and the message He wants people to hear. He is seeking only the pure-hearted.

December 11th, 2010.

First a letter from the LORD JESUS told to and written down by Sabrina and a second letter dictated to Susan. In Sabrina's letter the LORD makes reference to the occult and I have included a link to an article about GOD's views on the occult.

A good friend of ours said the LORD specifically gave her the verse "Jeremiah 1:17" to give to Sabrina and me and she had no idea of the content when HE gave it to her for our benefit. Here is the content:

Jeremiah 1:17. Thou therefore gird up thy loins, and arise, and speak unto them all that I command thee: be not dismayed at their faces, lest I confound thee before them.

I was amazed. The message was clear. I hear GOD saying to us just don't worry about what people think, OBEY ME. So then I ran across this Scripture in MY Bible study this week John 12:42-43 and another friend also sent me Isaiah 30:8-14 to consider.

John 12:42-43. Nevertheless among the chief rulers also many believed on him; but because of the Pharisees they did not confess him, lest they should be put out of the synagogue: For they loved the praise of men more than the praise of God.

Isaiah 30:8-14. Now go, write it before them in a table, and note it in a book, that it may be for the time to come for ever and ever: That this is a rebellious people, lying children, children that will not hear the law of the LORD: Which say to the seers, See not; and to the prophets, Prophesy not unto us right things, speak unto us smooth things, prophesy deceits: Get you out of the way, turn aside out of the path, cause the Holy One of Israel to cease from before us. Wherefore thus saith the Holy One of Israel, Because ye despise this word, and trust in oppression and perverseness, and stay thereon: Therefore this iniquity shall be to you as a breach ready to fall, swelling out in a high wall, whose breaking cometh suddenly at an instant. And he shall break it as the breaking of the potters' vessel that is broken in pieces; he shall not spare: so that there shall not be found in the bursting of it a sherd to take fire from the hearth, or to take water withal out of the pit.

If it were not Sabrina and myself putting out these WORDS of the LORD, it would surely be someone else of course and if not anyone else: Luke 19:40. And he answered and said unto them, I tell you that, if these should hold their peace, the stones would immediately cry out.

Letter dictated by JESUS our LORD to Sabrina December 11, 2010. Please be aware that Sabrina is Belgian and English is not her first language.

MY dear children, how I love you all. I have created you for MY Glory, to enjoy you and you ME, to have an everlasting intimate bond for eternity. I have prepared so much beauty for you, so many delicious things you will enjoy forever if you enter MY Kingdom.

The problem is many are still holding on to their lusts, to their own desires, to their own affairs. Is it really worth it to lose your eternity with ME for that? For what is only temporarily available to you will eventually lead into total destruction. This is the enemy's plan. He loves it when you enjoy the affairs of the world, the more, the better. And one day, he comes to strike you with death and there is nothing I can do for you any more. You will suffer greatly for eternity in that place they call hell. I am telling you, it is a real place, a real existence.

Oh MY dear people, why do I have to plead with you so much? Why are the affairs of this world so much more attractive to you than a Holy life with ME? A Holy Life with ME begins here on earth and lasts until eternity. There is no end.

Another thing I see is adultery. Many ways are being presented now to heaven. The sun comes up, she goes down again. The birds sing their song. The fields give their fruit in their time. You say, "This is nice, let's live happily and enjoy life while we still can." Don't you know that I, GOD hold everything together? Don't you know that the birds sing their morning song for ME? And don't you know that the sun, which I have created, will lose her gloss very soon? All the beauty of heaven will disappear together with MY bride. You will have nothing then to all your other ways to heaven, as there is only one way.

I AM THE WAY, THE TRUTH, AND THE LIFE, besides ME there is no GOD. I AM is a jealous GOD and I will, and do, not tolerate other gods to replace ME. Is that clear? Is that clear MY children? Do not follow after other gods that in fact, are no gods. They are a false illusion, created by satan to mislead many. So don't go into his game. Follow only ME. If you follow now your false gods, you will serve them for eternity. They will have you for eternity. They all exist in hell, where they are created.

Don't be fooled MY children, please don't be fooled. Lay aside and repent from every form of witchcraft, astrology, every way presented to heaven that has not the only name JESUS. There is only ONE way and that way is ME. I came to provide the way for you to heaven. I died for you the most horrible death and suffered for you in the most horrible pain. All, so you can be free.

But it's a choice. You must clothe yourself with this freedom and not with the other false ways that are only leading more to death. They did not die for you, did they? So why do you even consider their beliefs, their teachings, their masking temptations?

I am telling you people, if you want to be part of the bride, you must turn now. MY love is big, but there is an appointed time for everything, also for the homecoming of MY bride, called the rapture of MY bride.

Open your ears now and listen. Listen and obey MY Voice, as it is the only Voice that will lead you to eternal LIFE. Life in overflow, where the waters will run in perfect beauty, where the fruit will never exist to produce, where you will never thirst again. Behold Your Lord, Your King is coming for His bride! Be ready, as I am ready."

Hosea 4:14. I will not punish your daughters when they commit whoredom, nor your spouses when they commit adultery: for themselves are separated with whores, and they sacrifice with harlots: therefore the people that doth not understand shall fall.

Revelation 2:22. Behold, I will cast her into a bed, and them that commit adultery with her into great tribulation, except they repent of their deeds.

John 14:6. Jesus saith unto him, I am the way, the truth, and the life: no man cometh unto the Father, but by me.

2 Corinthians 5:3. If so be that being clothed we shall not be found naked.

Letter 51. Given by JESUS on December 9 & 10, 2010.

Write MY words down Susan, This is your LORD JESUS.

I am coming very soon. The people don't seem to grasp this truth. They have all sorts of things worked out in their minds, but the truth that I could be coming so soon.

Susan, write this down.

I am a patient GOD, very patient. I wait and wait on MY people. I see the works of men. I know the hearts of men. I see their comings and goings. I know all about men, their inner most thoughts. I know where men think they are going next. I know what they think they are doing, but I, GOD, I, JESUS will tell you that men do not really know what their plans will be in the next hour. They do not even know in the next minute. Their lives are up in the air. They think they have it all worked out, but their future is unknown to them. Only, I, GOD, know the future of all men, every man. I know what will happen next. I know what is going to happen.

Very soon I am coming to retrieve MY bride and the plans of humanity will change in a moment. The bride will be removed in a moment and she will come into a new existence with ME, her BRIDEGROOM. Those left on earth will face a different reality. All plans will come to a screeching halt.

Nothing planned before will come to pass. The world will be turned upside down. Still men make their plans and are confident in their planning. They say I am in their planning. I tell you the only thing I am telling MY people is to get ready and to be ready for MY move on the earth to rescue MY bride. All other plans are not MY plans. MY people need to stop worrying about their planning and seek MY Face, find out if they are prepared to be worthy to be taken out when I call MY people home. They need to do some inner searching and find out if their hearts are right toward ME. Repent, surrender, and come to ME in this late hour.

Have I not been clear in all MY Words? Have I not been clear in all MY Scripture? I have outlined the things to look for in these last days. MY Book is very clear. I know you MY people. I know it does not suit your purposes to face up to the change. Many will be left as a result of your lack of preparation. Your lamps are low on oil, HOLY SPIRIT oil to understand the times. Quickly get your lamp filled. Make your way to MY Heart. Be filled with MY SPIRIT. Surrender , repent, and turn to ME and I will give you the HOLY SPIRIT.

I want you to see the lateness of the hour. MY SPIRIT will reveal truth. Prepare to meet your MAKER. I am coming to take out a pure bride who knows the lateness of the hour. What is your plan? Do you plan to come before ME and listen to MY plans?

I will give you some words. Let us proceed. Susan, the hour is late. The people are not watching. The news is raging on and the headlines shout that we are in the end times. The people are just digging their heels down and refusing to listen. The time has come for the people to sit up and pay attention. I cannot make them regard MY Words if they refuse.

The truth can be heard if the people would humble themselves, open their eyes, block the voices around them, and focus on ME, JESUS. If only they would keep their eyes fixed on ME, if they would seek ME, seek MY Face, seek MY ways, seek MY Truth. Their love of this world has overtaken them. They love the approval of men. It is not popular to follow GOD. This is nothing new. Time and time again this repeats itself. The people are following after each other not what GOD says. If men don't approve then they won't listen to the leadings of GOD. This is as if men know what GOD knows. Men following after men, men leading each other astray, the world goes on as it always has, they say. These men will lead each other off a cliff.

The hour is at hand and soon the world will be run by men only. GOD will step away and allow men to rule and the result will be catastrophic, dismal, man's most desperate hour. I, GOD will let this happen. The world is coming to the end of itself soon. This world will not seem like the same world at all. Very soon, all will change. I am approaching earth and the people better make ready. The clock is ticking. Time is marching on. Very few are really taking heed. What do you need MY people to wake up to the truth? What is the message? Do you have something GOD should do to get your attention?

I have been clear in MY Word. I have been straight forward and up front about MY warnings. You know the time is here, but you listen to the words of the ill-informed and ill-advised around you and that seems like truth. The only truth is MY Truth and it is all outlined in MY Book. You don't need any other book to see MY Truth.

The times are here. I suggest you make time to read MY Book and approach ME with a humble heart and repentant spirit. Why is this so hard to see? The hour is at hand. I have chosen this as MY time to rescue MY people. MY people, follow ME and come to ME. I will receive you. You can find relief from the storm to come. The sand in the hourglass is shifting down. If you only knew how close the hour was, you would kneel down to ME to show you truth to save you from the coming evil.

I do not know what you need to respond to MY offer. Take this time to evaluate your position toward ME, your GOD. Where do you stand toward ME? Are you ready to be taken or are you unprepared? Wash your robe in MY Blood quickly. Receive MY Grace, MY Blessings, MY Love. Take MY Hand and run away with ME to the heavenlies, where we will all soon fly to. We will fly off together homeward to your new home in a beautiful Kingdom prepared for you to spend with ME in eternal bliss.

I only want the pure-hearted followers. What is this you ask? Those who have humbled themselves, surrendered fully, and come to know ME as their ALL in ALL, LORD and MASTER. I have no other kind of follower. This is who may enter MY Kingdom, the meek and tender-hearted toward ME and those around them. These qualities can only be found by surrendering to a HOLY GOD who will guide you by SPIRIT through the aid of the SON of GOD and blessed by the love of the FATHER, called out, chosen, sanctified, and made ready as a beautiful pure bride for her worthy GROOM, JESUS.

The wedding party is about to take place and the location of this event is ready to receive the guests. The hour is set and the time appointed. The guests are made ready. Be among them. Lay down your pride, sinful lusts, and worldly love affair. Set aside your personal desires and give them back to your MAKER. Let your CREATOR take back your life and make beauty of it, fill your being with light from above. Dance in the skies with the one true LOVE of your life, the GOD Who brought you into the world, Who will take you out to safety. Play among the stars with the ONE Who created you, who knows the details of your inner most being and loves everything about you, knows the number of hairs on your head.

Be at eternal peace with the ONE Who brought you into being. Return to your MAKER and live in bliss and indescribable beauty. Why miss this invitation? Now is the time to consider your choice. The enemy has made his offer: death. I make MINE: LIFE. Who will you choose? You alone can choose. I put life before you. These are MY pleas, MY warnings. Heed them. I adore you. Don't leave ME for eternity.

Love your BRIDEGROOM,

JESUS.

Matthew 24:42. Watch therefore: for ye know not what hour your Lord doth come.

Matthew 25. 1Then shall the kingdom of heaven be likened unto ten virgins, which took their lamps, and went forth to meet the bridegroom. 2And five of them were wise, and five were foolish. 3They that were foolish took their lamps, and took no oil with them: 4But the wise took oil in their vessels with their lamps. 5While the bridegroom tarried, they all slumbered and slept. 6And at midnight there was a cry made, Behold, the bridegroom cometh; go ye out to meet him. 7Then all those virgins arose, and trimmed their lamps. 8And the foolish said unto the wise, Give us of your oil; for our lamps are gone out. 9But the wise answered, saying, Not so; lest there be not enough for us and you: but go ye rather to them that sell, and buy for yourselves. 10And while they went to buy, the bridegroom came; and they that were ready went in with him to the marriage: and the door was shut. 11Afterward came also the other virgins, saying, Lord, Lord, open to us. 12But he answered and said, Verily I say unto you, I know you not. 13Watch therefore, for ye know neither the day nor the hour wherein the Son of man cometh.

PART 26

Along with the letter below from the LORD is a word from the LORD to our little 10-year-old friend Philipa, whose parents are missionaries for the LORD in Guinea. Philipa began to hear from the LORD and receive visions after she communicated with Sabrina about these letters from the LORD. She expressed enthusiasm for hearing from JESUS to Sabrina and then it was right after that she did in fact hear from the LORD. The letter below was told to Susan by JESUS along with a Scripture confirmation. The last three letters Susan copied down at the dictation of JESUS, HE followed each letter with a single Scripture verse. Each time the Scripture that was given, amazingly it coordinated with some of the content HE had dictated in each letter. This letter is the same. JESUS dictated these words in this letter to me (Susan): Be HOLY as I am HOLY. Then at the end of the letter, I asked if HE had a Scripture verse to include and HE simply said LEVITICUS 19 which starts out with this verse to MY amazement: 1 The LORD said to Moses, 2 "Speak to the entire assembly of Israel and say to them: "˜Be holy because I, the LORD your God, am holy.' (I have included the entire section of Leviticus 19 at the LORD's request below HIS letter.) So in this letter the LORD stresses that His people need to be holy. He also talks about being second to the world in the hearts of the people.

December 14th, 2010.

Along with the letter below from the LORD is a word from the LORD to our little 10-year-old friend Philipa, whose parents are missionaries for the LORD in Guinea. Philipa began to hear from the LORD and receive visions after she communicated with Sabrina about these letters from the LORD. She expressed enthusiasm for hearing from JESUS to Sabrina and then it was right after that she did in fact hear from the LORD.

The letter below was told to Susan by JESUS along with a Scripture confirmation. The last three letters Susan copied down at the dictation of JESUS, HE followed each letter with a single Scripture verse. Each time the Scripture that was given, amazingly it coordinated with some of the content HE had dictated in each letter. This letter is the same. JESUS dictated these words in this letter to me, Susan: Be HOLY as I am HOLY. Then at the end of the letter, I asked if HE had a Scripture verse to include and HE simply said LEVITICUS 19 which starts out with this verse to MY amazement: 1 The LORD said to Moses, 2 "Speak to the entire assembly of Israel and say to them: 'Be holy because I, the LORD your God, am holy.', I have included the entire section of Leviticus 19 at the LORD's request below HIS letter.

Letter 52. December 12, 2010, JESUS' Words given to Susan to send on to you.

Susan I will give you words. This is JESUS. I am going to give you words.

The world is slowly, but surely coming to a close. All is winding down. Soon the world will reach a point of no return. The climax of the end is approaching. I am about to make MY move. The world will be amazed at the events that are culminating.

I have been clear about MY plans. This world is reaching the end of what GOD will tolerate. It is funny that so many believe that I, GOD, will continue to tolerate so much evil. The people, even MY own people, have slid so far away from MY standards of Holiness that all seems fine and normal. It seems perfectly fine to them. They think that what they see going on in the world is no problem. The people come and go as they always have. The people have lost sight of what is fine and good and acceptable to a HOLY GOD. The world has degenerated to a point where even the Christians walk amongst the world and partake of the same activities and blend so easily.

There is no discerning the people of GOD with the heathens. MY people participate in the same vile activities and language and then come to ME one day a week and expect to find ME waiting for them with open arms as if all is well.

MY people engage in the same daily events and then turn to ME and assume I will accept their visit with ME as fruitful. Then they turn back to the world and play with its evil as if all is well. Well, all is not well. I will not call these MY people when I see them participating in worldly games and activities. Why do the people believe that MY standards as outlined in MY book have fallen so low to accommodate a world that does not respect or revere a HOLY GOD? Why do MY people regard MY Rules and Standards so little?

MY people who call themselves by MY Holy Name: why do you go into the world and look so much like the world? I cannot see any difference between you and the world. You walk among those of the world and you seek to be like them in every way. You want all the good things you think I, GOD offer, but you also want to play and engage with the ways and things of the world. It cannot be.

The things of GOD that you so desire are not to be given out to those who treat them commonly and with such disrespect. I am a HOLY GOD and MY Kingdom is pure and HOLY, untouched by evil. MY people need to walk away from the world. Come out. be separate. come away from the world. Stop engaging with the world: and believing that you will inherit the pure and HOLY things of GOD in the life to come. The road is narrow. Few find the narrow path. Those who find it have come away from the lusts and love interests of the world and all it offers. MY people, you cannot handle the unclean and see the impure and also walk the path to MY Kingdom with ME.

You must come to ME now in this late hour and surrender, repent, and turn to ME now so that I can wash your garments white and prepare you to come into MY beautiful, pure Kingdom. All is ready, but now is the deciding hour for ME to receive a pure, untouched, clean bride for MYSELF.

You cannot come with ME if you persist in following the wide path of the unclean things of the worldly. You may have your way with the world, yes, this is your choice, but I cannot bring you with ME into MY pure, white precious home I have prepared for MY sweet bride. I must leave you and the hour is closing in.

If you wait too long, I have no choice but to leave you behind. Sad though it may be, you will give ME no choice. I love you and I want you to come to ME, receive MY SPIRIT and be made ready. But you must receive ME as your LORD and Savior. Repent of your eagerness to be part of the evil world and turn back to MY HOLY Ways.

The things of this world are leading you astray. I cannot have you in MY World with MY people if you persist in following after your lusts for the unclean things of the world. I am a HOLY GOD and I ask no less than the same of MY children. Be HOLY as I am HOLY. Did I not say this in MY Book? I can bring you to this place MY dear children only if you surrender and repent of your sin to ME, JESUS your SAVIOR. Then I can give you MY SPIRIT, the HOLY SPIRIT. He will then show you the narrow path and lead you into righteousness. This is the only way to enter MY Kingdom, to leave this planet, and be saved in these last minutes when I come for MY bride.

You are down on the wire and now you must choose. Do you stay in the world and follow after the pattern of evil or will you turn to ME and take MY safe route out and come home to the Kingdom? I have many mansions for you. They are planned out with you in mind. I have spared nothing to bring you great pleasure in this life, life abundant, life eternal. What must I do to pull your grip off of a dying, fading, crumbling sin-ridden world to MY LIFE of unexpected, uncalculated intense beauty? Your mind cannot comprehend the incomprehensible. You cannot dream dreams that your mind cannot conceive of the world that is prepared for those who love ME.

Now you can stay and choose for the world, but it will be a sad ending for you. You will face the worst. The world is changing rapidly. The enemy will consume the world and his ways will reign supreme. You will either, fold into his ways, and ultimately separate yourself from ME your LORD and MAKER for eternity OR you will have to reject the system of the enemy and then you will be at his mercy. It will not be an easy choice for MY lukewarm church on the earth. The enemy is savage and he will make it difficult to choose against him. Death will be the only escape from his grip. Death would be an easy escape, but he won't make it so easy for the ones who choose for ME after the bride is removed from the earth. I, GOD am trying to outline the options you have in this closing hour. I want you to know the consequences of your choices.

Soon, very soon this world will go dark. You won't see it because you refuse to look, but the truth remains: I am coming to get MY bride. She will be safe, but the world will come undone. I bring truth. This truth is hard to find anywhere else. The enemy does not want you to have the truth. Even those who call themselves Christians are afraid to tell or believe the truth.

I am trying to warn you in this late hour. MY Book has been clear that a day would come for ME to remove MY bride. I have stated the things to look for when the hour approached. I have been exceeding upfront that you should watch, be vigilant, and not slumbering when the time was close for those events to take place. Yet most are sleeping, most are occupied, most are even angry at the thought that MY return could be so near. Why are you so angry? Why are you so sad at the idea that MY coming has now arrived? Could it be that MY coming is spoiling your plans? Could it be that you are so busy lusting after the world that MY coming is wrecking your plans to engage with the world?

Don't you know that this world is an enmity to ME? Then why are you so displeased when you hear MY coming is now? You evil generation, you disgust ME. I am a jealous GOD. Choose for ME or choose against ME, but I won't have you as MINE as long as you have a roving eye that lusts for the evil of this world. I offer you a Kingdom that is so superior to this evil world and yet you must have this world as if it reigns supreme in your heart.

You have put ME way down on your list, way toward the bottom. I, GOD, your MAKER, your CREATOR, comes down below your children, your work, your hobbies. I am second fiddle in a long list of worldly pursuits. You make time with everything but ME. You have many gods before ME. You worship your church programs and your riches. Do you not believe I had anything to do with the things in your life that you put before ME? Do you not know that I, GOD have given you these blessings, yet you have no regard for ME, for if you did I would not be so distant from your heart. You need eye salve only I can give. You need ME.

I ask you again plainly: will you surrender, repent, and turn to ME? You have precious little time left. If you accept MY offer, I will keep you from the coming hour of destruction. But soon the offer will not be there any more. Waste no time, the hour is at hand. I am being generous even now with MY warnings to the earth. MY compassion is great and MY longsuffering and tolerance for this evil generation has been great, but there is a limit to MY patience as I am about to make MY pick up of the bride and delivery to her new home above.

I am waiting briefly. Stop stalling. Make a choice. The hour is winding down.

Please choose for ME. You will never be disappointed. MY Love is great.

I am JESUS. the one true WAY to life everlasting.

Leviticus 19:

Various Laws.

1 The LORD said to Moses, 2 "Speak to the entire assembly of Israel and say to them: 'Be holy because I, the LORD your God, am holy.'

3 "'Each of you must respect your mother and father, and you must observe MY Sabbaths. I am the LORD your God.

4 "'Do not turn to idols or make metal gods for yourselves. I am the

LORD your God.

5 "'When you sacrifice a fellowship offering to the LORD, sacrifice it in such a way that it will be accepted on your behalf. 6 It shall be eaten on the day you sacrifice it or on the next day; anything left over until the third day must be burned up. 7 If any of it is eaten on the third day, it is impure and will not be accepted. 8 Whoever eats it will be held responsible because they have desecrated what is holy to the LORD; they must be cut off from their people.

9 "'When you reap the harvest of your land, do not reap to the very edges of your field or gather the gleanings of your harvest. 10 Do not go over your vineyard a second time or pick up the grapes that have fallen. Leave them for the poor and the foreigner. I am the LORD your God.

11 "'Do not steal.

"'Do not lie.

"'Do not deceive one another.

12 "'Do not swear falsely by MY name and so profane the name of your God. I am the LORD.

13 "'Do not defraud or rob your neighbor.

"'Do not hold back the wages of a hired worker overnight.

14 "'Do not curse the deaf or put a stumbling block in front of the blind, but fear your God. I am the LORD.

15 "'Do not pervert justice; do not show partiality to the poor or favoritism to the great, but judge your neighbor fairly.

16 "'Do not go about spreading slander among your people.

"'Do not do anything that endangers your neighbor's life. I am the LORD.

17 "'Do not hate a fellow Israelite in your heart. Rebuke your

neighbor frankly so you will not share in their guilt.

18 "'Do not seek revenge or bear a grudge against anyone among your people, but love your neighbor as yourself. I am the LORD.

19 "'Keep MY decrees.

"'Do not mate different kinds of animals.

"'Do not plant your field with two kinds of seed.

"'Do not wear clothing woven of two kinds of material.

20 "'If a man sleeps with a female slave who is promised to another man but who has not been ransomed or given her freedom, there must be due punishment.[a] Yet they are not to be put to death, because she had not been freed. 21 The man, however, must bring a ram to the entrance to the tent of meeting for a guilt offering to the LORD. 22 With the ram of the guilt offering the priest is to make atonement for him before the LORD for the sin he has committed, and his sin will be forgiven.

23 "'When you enter the land and plant any kind of fruit tree, regard its fruit as forbidden.[b] For three years you are to consider it forbidden[c]; it must not be eaten. 24 In the fourth year all its fruit will be holy, an offering of praise to the LORD. 25 But in the fifth year you may eat its fruit. In this way your harvest will be increased. I am the LORD your God.

26 "'Do not eat any meat with the blood still in it.

"'Do not practice divination or seek omens.

27 "'Do not cut the hair at the sides of your head or clip off the edges of your beard.

28 "'Do not cut your bodies for the dead or put tattoo marks on yourselves. I am the LORD.

29 "'Do not degrade your daughter by making her a prostitute, or the land will turn to prostitution and be filled with wickedness.

30 "'Observe MY Sabbaths and have reverence for MY sanctuary. I am the LORD.

31 "'Do not turn to mediums or seek out spiritists, for you will be defiled by them. I am the LORD your God.

32 "'Stand up in the presence of the aged, show respect for the elderly and revere your God. I am the LORD.

33 "'When a foreigner resides among you in your land, do not mistreat them. 34 The foreigner residing among you must be treated as your native-born. Love them as yourself, for you were foreigners in Egypt. I am the LORD your God.

35 "'Do not use dishonest standards when measuring length, weight or quantity. 36 Use honest scales and honest weights, an honest ephah[d] and an honest hin.[e] I am the LORD your God, who brought you out of Egypt.

37 "'Keep all MY decrees and all MY laws and follow them. I am the LORD.'"

FRESH REVELATIONS TO A 10-YEAR-OLD GIRL FROM THE LORD:

A few days ago, November 19, a young girl contacted me, Sabrina, through email. Her name is Philipa and she is 10-years-old and though she is still young, she is very smart and loves JESUS so much. Philipa said she was open for any advice/words. I wrote her back that same day and to MY surprise the Lord had a beautiful word for her. I will share the last sentence: "I long to hear your voice MY beautiful child, so come, come! I will surprise you with MY presence and you will hear MY Voice. I love you deeply, Your Father and friend forever, Jesus." After this word from the LORD Philipa began to have visions and hear from the LORD herself. Philipa's parents are missionaries for the LORD in Guinea.

Philipa, our 10-year-old friend from Guinea, received 2 more visions from the Lord, Dec. 12, 2010.

Vision 1:

ON THE 10th OF DECEMBER 2010, WHILST PRAYING WITH MY PARENTS, THE LORD SHOWED ME ANOTHER CLOCK REVEALING ONE SECOND MORE FOR JESUS TO COME.

THE SECOND WAS ABOUT TO MOVE, AND EVEN PEOPLE LIKE MOSES, NOAH, etc. WERE WAITING AT WHERE THE CLOCK WAS.

THEN, AFTER THAT I SAW A MAN OPENING THE GATE FOR THE BRIDE.

THEN LATER ON, I SAW MYSELF IN THE MIDST OF SO MANY WORSHIPING PEOPLE, THEN I JUMPED INTO THEM.

PHILIPA.

Vision 2, Philipa sent Sabrina this on December 12:

Please THE LORD gave me another message and please here they go:

"Do not waste this good time MY children, I am coming very, very soon it is almost 12:00, Midnight. I am giving you very short warnings now! that I shall not give out again for I am coming. I am almost there MY foot is about to move for MY bride. These are MY last warnings.

YOUR BRIDEGROOM,

SAVIOUR,

YESHUA.

More information about Philipa:

November 21 I, Sabrina, received this mail from Philipa, translated to English:

LAST NIGHT, I HEARD THE LORD TELLING ME THAT HE

WOULD USE ME FOR HIS WORK. SO WHEN I WENT TO CHURCH GOD SHOWED ME A CLOCK AND TOLD ME THAT IT IS LEFT WITH ONE MINUTE MORE FOR HIM TO COME. AND HE SAID THAT MY CHILDREN REPENT, REPENT. AND HE SAID THAT DARKNESS WOULD SOON TAKE OVER THE WORLD AND THAT HE CAN NOT BARE THE SIN OF MAN ANY LONGER. SO I SHOULD SPREAD AND TELL THIS WORD TO PEOPLE. AND THIS AFTERNOON, HE TOLD ME, "MY CHILDREN CHANGE. FOR ONE MINUTE IS NOT ANY LONG TIME. HELL IS BEYOND ANY HUMAN KNOWLEDGE. HUMAN KNOWLEDGE IS NOT ANY GOOD KNOWLEDGE. HELL IS NOT A GOOD PLACE. MY CHILDREN CHANGE, CHANGE! MY CHILDREN WHY HAVE FORSAKEN ME? GET OUT OF THE DARKNESS."

I, Sabrina, wrote Philipa back that same day and the Lord had another personal word for her to encourage her to share these words with her parents, church, friends, and family. I had communicated with her mother before and she shared that they are preparing for the rapture and are missionaries in the French-speaking country Guinea with 92% muslims.

Philipa has asked me to pray for her, so that God will use her for His work as He has started. May I ask all of you to pray for this little girl and her family, who is so open and willing for the Lord and truly an example for me?

November 22: Another vision given to Philipa:

I HAD ANOTHER VISION ALSO TODAY. I SAW A MAN ON A HILL HOLDING A STAFF WITH HIS HANDS AND THE STAFF UP WHILE THE PEOPLE WERE DOWN THE HILL. AND THE MAN WAS SAYING, "REPENT FOR THE KINGDOM OF GOD IS NEAR." BUT, THE PEOPLE STARTED LAUGHING. –PHILIPA

New messages received by Philipa from the LORD JESUS:

HI SIS, SABRINA, November 25, 2010.

PLEASE, TODAY AS I WAS AT SCHOOL THE LORD TOLD ME:

"I AM COMING SOON MY CHILDREN. LEAVE ME AND YOU WILL FACE ETERNAL DEATH FOR LIFE. I TELL YOU HELL IS GREATER THAN ANY HUMAN KNOWLEDGE. I TELL YOU, I WOULD LOVE AND CHERISH THOSE WHO LOVE ME. I AM EVERY THING THAT MAN WOULD EVER LIKE. HELL IS ETERNAL. LEAVE ME AND I WILL PUNISH YOU SEVERLY. YOU DO NOT KNOW WHAT IT IS LIKE AND WOULD BE LIKE. I KNOW THE SIN OF MAN AND I SAY: COME TO ME LIKE THAT! COME! COME! AND YOU WOUL FIND ETERNAL PEACE. THIS IS MY WARNING. COME! COME! I LOVE YOU SO DEEPLY. I AM EVER READY TO LISTEN TO YOU. NO ONE SHALL FIND ETERNAL PEACE WITHOUT ME. REPENT FOR THE KINGDOM OF GOD IS NEAR. I LOVE YOU. DO NOT BLAME ME WHEN I PUNISH YOU. THESE ARE MY WORDS. JESUS."

DEAR SIS, SABRINA, November 26, 2010.

PLEASE, I ALWAYS GO WITH MY BOOK, JOURNAL, EVERYWHERE SO IMMEDIATELY, WHEN I HEAR GOD'S VOVICE, I WOULD WRITE IT. PLEASE, TODAY I HEARD THE LORD TELLING ME:

"MY CHILDREN THE TIME IS UP. COME! COME! DO NOT LISTEN TO FALSE TEACHINGS, FOR TIME IS UP! I AM COMING SOON. NO ONE CAN TELL WHEN. FOR THIS TIME, I AM COMING SOON. TAKE MY WORD OR LEAVE IT, FOR MY WORD IS PERMANENT. MY BRIDE, CONTINUE WITH YOUR WORK, BUT IT WILL NOT BE FOR LONG BEFORE I COME. JUST WORSHIP ME FOR IT IS JUST A LITTLE TIME LEFT. WAIT JUST FOR A LITTLE TIME MORE, FOR I AM COMING SOON!

TAKE MY WORD OR LEAVE IT, FOR MY BRIDE IS READY AND THOSE WHO WILL LEAVE ME, WILL FACE ETERNAL DEATH, ETERNAL TORTURE.

THESE ARE MY WORDS TAKE IT OR LEAVE IT. THERE ARE TWO OPTIONS: GO TO HEAVEN OR GO TO HELL. IF YOU DISRESPECT ME AND GO TO HELL, YOU WILL HAVE NO

OTHER OPTION THAN TO FACE TORTURE.

WHY HAVE YOU TAKEN THE PATH OF STAIN MY CHILDREN? WHY? WHY? WHY? WHY HAVE YOU FORSAKEN ME? ISN'T MY WORD ENOUGH FOR YOU? HOW MANY TIMES SHOULD I WARN YOU! GO ON AND MAKE THE devil your new god. IF MY WORD IS NOT ENOUGH FOR YOU, CONTINUE TO DEPART FROM MY WORD. THEN YOU WILL HAVE NO OTHER OPTION THAN TO PERISH FOR GOOD, FOR ETERNITY. FORGET ME, AND DIE AND SUFFER. THESE ARE MY WORDS. JESUS."

DEAR SIS, SABRINA, November 28, 2010.

PLEASE, TODAY BEFORE I WENT TO CHURCH THE LORD GAVE ME HIS WORDS ENTITLED "THE GREAT STORM"

HE TOLD ME: "BEFORE I COME, THERE WILL BE A GREAT STORM. NOBODY KNOWS WHAT KIND OF STORM. I AM A MIGHTY GOD. I CAN DO ANYTHING. JUST TAKE THESE WORDS. LET THEM BE YOUR ADVISOR. LEAVE YOUR ADVISOR OR TAKE IT, OR ELSE YOU WILL FACE YOUR OWN STORM. I REPEAT: NO ONE KNOWS WHEN THE STORM IS COMING AND HOW IT WILL BE. I TELL YOU I WILL NOT SHOW ANYONE HOW IT WILL BE, FOR MY WORD IS PERMANENT."

I ASKED JESUS HOW AND HE TOLD ME: "THERE WILL BE STORM ALL OVER THE WORLD. I WILL NOT EXPLAIN HOW."

AFTERWARD HE TOLD ME: "MY CHILDREN ARE DISOBEDIENT TO MY WORD. THEY HAVE FORSAKEN ME. I WILL NOT TALK, BUT JUST PUNISH. I JUST GIVE MY WORDS, WHETHER THEY TAKE IT OR NOT, I AM COMING SOON. TIME IS UP. I TELL YOU, TIME IS UP. TIME IS REALLY UP. YOU HEARD I WAS COMING LONG AGO, BUT NOW I SAY, TIME IS REALLY UP. I AM COMING SOON. I TELL YOU NO ONE CAN TELL WHEN. MY SONS AND DAUGHTERS, I AM COMING SOONER. TIME IS UP. I LOVE YOU, BUT YOU HAVE FORSAKEN ME. WHY? WHY? MY CHILDREN HAVE YOU DONE SO? TIME IS UP."

Acts 2:17: And it shall come to pass in the last days, saith God, I will pour out of MY Spirit upon all flesh: and your sons and your daughters shall prophesy, and your young men shall see visions, and your old men shall dream dreams.

PART 27

I (Susan) would like to share an amazing story about this letter I received below from JESUS. The same morning I received this letter below, I woke in the early morning three different times and I heard very clearly the name "HEZEKIAH." Well honestly, I knew I had heard this name before and that it was probably from the Bible, but I couldn't place who it was or where I had heard of it. Well later that morning, I had been praying and I asked the LORD for a Scripture to look up and HE simply said, "MICAH." I had not yet looked up the name HEZEKIAH in the Bible yet that day, but instead I turned to the book of Micah the LORD suggested and I was amazed to discover that "Hezekiah" was actually the King reigning during the era that Micah was a prophet. Well that same morning, the LORD had dictated this letter below to me, I was stunned to discover that Micah addressed the rise of religious infidelity and idol worship as this letter also addresses and this confirmation suggests that the people still turn their backs to GOD now, just like they did during Micah's era. In this letter JESUS addresses the doubts of the people about the end coming. He speaks on hell, and the church doing things only for their benefit and not GOD's in worship.

December 17th, 2010.

The series of messages were dictated to us, and other people as well. First is a letter dictated to Sabrina by JESUS. Below it is a letter from the LORD as told to Susan for you.

I, Susan, would like to share an amazing story about this letter I received below from JESUS. The same morning I received this letter below, I woke in the early morning three different times and I heard very clearly the name "HEZEKIAH." Well honestly, I knew I had heard this name before and that it was probably from the Bible, but I couldn't place who it was or where I had heard of it. Well later that morning, I had been praying and I asked the LORD for a Scripture to look up and HE simply said, "MICAH." I had not looked up the name HEZEKIAH in the Bible yet that day, but instead I turned to the book of Micah the LORD suggested and I was amazed to discover that "Hezekiah" was actually the King reigning during the era that Micah was a prophet. Well that same morning, the LORD had dictated this letter below to me, I was stunned to discover that Micah addressed the rise of religious infidelity and idol worship as this letter also addresses and this confirmation suggests that the people still turn their backs to GOD now, just like they did during Micah's era. Here is more info about Micah and King Hezekiah:

http://www.lovethelord.com/books/micah/01.html

How many more letters will we put out you may wonder? Well we do not know. All we know is that as long as the LORD continues to give us these letters to send out, we will do it. We've gotten lots of mail because of these letters. Thank you for all your wonderful notes and prayers. I think I speak for Sabrina also when I say this: if I thought we could see one person saved by the LORD JESUS who would avoid an eternity in hell, it would all be worth it to us, whatever people think or say. If we saw just one person in heaven who would have gone to hell saved, it's worth it. Are you that one person? We hope so.

Letter Dictated to Sabrina of Belgium by JESUS, December 16, 2010.

"I want MY people to come to ME before MY Throne of Grace. Take the time to come to ME and to seek ME in your prayer times. If you have to do it in a rush, it means nothing to ME. Get up in time and seek MY Face.

This age is about to end, the age of grace. If you seek ME now, you can find favor with your GOD in heaven who has ears to listen and eyes to see. Don't give ME your daily rushed prayers. Give ME your best quality prayers, prayers that involve your complete heart, soul, spirit.

Give ME all. I want it all. Surrender all to your Holy GOD in heaven. Being too busy is just an excuse. I created you to worship ME. This should be the most important task of your day. I can only have your heart if you give it to ME. Seek ME now in the private hours, come to ME now to dine with ME. Create a deep intimacy with Your GOD in heaven who hears the cries of His people on earth.

Come to ME now, now is the time. There has never been such a time as this. A time where I am collecting MY bride into the secret chambers of MY love and safety. Come MY bride, the time has come. Lay aside your worldly affairs and seek ME, only ME. The time has come to take you up in heaven, where you will dine with ME forever.

Make sure your household is in order and ready to meet ME in the air. Warn the ones close to you, so they will know what has happened. Still many are coming to ME in this late hour, for the hour is very late. I am telling you, the clock does not stand still, and it is moving to midnight. When it strikes midnight, you will be with ME in heaven. So warn your loved ones and your neighbours.

I am running out of time, but I will not be too late. I, GOD am always in time, so make sure you will be too. MY heart is running over with patience to this dying world, this sick world full of awful sin that hurts MY eyes and MY BEING. I died for this, MY bride, still many do not want to accept MY offer. The time is about to end. The time of grace has been long.

The people will know what has happened, but they will try to deny it. Much grief is coming to this dying world and if I, GOD would not stop it, nobody would be left. So still, MY grace will come in action, but woe to the men and woman who die in their sins during this time. Woe to the men and woman who refuse to listen to MY Words now and keep their blinders on.

MY heart goes out to MY bride, she is so beautiful. She is MY special reward. She and I will have a unique bond in heaven for eternity. She will have a special place with ME in heaven. She will have a special access to ME in heaven. Her reward will be ME, JESUS. Are you ready MY precious bride? I AM is ready. Be ready! Your GOD is coming! The angels sing Alleluia, Alleluia, Alleluia, for the KING has come to collect His bride! This says, the I AM and the AMEN!"

Hebrews 4:16 . Let us therefore come boldly unto the throne of grace, that we may obtain mercy, and find grace to help in time of need.

Song of Solomon 1:4 . Draw me, we will run after thee: the King hath brought me into his chambers: we will be glad and rejoice in thee, we will remember thy love more than wine: the upright love thee.

Matthew 25:6. And, at midnight there was a cry made, Behold, the Bridegroom cometh; go ye out to meet him.

Revelation 19:6. And I heard as it were the voice of a great multitude, and as the voice of many waters, and as the voice of mighty thunderings, saying, Alleluia: for the Lord God omnipotent reigneth.

Letter 54. December 15, 2010. A letter from JESUS as told to Susan for you.

Yes, Susan I have words. Susan This is your LORD & MAKER JESUS.

These words are for all who will hear them. I have many words.

I, JESUS, am ready to speak to the people. MY people who call yourselves by MY Name, MY Holy Name, I have given you this gift of MY Love. I have given you MYSELF. Now, MY people who I love and call MY own, we are entering into a new phase, a new hour. Soon I will bring MY bride home. Soon she will come home. I will carry her across the threshold and show her, her new home of beauty and love everlasting. This is MY promise to MY people I am about to fulfill that promise.

I, GOD, I JESUS am true to MY Word. When I say I will do something, I do it. Even MY people doubt this about ME. They have doubts. I know your doubts. You see the signs as defined in MY Book, yet you do not believe. You think the hour is much later, perhaps for future generations even. I tell you the truth, this generation will not withstand the evil coming on the earth and there will not be forthcoming future generations that would survive the ever-growing evil that encompasses the earth. I am a HOLY GOD and I cannot continue to look upon such a grand-scale of evil that has permeated the earth much longer. I must rescue MY bride and release MY grip of the earth, depart, and allow the evil to abound apart from MY protection. This is what is coming on the earth shortly.

MY people you have lost sight of what a HOLY GOD stands for and what I represent. You have become jaded by your engaging in the dealings of evil men. You cannot see the evil around you. You have become so accustom to the evil abounding that you cannot discern for yourself anymore. You watch what heathens see and you fold into the same activities and it looks all so normal to you. You have forgotten about your GOD's Holiness and Holy Ways. You are filthy and covered in filth. What must I do, for you to see that your robes are dirtied from your love and lust of the world?

MY people, I cannot bring you into safe passage because you choose against ME. You ask, "How is that?" I know your hearts. I see within. I know your inner most thoughts. I know how you lust and engage with the world following closely after its heels. When you chase after the world and the things of the world you also run from ME. You have run so far from ME, I will lose you if you don't turn and run back into MY arms, surrender, repent, and turn back to ME.

The enemy is clever. He awaits you at every turn to entrap you, to entice you, to ensnare you. Your foothold is loosening and soon you will fall and there will be no recovery. He wants this desperately and so many have fallen into his cleverly sprung trap and they will never return to ME. I will never see them again. Hell is eternal.

Come to your senses, MY people. See the sin you are engaging in, see the lukewarm danger you are captivated into. See that you are standing at the brink of eternity about to plunge over the edge. Please turn back. Come to ME in this late hour. Wake and see what is forming around you.

I want to speak of hell. It is a never-ending nightmare of oppression. I cannot be near you in hell. You will be without a Holy, Just GOD in this place of terror and torment. You will long to cry out for love, justice, beauty, hope, and it will never appear to you again.

So many go to hell from this life because they choose to fill the hours in this life with the things that distract them from seeking a relationship with ME and to understand and read MY Book. This time you waste with these worldly pursuits you are drawn to will lead you to hell. I am sorry to tell you this, but I must tell you the truth.

Most people will go to hell because I require a full commitment of complete and total surrender and so very few do this. Their daily hours are consumed with worldly pursuits and there is no time left for their CREATOR. This lackluster commitment and lukewarmness will lead you to hell. This eternal choice is unending and there can be no turning back. The separation from GOD is final along with love, tenderness, kindness, beauty. These things will never be experienced again.

MY Words and MY Book are clear on these matters. You choose not to see, but your refusal to look is not an excuse when you face MY judgment. Mark MY Word, you will face ME and if you make no choice or choose against ME, we will meet face to face and you will know the sorrow of your choices. It will then be the beginning as you make your first step to eternal hell, a very long existence apart from a HOLY GOD of peace and salvation, love and beauty.

You do not like these words but the truth must be told. Mankind now has a moment of decision. Come with ME, your LORD JESUS to safekeeping or stay apart from ME and face the unknown of the enemy. I am looking for hearts turned completely to ME. I want your surrender and to humble yourself before ME with true remorse over your lust and affection for evil.

I do not want your ritual cold worship of ME anymore. You come to ME and worship in a cold, rote way. You do not even know ME. You look around and see others worshipping and you follow along. But who are you worshipping? We have never met. You have never even taken time to know ME, to discover ME, and MY Ways. You follow blind sheep and you call this worship. This is a stench, it is an outrage. Stop this empty worship. Get on your hands and knees and repent for worshipping a GOD you don't care to really know. I don't know you. When did we meet? When have we spoken?

You play church with each other, but you are far from ME, your GOD, your CREATOR. I won't have it. I will leave without you soon, O' church of the lukewarm worshippers. I am a HOLY GOD and I hold no place, no time, no reverence in your heart.

Your display of worship is for each other, not ME! If it were for ME, I would know you. I would hear from you often. You would seek MY Face. But you seek the world and all it offers. You even participate in the world and use MY Holy Name to do it. You bring the world into MY Holy Sanctuary to appease the heathens and you care nothing for your LORD JESUS. I DIED FOR YOU! Who else will love you and care for you as I do?

The time is almost up, O' church of the lukewarm. Soon you will see you have been left behind when MY bride is removed and you will be in shock. Then you will seek MY Face, but the door will be shut. It is written. This is not a new word. Open MY Book, I do not change. I am TRUTH. TRUTH is about to come for HIS beloved. You have precious moments remaining to seek TRUTH. Come to ME, JESUS. I am the only TRUTH. I will save you with MY Blood Covering.

I am the ALPHA and OMEGA.

I am the I AM.

MIGHTY GOD EVERLASTING.

PRINCE OF PEACE.

LORD OF LORDS.

KING OF KINGS.

GOD OF THE UNIVERSE.

THERE IS NO OTHER GOD.

I AM JESUS.

Micah 6:8. He hath shewed thee, O man, what is good; and what doth the LORD require of thee, but to do justly, and to love mercy, and to walk humbly with thy God?

PART 28

In this letter once again JESUS says that if you are making plans apart from HIS plans you are going to miss HIM when HE returns. He addresses how focus off of HIM will leave you behind to face the worst. This letter is about making choices and the consequences of the choices we make.

December 20th, 2010.

Below it is a letter from the LORD as told to Susan for you. We have included this time also words given to a good friend of ours, Edmond Ergut, by the LORD, below this letter. God bless you Edmond!

I asked for a Scripture to go with this letter below and amazingly the LORD gave me Joshua 3:16 and this is what I discovered:

Joshua 3:16 . That the waters which came down from above stood and rose up upon an heap very far from the city Adam, that is beside Zaretan: and those that came down toward the sea of the plain, even the salt sea, failed, and were cut off: and the people passed over right against Jericho.

Interesting the LORD chose a "rescue mission scenario" from the Old Testament for this letter below. One writer likens the Joshua 3:16 Scripture to a kind of rapture describing it this way:

Joshua, Jesus, led Israel, man child, over Jordan to the Promised Land, heaven. The Israelites entered the Promised Land without being touched by the waters of Jordan, death, and then the waters returned and all those entering the Promised Land after them would have to ford the river.

Letter 55. December 18-19, 2010.

Yes Susan I have words. Copy this down.

I want to tell you about this new phase the world is going into. The world is approaching a time of evil that is unrivaled by any other time known to mankind. The people slumber, they are snoozing. The world is falling into complete disaster while the world around sleeps. Leaders have no idea how to cope. They see it coming, but they keep their thoughts silent while their people are dying from not having the truth. I am sad for their loss.

The day is closing in and the people will be amazed at the nearness of MY coming. I am very near. MY people who are watching now, MY sheep hear MY voice. They know I am close. They see the signs. They are watching. These are the children who will be taken. If you are not watching, your lamp is not full. You will be left to face the worst. I cannot save you if you cannot be interested enough to watch for MY coming.

I am looking for those who are anxiously awaiting MY return. If the cares of this world captivate you so and you cannot see the signs of MY coming and watch for ME even, I cannot bring you out to safety. I have made MYSELF clear in MY Book to watch for MY coming and to be vigilant in being ready when the signs that have been foretold unfold before you. The hour is now. You are either not watching or you see it, but want to deny what is happening around you. You think if you can deny what you see then perhaps this will all go away. You watch all the people around you who are also not watching or not caring and you follow suit. You are looking in the wrong direction for your salvation. Your family, friends, neighbors cannot save you. I am your only SAVIOR. Keep your eyes fixed on ME.

How can you keep your eyes fixed on ME when you are caught up in all your worldly planning and programs? I am not in your thoughts. You are going to miss it. I am your safe passage. If you do not find ME in your daily activities. if I do not come up in your mind, you will not know what is coming and the future will blindside you as the unexpected is about to happen.

MY people will know and not be surprised because I am close and they are watching. They are ready and so their escape is assured. I am that narrow escape. I am the WAY, I am the TRUTH, I am the LIFE. I am pulling MY people out of the line of fire very soon and taking them to safe keeping while the world sinks to an all-time low and the enemy takes over the planet. Avoid disaster MY people. I am your SAVIOR, RESCUER. I will keep you safe.

You do not have to go this alone. I will bring you into MY safe secure arms, cover you with MY loving wings and we will fly away to everlasting safety. I am the RESCUER. I am the One who will bring the salvation. I will bring you to MY home and put you in a secure eternal place.

Choose for ME and avoid pain and suffering. I long to rescue and keep you safe. I have a beautiful life planned for you. You cannot comprehend it. It is great spectacular beauty. This vocabulary lacks the words to describe your home. MY FATHER waits to greet the bride and the banquet is prepared, a large banquet set and ready for your presence. I have brought together a magnificent offering of food and place settings for MY children and to share together at this lovely table. We will celebrate our marriage and our everlasting life together. It will be the greatest celebration ever held.

Susan, yes I have words.

Tomorrow is coming fast.

MY world is one of everlasting untold beauty. Marvelous and lovely is the world I have prepared for those who truly love and seek ME in this world. MY sheep, this is not your world. You are made for another life, a better eternal life. I am coming soon to put you in safe keeping apart from the evil of this world. You must wash yourself clean in MY Blood and through MY Word in MY Book. Surrender and turn your life over to ME. Repent of your sins. I am waiting MY people, MY sheep, the hour is closing in.

Very soon, I am coming to get the people. I will bring them out. I have planned this for a very long time and the hour is approaching. I am coming to that point and I will snatch the people out of the grasp of MY enemy. I know who is coming.

You must choose. The choice is yours. I cannot do this choosing for you. I am clear about the choices. I have made it very clear. The masses will refuse MY offer of escape. They will remain to face an evil that is beyond anything man has witnessed or encountered before. I want MY people to avoid the terror coming, but they cannot imagine how bad it will be. The suffering will be immense for the ones who choose against MY enemy. He will punish those who choose against him and the choosing for ME will be a difficult one. Now is the time to choose for ME. Come to ME now and be part of MY bride and I will make you ready to be received into MY beautiful Kingdom. If you choose for ME after I remove MY bride your choices will be most difficult. The world will go on, but if you want to choose for ME you won't be able to join back into the world. The alternative will be suffering and death. It will be hard to face. If you join in the world system, you will see eternal suffering. Many will lose their lives after I come for MY bride.

I am coming for a pure bride. One who loves ME before anything else, above all others, above all things. I am sorry, but these are MY stipulations. I have made this clear in MY Word, MY Holy Word. I do not deviate from MY Word. MY Word is clear and uncomplicated. Love ME above all else. I did not create you to put ME in second or third position in your heart. If you believe this, you are mistaken. You have heard this from someone other than ME. I am a jealous GOD. I do not create MY people to follow after other gods, other lowly, worthless gods.

If you want to be with ME in MY Holy Home in Heaven, you must count the cost in this life. You must evaluate your position and decide for yourself what direction you want to move in. You either come with ME and understand that I, GOD want nothing but first place in your heart or choose to put ME in an inferior place in your heart and I will allow you to live out the consequences of your choice for eternity and without a loving, divine GOD. It will be a bleak eternity. You decide.

You put all your life interests before ME your GOD. You spend no time communing with your GOD. I long for relationship with you. I long to share conversations with you, to hear your heartfelt words toward ME, your GOD. I am remote to you. You seek ME when you are in dire circumstances. Suddenly you remember MY Name and call out to ME. After your crisis is over, I go to the bottom shelf of your heart. You remember ME not, as if I don't exist. Why do you suppose I will want you in MY eternal home when you have no regard for ME at all? I will spit you out. What, this shocks you? Read MY Word. Your love for ME is lukewarm and when you come to ME in the next hour, if you do not embrace ME now, I will not know you or acknowledge you to MY FATHER and HIS Holy Angels.

What has MY sacrifice at Calvary meant to you? Do you not care what I, GOD did to save you from eternal hell? I, GOD, I, JESUS was humbled in a violent way to bring you life eternal and you reject MY work on the cross to save you. I do not take this rejection lightly. This is a serious matter. Your lack of regard for MY sacrifice is belittling of MY Holy Name and MY Work on the cross. I endured evil men to save all men, but I will not force this salvation. I only make it available to all who want it. If you do not care for MY sacrifice, MY ransom than you can reject ME, but know this. MY FATHER will reject you. You will stand before MY FATHER and HE will not accept your explanation for this sinful way you have led your life and you will receive eternal punishment. You will have nothing to say apart from MY sacrifice. There is no atonement for your evil works. You will be sent to hell for the evil you have done against a HOLY GOD.

Accept MY free gift of salvation. Surrender all and repent to your GOD and live.

Your time is running out. You have moments left on the clock. Choose salvation through ME or lose your life to the enemy who is ruthless.

Follow ME, LORD JESUS. JESUS CHRIST.

"I am the Son of the Living God, and no man comes to the Father but through me, and all those who reject me, Jesus Christ, they are condemned! There is no way out for them! Their sin is that they reject me, they reject me, the Son of God, they deny me, and those who deny me I shall deny to the Father.

They deny MY crucifixion. They deny that I died for their sins and that they can live with me in paradise as long as they come to me and believe in me. They deny that I can give them everlasting life; they deny me, this is their sin, that they deny the Living God, the Son of the Living God, and that they are wicked, they choose evil, and they choose wickedness.

This is their sin, they deny the Living God. They deny the Son of the Living God. They deny Jesus Christ, for I am all truth, I am all righteousness, and without me there is no way, they shall perish, this is the truth, that if they come to me, the Son of the Living God, I shall give them everlasting life.

It is me that shall save them, I am the Savior of the world, I am the Redeemer, I am Everlasting Life, I am green pastures, I am everlasting, and I shall give them everlasting waters so that they will never thirst and they shall never hunger.

For MY Father so loved the world that He sent me on earth to walk the earth and to set sinners free, to set the down trodden free, to give sight to the blind, to heal the wounded, to heal the sick, to set free the captive.

I came to save sinners; I came to save sinners from the fires of everlasting hell; I came to set them free; I came to give them everlasting life; that they might have life abundantly, that they may live with me and MY Father in MY Father's mansion. I came for all. And for those who accept me and for those who serve me, they shall be given abundantly; they shall be treated as sons of God and kings of heaven!

But for those who reject me, for those who reject the Son who the Father has sent, there is only fire left. For I came, for I came to save them out of the pit, for I came to save them, for I came for them that they may live with me.

But if they reject me, if they reject me, woe! For I only can send them to hell. For that is all that is left for them, for that is all that MY Father has left for them. He has done all that He can. He has sent them His only Son, to serve, to serve them, to save them, to bring them to the truth, to bring them to the life, but they would rather choose darkness.

I am the light, I am the way, I am the truth! No man comes to the Father but through me. I am the Son of God and only through me can they see the Father; I am the Son of god, I lay down MY life for them, and if they reject me there is no other way; I am the way, I am the truth, I am the light; MY Father sent me to save the world, and those who receive me I will receive, I will accept, I will tell of them to MY Father, and they shall be in heaven with me and they shall be in paradise, their name shall be written in the Book of Life and they shall have everlasting life.

But those who reject me there is no way but hell, there is no other way, for I am the way, I am the truth, I am the light; I was sent to save sinners, I was sent to save them."

INDICTMENT AGAINST GOD'S PEOPLE.

"MY people are estranged, they have left me; I ask you to share MY burden, for I am grieved and I am heavy hearted, and the time is come, the time is come for me to bring forth MY judgment for they have not turned their heads towards me."

"Religion today is like leprosy; the people are indwelling in this false religion. It is like a leprosy that has grown on them and is ready to kill them and break them; and they are dying, they are dying and they do not know it. They are in the pit and they do not know it, they are blind and they do not know it. Religion is killing them, it is suffocating them and it has blinded them to the truth, the truth of MY Word and of MY vision for them."

"The institutions of righteousness are corrupt, full of extortion, full of filth, full of strife."

"For MY axe is laid bare to every tree that bears not fruit; it shall be hewn down and cast into the fire; not one of those will be left for they bear not fruit, for they shine forth not MY light, they are but a hindrance. They shall be hewn and cast down to make way for those who bear fruit and who shine forth MY light; who bear fruit and water and feed the rest, those they shall make a way for. The rest shall be cut down for they are wicked and they thrive on their own juice that that juice will kill them."

"From the most grievous sinner to the most righteous of God's children, I have all given them a chance, I have all at one point called them; I have called them and asked them to come out and to serve me."

"I have called them; I have searched each one's heart and I have called them, from the most grievous, from the most terrible sinner, to the most righteous."

"But I tell you! I have gone to each one of them. I have searched each one of their hearts and they have known that I have called them and I have tried to woo them to me and talk to them. But yet they turn not to me, yet they turn not to me."

"I have given them a chance; I died on the cross for all sinners, I died on the cross for all without respect of persons, that all may be saved, that not one should be perished except the one that betrayed me."

"They reject all that I have for them, so they shall see MY judgment! For now they shall see what I have in store for them! For they chose the world, they chose the world!"

"I came for them all, without respect of persons I died on the cross; I bled for them! I bled and I died and I was crucified for them; and they know this! And they know this in their heart that I came to save them from the evil one, but yet they turn away, because they look at this world and they are choked by the cares of this world."

"Woe be unto them! For I came to them just as I came unto you. I pleaded and I wooed them; I asked them to turn their hearts, I asked them to turn their face, that I would take care of their problems, that I would take care of their anguish and their grief and their troubles."

GOD ALWAYS WARNS HIS PEOPLE.

Oh Zion, Zion, do not let your faith wander and be overshadowed by your own desires. For Zion is MY body, MY Church, MY Spirit. It is I, your Lord Jesus, who has reached out and touched every heart and every soul that enters through your doors of fellowship. For I have a special purpose and task awaiting all those who will stand firm and believe this message. It is not MY pleasure that you build walls, rules, and doctrine, other than what is written. I know each and every heart that bears MY name and longs for MY coming. Won't you open your spiritual ears and spiritual eyes to see and hear of what a mighty thing I am about to do? I want you to trust, fully, in me, for you look at the sky and predict tomorrow's weather and you table the tides, but you won't look at the warnings of the changing times. There is a cloud of judgment hanging over the United States, and, in fact, hovering over California. In January 1980, the very ground you dwell on shook by MY hand. Then in May 1980, to your far north, a mountain exploded and the ground shook all about. Then in June 1980, to the direct east of you, the earth shook the strong high mountains of the Sierras. Within weeks, your southern borders shook. And then, centered off the West Coast, the earth and seas were shaken. Why are you sleeping Zion?

Can you not see MY anger? Can you not see all about you the rebellious masses eagerly worshipping all their man-made idols? Sex-sin is rampant; lust for power and self-righteousness are the talk of the times. Above every nation of all history, America has been blessed. But in the last 30 years she has walked away from MY covenant. Even the most wicked generation of Israel was not as evil as yours. Sodom and Gomorrah were small compared to the evil ways of this Nation. Awaken to MY calling Zion, lest I find you sleeping, not guarding what little faith you have. Catch hold! For in less than two minutes of time the riches and man, made idols will be swept away.

Wake up, Zion, for the Glory of God is at hand. Listen carefully, open your hearts, plant your feet firmly where you stand. For I, your Lord, am going to shake MY Church and scatter MY flocks and those with faith will hear your singing and your worship and know I am with you. Yes, you, Zion will be MY guide to MY lost sheep; you will be the compassion of MY Spirit; you will be the rallying point after disaster strikes. Yes, I will be with you and lead you, and the weak of heart, the broken spirits, the torn flesh, and even the dead will hear your voices lifted up to me, and MY healing power, signs and wonders will abound to lead them back to me.

There will be no dwelling large enough to hold all the repentant hearts and, in fact, the green fields surrounding your place of worship on Zion's hill will be amassed with souls bearing MY name. Lay hold of your faith, Zion, for as surely as you hear this Prophesy, all of this and much more is about to happen. Do not move from where you are, but rather pray for the strength of MY spirit: pray for your roots to be deeply immersed in MY word; prepare for the work I have for you. Know this, since MY ministry began, I have not come seeking the righteous but rather the lost, those living in darkness; yes, those even now seeking for someone to tell them the truth. But, MY church bodies, selfishly, have turned inward to themselves and I must pull them down and scatter the flocks for they are full of thistles and thorns not fit for MY high purpose. Lay hold, Zion, lest this happens to you. Cast away your bolted doors; prepare to move into the open fields on Zion's hill. For even the building you are dwelling in will be gone. I tell you this, even if just two of MY beloved remain faithful to this Prophesy, I will unfold all of this around them, for MY will be done.

The very Glory of God is and always has been the repentant heart, those seeking the truth and salvation, and entering in. MY ministry is the whole world and you who have faith are to gather the harvest of MY hand. All the promises of MY written word are available to you who believe. In that time, when Zion gathers, and the weather is foul, just a mighty shout of praise, in MY name, will part the clouds, stop the winds and gales, and MY light will burst forth and abundantly refresh you; and when you hunger, the bread of life will feed your souls, and your faith and worship shall glorify the Living God.

MY servant, who now gives this Prophesy to you, is anointed by MY hand and Spirit to warn all the churches and Christian meeting places round, about. He will be abused, scoffed at, and ridiculed by those claiming to be mine, but MY Holy Spirit will precede him, and MY signs and wonders will follow him. I always warn MY people! Anoint him with oil, Zion, any of you who believe, and swiftly send him on his way. For before he can finish his task, all of what he has told you, this day, will come to pass. Amen. Behold, I come quickly, Amen. Yes, I come quickly, Amen.

RESTORATION.

"The children of God shall be united under one Spirit, the Spirit of truth, the Holy Spirit. The Spirit that reveals all truth from the throne of God, the Spirit that reveals the beginning from the end, the end from the beginning; this is MY Spirit, the Holy Spirit, it will unite all the true children of God."

"There will be many who are hungry for the Word of God. There will be many who are hungry for the truth. There will be many who will come to the truth, and there will be many who will come to hear you preach the Word of God in all its purity; they are hungry for the truth; they are hungry for their God; and they will come to the light."

"They must become warriors for Christ; they must proclaim the name of God; the light must shine forth, and the Word of God must be proclaimed."

"The truth must go forth, the light must shine; the Word of God must be proclaimed; the evil spirits must be smashed; the saints must come out of their caves."

"I say, go forth! Go forth and be a light! Show them! Show them that they can be healed, if they but come to MY throne, if they but shed this falseness, the lies, the hypocrisy. Just come to MY throne and I shall heal them and they shall be with me and we shall live in MY Father's mansion as one, as one family."

"Only those that turn to me, and realize that I am supreme, and that only in me is there true reality, and that this world is not reality, that this world is just a stage; only those who turn to me and see me as their only hope, as their only salvation, as their true reality, them I shall pluck from this earth and they shall be with me in paradise."

"I came that all may know me; I came that all may have the knowledge that you have; I came for all that I should reveal wisdom to all."

You will be MY light. You will be MY beacon. You will be the light in the world in these latter days. And you will show them that the Holy God is pure without blemish or spot, and that He wants them to be pure without blemish or spot; that they should come to me as a pure bride, a bride that I am proud to show to MY Father, that He will accept and say, "Yes, they are right, bring them into MY mansion."

"The bride will know, the bride will see that you are pure and holy; I ask that you be holy as I am holy, perfect yourselves, cleanse yourselves, make your paths straight, make sure that you are holy."

"This is one of your missions, to bring about the Restoration; as they come to you they will see the truth and they shall perfect themselves through your word and your admonitions and your doctrine, they shall perfect themselves with spot or without blemish."

"And, when they hear your voice, they will know that this is the voice of the Lord, this is the voice of their Shepherd. And MY sheep will come, MY sheep will come out of their hiding, MY sheep will come out of their sins, MY sheep will come out of their works, MY sheep will come out of their vanity and frivolity and their programs!"

SAN FRANCISCO.

"MY heart is heavy, as I see all that goes on in this city MY heart is heavy for all the sins and all the abominations and all the wickedness and evil that I see, I cannot bear, I cannot bear! I see sins that you don't even know about, that you cannot even imagine, and MY heart is weary; I ask you to look at this city the way I look at it.

This city is evil and wicked and MY judgment is so right for this city; every citizen, every citizen hates God, they walk in their own ways, they walk in their own lust, they walk in their own depravity, they are wretched and they are naked and they are hungry and they don't even know it. Their face they turn towards themselves, they try to glorify themselves, they try to adorn themselves, they try to cover up, but I see their hearts, their heart is far from me, and MY heart is heavy, I am very sad and I am very heavy hearted.

This city hates God and it hates me; the mention of MY name and they turn their head and they harden their heart and their back stiffens and they do not want to speak of me; MY name itself is like a bad word in this city; this city hates God and this city hates me.

The sins of this city cry out to me to avenge this city with MY wrath; this city is evil! The sins of this city are worse than Sodom and Gomorrah! The wickedness that prevails! The wretchedness! The emptiness!

This is why I have brought you to this city as a light, that you will show this city that the Living God sees their sins and He is ready to avenge them!

I cannot speak of their sins, I cannot speak of their wickedness and evil; I am so heavy! I am so heavy hearted! But this city grows in wickedness and evil every day and I am ready to lay MY hand bare! I am ready to pierce MY sword through their hearts! So they know that I am alive and that they are hurting me, and they are hurting who gave them the very breath which they breath is from me, and they turn their heads away from me, they turn their hearts away from me!

I am grieved! I am very sad! But MY justice I will mete out with MY wrath and MY judgment! I ask you to see this city! I ask you to see their eyes! I ask you to see their hearts the way that I see them! I am grieved! You must see this city the way I see it. So that when you bring forth MY judgment you will know it comes with all justice! I ask you to see this city the way I see it!

Raise your arm and take MY sword; you will be MY instrument to bring forth MY vengeance, MY wrath.

This is the day, this is MY day of fury, for I am very angry with the wicked and MY wrath shall come upon them.

When the sun shines brightest, that is your time, when the sun shines brightest and is right over head, you shall enter the crowd and you shall stand in their midst, you shall proclaim MY name, you shall uplift MY standard and you shall call MY fire, you shall bring down MY sword and they shall burn!

MY fire shall come down and burn the wicked, they shall be as stubble; they shall burn as tares but the righteous shall stand; you shall tread the wicked and they shall not hurt you.

The wicked shall be stamped like pulp on the ground and MY wrath shall be manifest; the day is at hand and you shall manifest MY wrath! The fire of the Lord shall burn bright!

As the Lord moves in with judgment and wrath, the demons shall move out with anger and fury, and there shall be fire and there shall be smoke and there shall be stench so strong that the righteous will have to turn their head because the stench will be so bad; the judgment of the Lord will fall strong upon this city.

This city is San Francisco, this "pretty", this so-called "glorious" city of San Francisco shall be abased, shall be abased, shall become like cinders, they shall burn, this city shall burn, this city shall be abased, because MY Word will cut their lies, their hypocrisy, their sin, and their evil, shall cut them asunder, and this city will be abased.

I have looked upon this city and it is wicked, it is wicked; and as you go forth in the gap, and as you confront the enemy, you will tell them, you will tell them of the coming wrath and doom that this city will experience, you shall tell them that not one stone will be left unturned.

And they will look at you and they will think that you are mad; but you will tell them that the Living God has said that this city will be destroyed, not one stone will be left unturned, because I have visited this city and I have seen no good."

AMERICA.

"As I have given you visions and messages of MY judgment and wrath, so will you go forth. And so will you proclaim in graphic detail of MY judgments, and of MY fire, and of death all over this land; and of waters that will rise, and of the stars that will darken, and of the wind that will rush."

"You shall prophesy of this, and I will give you power over the waters, I will give you power over the fire, I will give you power over the weather, I will give you power over the wind, and you shall prophesy of this judgment over this nation."

"I have forsaken them now, MY wrath shall come and you shall prophesy in graphic detail of their judgment, of their death, of their sure doom, and of the dead that will be from one end of this nation to the other."

"This whole nation shall see MY fire, this whole nation shall be in confusion, this whole nation will be under strong delusion, they will not know, I shall shake their very roots, I shall shake their very roots and they will not know what has happened."

"For the fire will sweep through this nation. And there will be strong confusion and strong delusion. And there will be panic everywhere, there will be panic everywhere, people running to and fro, trying to hide with no place to hide; they will jump into the sea for they will not know where else to go; and they will drown and they will kill themselves."

"MY fire will sweep through this nation. And there shall be turmoil; and there shall be chaos; there will be no place to hide, no place to hide. For I will seek them out of their dark corners and I shall pull them and I shall kill them; for those that reject me, there shall be no place to hide, no place to hide."

"They will look at you as a fool. They will look at you as a fool masquerading in a fool's paradise. For you speak of death; for you speak of judgment; for you speak of darkness; for you speak of fire; for you speak of MY wrath. And they, all they see is sunshine, green trees, fair weather, and they frolic in their folly, and they have fun, and they enjoy, and they laugh, and they drink, and they become drunken, and they sleep."

"For all of a sudden MY fire will come! For all of a sudden MY judgment will come! For all of a sudden when they are asleep and when they are drinking and when they are frolicking in their folly, MY judgment will come! And they will know that a prophet has been among them, for he has spoken of it, of MY judgment, and MY wrath."

These words above in bold were given to Edmond Ergut.

PART 29

First is a letter from the LORD JESUS as dictated to Sabrina and also a special letter to the bride of Christ specifically from her GROOM JESUS. Below it is a letter from the LORD as told to Susan. Below this letter is a Section written by the evangelist and author Charles Spurgeon about topic: "The Form of Godliness Without the Power."• Susan included this writing of Charles Spurgeon since in the letter the LORD mentions this particular phrase. Sabrina's letter speaks of the people rejecting the LORD for the world. In the letter to Susan, the LORD talks of His compassion; patience with a world that is rejecting Him, but He still wants a pure bride.

December 23rd, 2010.

First is a letter from the LORD JESUS as dictated to Sabrina and also a special letter to the bride of Christ specifically from her GROOM JESUS. Below it is a letter from the LORD as told to Susan. Below this letter is a Section written by the evangelist and author Charles Spurgeon about the topic: "The Form of Godliness Without the Power." I included this writing of Charles Spurgeon since in the letter the LORD mentions this particular phrase.

God bless, we love hearing from you, kindest regards for your prayers and love.

Letter dictated to Sabrina by the LORD JESUS on December 22, 2010.

"These are MY last pleas. I am done with this generation. I am pleading to this lost world forever now. I am an all-consuming GOD, a very patient GOD, but MY pleas have no effect. Only a few are repenting and turning to ME. This is so sad. Why do you forsake ME, MY people? Have I not suffered enough for your redemption?

In the way you reject ME now, you will suffer for eternity, if you don't

212

turn your ways to ME. I died for all. I suffered for all. Yet you live as if this never happened. 'Oh we have one more day, than I will think about MY ways. Let me first enjoy MY life a bit longer, let me first take care of all MY plans in this world, then if there is any time left, I will consider to think about MY God.'

Whose God? Don't call me your God. I am only the GOD of MY faithful children who seek ME in all their ways. I am done with you world. Go and have your way. GO ! This GOD who is in the back of your mind has created you. He has given you the very breath you use now to read this letter, to do your daily things. Did you know that? I have made you so perfectly beautiful, so everything fits together nicely, so everything operates in your body in a most wonderful way. Yet you take it all for granted. I thought it all out. I thought about you and you were there. Everyone of MY people is an unique creation and I had plans and ways for all of you.

You will never see the beauty of heaven I have made for you, so you could enjoy ME for eternity. There is no greater joy then to know your GOD in heaven. Did you know that? The love affaires of this world are calling you, so go and enjoy your life on earth while you still can. I have called you over and over. I see sin all over you. I don't see a repented, surrendered heart to ME. You are filthy, MY people. You choose this yourself. You can be beautiful through ME, I, JESUS who bought you freedom from this sinful bondage.

But the choice is yours. I created you with a freewill, so I cannot do otherwise than to accept your choice. But I want you to know it breaks MY heart. Over and over again you have broken MY heart. And yet, you can always come to ME. I always forgive you. But don't play with ME. Even I have MY boundaries, although MY grace is big. If you continue to choose this sinful, playful lifestyle, you will give ME no other choice than to send you to hell. It's written in MY Word.

You can do nothing good out of yourself. Nobody can. The only good thing comes from and through ME, as I AM love and love has created you. This world is running to its end. So what will you do?

Will you continue and go on as every day? Thinking the sun comes up every morning and I can enjoy MY day? Nothing major will happen? And tonight, I will sleep well? Don't be mistaken.

In one split of a second, this whole world will turn into a darkness you have never experienced in your whole life. There has never been and will never be again such a darkness on earth. Demons are waiting to be loosed. They will have no mercy. Then, you will know I have spoken the truth and you will remember how much I warned you.

The time is not over yet, but it sure is striking almost midnight. MY finger is about to move the clock. So, what will you do? Look at yourself and ask ME to reveal MYSELF to you. Ask ME to show you the real you. Ask ME to come to you and fill you with MY love and grace. I can still save you. For some it is already too late, they have made up their mind. For some, there is still hope. I, GOD will judge your heart. So don't delay any longer and come to ME. There has never been a more urgent time than this."

I, GOD have spoken.

Hebrews 10:26-27. For if we sin willfully after that we have received the knowledge of the truth, there remaineth no more sacrifice for sins, But a certain fearful looking for of judgment and fiery indignation, which shall devour the adversaries.

The Lord wanted Sabrina to write this letter for the bride in white bold.

"This is a special message for MY bride. I have bought you with MY blood. MY precious blood runs through your veins. I am so proud of you MY bride. I see you are ready. MY bride will have a special place with ME in heaven. You will never regret all the longing and waiting for ME.

I am your BRIDEGROOM. Your BRIDEGROOM is waiting with the same longing, MY bride. Can you just hold on a little longer? Don't be disappointed. You are MY light in this world. Those who truly love ME, spread MY word. They cannot do otherwise than to speak and testify of MY love for them. This is MY bride. I love her. I treasure her. She was MY joy at the cross. The joy laid before ME.

MY precious bride, hold on, I am coming. I am doing a mighty work in this world and in people's hearts and it's worth the waiting. You won't have to wait much longer now. I AM is coming. I am on MY way. Just a few finishing touches here and there, and then you will see ME coming in the sky. It will all happen very fast. It will be the most glorious moment for you and ME when you enter MY Kingdom and settle yourself at the wedding table that I have prepared with so much care.

I have thought of every detail for you. It's all so perfect. Can you feel the joy and love? I can. Encourage each other and don't give up. MY FATHER is about to give the sign. It won't be much longer. Please be patient. Your rewards shall be without measure. You are MY shining stars on earth. So keep shining! You are washed in MY blood. You are pure and clean.

Keep yourself from this world. Distance yourself, so you won't be polluted. Keep MY Words, worship ME and stay close to ME. Never stop praying for MY coming. I love to hear those prayers. They move MY heart. Be patient. The time is almost here. I, JESUS your BRIDEGROOM, am waiting and longing for you, so bless MY heart and stay close to ME in this last hour."

Hebrews 12:2. Looking unto Jesus the author and finisher of our faith; who for the joy that was set before him endured the cross, despising the shame, and is set down at the right hand of the throne of God.

Hebrews 12:22-24. But ye are come unto mount zion, and unto the city of the living God, the heavenly Jerusalem, and to an innumerable company of angels, To the general assembly and church of the firstborn, which are written in heaven, and to God the Judge of all, and to the spirits of just men made perfect, And to Jesus the mediator of the new covenant, and to the blood of sprinkling, thats speaketh better things than that of Abel.

Hebrews 10:37-38. For yet a little while, and he that shall come will come, and will not tarry. Now the just shall live by faith: but if any man draw back, MY soul shall have no pleasure in him.

Letter 56. given by the LORD JESUS to Susan. December 21, 2010.

I have words.

I have a message for the world.

Soon, I will be coming to earth to get MY bride. The hour is approaching quickly. The people remain in denial. This is not MY plan for them, but I cannot change their hearts. They must choose ME over the enemy. If they turn to ME and I receive permission through their surrender to ME, I can send MY SPIRIT to them and HE can prepare them to be ready for the escape from the evil coming to the earth.

I am a compassionate GOD. I want to save MY people. I long to save MY people. I want MY people to come to ME in this late hour. I know their hearts. They cannot believe that the hour is almost up. They cannot see what is right before them because they are not watching. They are too captivated by the things of the world, everything before ME, their GOD.

I am a patient GOD. I wait patiently. I see evil at every turn. The earth has grown cold toward its GOD. What do the people expect from ME their GOD? Do they expect endless tolerance of their evil running amok? This evil has been building up for many years and it is cresting to its peak. The enemy reigns in the hearts of the people supreme. They wish to serve a different master than I, their CREATOR. They have chosen to serve the creation: an inferior choice to their one true GOD. I offer love and peace, security, salvation. I offer an escape route to beauty ever-lasting.

The world is coming to a halt. All is going black, complete darkness, a world without its MAKER, its GOD. You have seconds on the clock. I am giving you these warnings, so that you can know and prepare your heart for ME. I am taking only a pure bride with ME to MY Home in heaven. If you are unprepared, I cannot remove you from the dark world ahead.

Do you want this purity? Do you want this larger measure of oil? You must be humble toward ME; surrender to ME; repent of your sin to ME; lay your life down before ME. I will accept these and MY HOLY SPIRIT will come into your life and prepare you to come with ME, your BRIDEGROOM. I will embrace you, call you MY own, and care for you always.

These are MY Terms. You refuse to believe MY Warnings. You reject MY Truth. I am closing in on the hour of MY return. These are precious moments. Open your eyes. Back away from your worldly pursuits and love affair. You are hypnotized by evil. Your passion for ME is lukewarm. Your passion for the world exceeds your needs for ME. You are lost. You are gravitating to outer darkness. You are moving away from ME. I cannot pull you back, if you never turn to ME.

The path to ME is narrow. Why do you refuse to believe this? You think otherwise, but this is not so. Many believe they are on the correct path. They delude themselves. The enemy has deceived them greatly. I am the ONE TRUE NARROW PATH. The deception about what I expect of MY followers is great. I ask for complete surrender, so many do not grasp this. They believe to have a form of Godliness but deny the power thereof.

MY people if you choose to be part in the world, consumed by the cares of the world and partially following ME, we have no relationship at all. Halfway is no way. You are in a dangerous position. You want ME a little when MY Presence pleases you, but this is no relationship. I cannot take you when I come. You will miss the narrow way, the narrow escape that is about to happen. It will come quickly and then you will realize you missed it. The second I remove MY children to safety will be the beginning of a new way of life on earth. Darkness will consume and the bride will not be on earth.

MY people, this brief moment is about to happen. In your heart you know this, but I am sorry you refuse to believe. You knew the day would arrive. MY Book and the signs I have given have been described and clear to you. Think about what keeps you from realizing this. What comes to mind first when you hear these warnings? Is it your future plans? Is it your pursuit of worldly possessions? Is it your ministry planning? What do you have as an idol that is blinding your ability to see truth? Your anger rises up when people speak of MY soon coming to you. Why? Will you be angry when you find out you have been left behind or will you be sad and filled with great sorrow? What causes you to be so resistant to MY pleadings and how the signs in the world are actually described in MY Book coming into reality?

Soon MY patience with you, MY people will be done. I cannot wait on you MY people forever. I must remove MY bride to safety as she waits patiently while you persist in handling the evil things of the world and refuse to return to your first LOVE your LORD JESUS. I am your first LOVE. I brought you into this world. I give you life every second of the day. I preserve your life while you reject ME. I bring the rain down for all. I bring the sunlight down for all. MY Love is toward all peoples. But very soon I must leave those who choose against ME to face the outcome of their choosing.

This has happened before and has been described in MY Book to happen again. I am a GOD of light. I am completely honest to MY people and true to MY Word. What do you need to see truth? I am taking the remnant home who are clean and prepared for MY retrieval.

The hour is closing in. The warnings are clear. The path is narrow.

MY Hand is extended. Grasp it and I will lead you out to safety. I want to do this for you, I long to do this. MY sadness is great that you will not come with ME, MY people.

Your BRIDEGROOM waiteth. Only seconds to go. Seek MY beautiful Face. MY Love is pure and perfect. You will never know anything more satisfying than ME, JESUS.

Turn to ME quickly, JESUS.

Charles Spurgeon writes about "The Form of Godliness Without the Power."

"Having a form of godliness but denying its power." A mere form of godliness joined to an unholy heart is of no value to God. The swan, although its feathers are as white as snow, yet its skin is black. God will not accept that 'external morality' which conceals 'internal impurity'. There must be a pure heart as well as a clean life.

The power of godliness must work within, or else God will not accept our offering. There is no value to man or to God in a religion which is a dead form. Sad is that man's plight who wears the name of Christian but has never been quickened by the Holy Spirit.

There is no use in a mere formal religion. If your religion is without spiritual life, what is the use of it? Could you ride home on a dead horse? Would you hunt with dead dogs? Is false religion any better? In the depth of winter, can you warm yourself before a 'painted fire'? Could you dine off the 'picture of a feast' when you are hungry?

There must be vitality and substantiality, or else the form is utterly worthless; and worse than worthless, for it may flatter you into deadly self conceit.

How shameful will such a fruitless, lifeless professor be in eternity, when the secrets of all hearts shall be revealed! What shame and everlasting contempt will await him when his falsehood shall be detected, and his baseness shall fill all holy minds with horror!

What will be the hell of the false professor! "Having a form of godliness but denying its power."

PART 30

This has one letter given by JESUS to Susan for all who will receive it. This letter speaks of lukewarm commitment and doing good works apart from GOD's consent. The world looks so normal, but it is not. No middle ground, only 100 percent commitment. There is only one path to GOD - not many.

December 26th, 2010.

This Part 30 has one letter given by JESUS to Susan for all who will receive it. This letter stands alone. The message is very serious. Please take time to read this message and even to get it out to others.

Please Note: with this message below are two links put together by our friend Jude of the Philippines of the LORD's letters in brochure format for public distribution and also some of our linking partners and the LORD's letters translated into other languages.

Letter 57. December 24, 2010. Words given by JESUS to Susan.

Susan, this is your LORD speaking. Yes, Susan, I have words for you.

The hour is closing in. The people think not. Even those who are MY own do not believe ME. They have no faith. They read MY Word. They see the times. They do not believe that the hour approaches for ME to retrieve MY bride. I do not know what they will need to see the truth. I have laid this out carefully for all to see and yet the majority, refuse to see and they refuse to look. They are so preoccupied with the world before them. They do not want to look, see, believe for themselves.

There are a few who are watching. There are a few who have noticed the times are lining up with MY Word, MY Words given so many years in advance by MY prophets. Yet they look the other way. This does not coordinate with their earthly desires. They run toward the unclean. They are captivated by the things of the world. I know you MY people. I know how you lust after the things that all the heathens lust after.

You have drummed up every excuse in MY Book to make yourself justified to pursue the world and the unclean things thereof. You use MY Book to give yourself license to pursue the world. You know what I speak of. You pursue wealth and possessions and you say, GOD doesn't want us poor. When did I even speak to you? You are so busy proving that it is in MY will that you have everything the heathens' possess, that you don't even talk to ME anymore. You don't know ME. You know the world. You know wealth. You know the lusts of the world, but you do not know ME. You are an enmity to ME along with the world. I cannot take you to MY Kingdom. Your lukewarmness will put you outside MY Kingdom and I cannot take you with ME when I come to remove MY bride.

I am a GOD of TRUTH and LOVE. Do you find these words to hurt? Well sometimes the TRUTH must hurt. I want to save you. Pull away from your lusting, clinging to the world around you. You accept MY offer of salvation and then turn back and blend perfectly with those in the world. I cannot have you in MY World as long as you continue to pursue your own agenda. If you surrender and repent of your sins to ME and give ME your life, your will, your all, then I can establish MY Will in your life and I can work MY perfect plans in your life. Your justification of your plans in your life using MY precious Word, yet never actually surrendering your all to ME is putrid to ME.

Your working of good without consulting ME disgusts ME. If you don't surrender to ME completely and make ME the undisputable MASTER over your life, then someday when you stand before ME, all your so-called good works will burn up because these were your plans and not MINE. You did not take time to become intimate with ME, to truly know MY Will for your life. You proceeded in the direction you chose.

If you continue to pursue your own path and spend little or no time with ME, getting to know ME, establishing intimacy with your GOD, then your chosen path will lead you straight to hell. This is harsh you say. WAKE UP, MY people. This is TRUTH. I AM GOD. I created you. Quit working in the framework of your own thinking and justifying your love affair and adultery with the world by using MY Words. I want to spit you out.

Come to ME in these closing moments. Turn from your unrepentant lusting after the things of the world. If you put down your lusts for the world and actually spent time with ME and MY Word, you would see that these are roads that all lead to hell.

The world says there many paths that lead to GOD. This is an outrageous lie of the enemy. The TRUTH in MY Word is that there is only one narrow path, one narrow way to the FATHER and it is I; JESUS CHRIST, the MESSIAH. You must make ME your LORD and MASTER, and if you do not give ME everything, including all your future planning, you serve another master. This master you serve tries to pose as light. His light is blinding you MY children, MY little ones. You are following him to hell.

The things of the world that you see others, who do not know ME engaging in look so right. They look so normal. This is the way the enemy deceives you. Step away. Separate yourself unto ME. MY Way leads you to freedom, peace, love, and satisfaction through ME, your ONE TRUE LOVE. The enemy wants to trip you up and he is succeeding. The path is thin and few find it. *MY Word is plain. The road to hell is wide. This TRUTH should be sobering for you. If you knew something was rare, unique, than you would know you must look carefully for it. The wide road by contrast is easy to find. MY people, lay down your life before ME now, the narrow path doorway is about to close and when I come to get MY beloved, it will close.

This is the moment of decision. The world around you seems normal, right. But you are falling into the enemy's hands and you are resisting MY TRUTH. I have made it clear in MY Word that it will be

222

as the days of Noah and Lot. Few will be found worthy to be saved when I come for MY bride. MY people this should be sobering for you, but you fear ME not and cling to the world as if it holds your answers.

The world is crumbling. It groans and creaks under the pressure of consuming evil that is taking over. Can you not see this? What do you not see about this TRUTH? The world is growing cold toward its GOD, even indifferent. It seeks after every explanation to disbelieve ME. Why can you not see this? Soon MY TRUTH will win out and what side will you be standing on? Will you be with ME in the end or will you be on the side of eternal regret, sorrow, loss, torment, and fire, cast into the final destination, the Lake of Fire.

You are either MINE, fully-surrendered or you are not MINE. There is no middle ground. Those who ride the fence and have a little love for ME and indulge themselves, they believe justifiably using MY Word, with the world are already dead and lifeless to ME. You belong fully-surrendered to your master, satan. He does not mind that you say you are MINE, as long as you are not fully-surrendered to ME. You can call yourself anything you want, you can visit MY House as often as you like, you can wear MY Name on your sleeve, but if you are not fully-surrendered to ME and engaging fully in the ways of the world then you belong to MY enemy and you are his slave. And when you stand before ME, I will know you are not MINE and you will join your master for eternity.

Choose quickly. I must leave soon with MY beloved. Join us. But choose now. No decision is also a choice against ME. I love you, but I am also always and eternally TRUTHFUL. Turn to ME. Make ME your undisputed LORD and MASTER and I will bring you to eternal safekeeping. Time is running out.

Let these Words stand.

I, JESUS have spoken.

After I took down the LORD's letter, HE said to add this Scripture:

Romans 1:19. since what may be known about God is plain to them, because God has made it plain to them.

I added this Scripture:

2 Corinthians 11:14-15. And no marvel; for Satan himself is transformed into an angel of light. 15Therefore it is no great thing if his ministers also be transformed as the ministers of righteousness; whose end shall be according to their works.

Luke 13:22-27. And he went through the cities and villages, teaching, and journeying toward Jerusalem. Then said one unto him, Lord, are there few that be saved? And he said unto them, Strive to enter in at the strait gate: for many, I say unto you, will seek to enter in, and shall not be able. When once the master of the house is risen up, and hath shut to the door, and ye begin to stand without, and to knock at the door, saying, Lord, Lord, open unto us; and he shall answer and say unto you, I know you not whence ye are: Then shall ye begin to say, We have eaten and drunk in thy presence, and thou hast taught in our streets. But he shall say, I tell you, I know you not whence ye are; depart from me, all ye workers of iniquity.

PART 31

This was dictated by JESUS to Susan for you. Again the message here is more focus on the world than the LORD. A lukewarm commitment and following men will lead to disaster. JESUS asks do the people even wonder who created them?

December 29th, 2010.

This Part 31 was dictated by JESUS to Susan for you. The time is only growing closer everyday to the LORD's return as HE describes in HIS words and the letters are each more urgent. We hope you find the courage to share these words with someone you care about, and if not these words, tell your friends that the time is now to make a commitment to the LORD.

Please Note: with this message below are five links put together by our friend Jude of the Philippines of the LORD's letters in brochure format for public distribution and also some of our linking partners and the LORD's letters translated into other languages.

Letter 60. December 27, 2010. This letter was told by JESUS CHRIST to Susan for you:

Yes, Susan I do have words.

These are final pleas. I am trying to capture the attention of MY children. MY children are so very caught up in the world. MY dear children, whom I created, what did you expect to see happen just prior to MY return for MY bride? What did you think would need to happen before I come to retrieve MY bride that would signal you to take these words seriously? What in your mind did you need to see before you would decide to sit up and pay attention? What can I provide you that I have not clearly outlined in MY Book?

MY dear ones, you also must be watching and you also must read MY Book, and seek ME through a surrendered relationship. If you cannot meet this criteria, than no, you are not seeing and all this talk of MY return to receive MY bride is absolute nonsense to you. MY Book is nonsense to most of MY people. They do not believe most of what I have set out in MY Book. If you believed MY Book and you received MY SPIRIT, you would know the lateness of the hour and you would believe these warnings. As it is, you are blinded to truth and caught up in the deluge of daily living. Everything in this world is more important than seeking a relationship with ME, your LORD and SAVIOR.

I find it interesting that I made you, I created every part of you, I breathed life into you, I gave you life and I keep you alive and yet, you won't look up from your paper once to find ME, your CREATOR. I wait on you. I wait for you to even ponder about where you come from and where are you going? You have all kinds of thoughts about your human existence. You write me off as an explanation for why you exist. Why? I know why. Because if I exist, than you need to follow ME and MY Ways, and you are happy following your present master. You don't think you follow anyone but your own ways? You are either following ME, your GOD, or you follow MY enemy. You are following him over a cliff, straight to hell.

You must surrender, repent, and turn back to ME, so I can save you. The direction you move in is one that is cursed. You have been moving in this direction from the start. If you don't change your course, repent to a HOLY GOD, and turn back, the direction you are following and the course you are on, will lead you to hell. All men must choose. They choose the direction they move in or they will turn around and follow ME to the narrow path. Stay on the course you are following, and I will lose you for eternity. Please change your course. Read MY Book and surrender to ME. I, GOD want you to believe MY Pleas, MY Truth. This is all written in MY Book. Nothing has changed.

I am JESUS, I am GOD. You can choose to follow ME. Open your eyes or stay on the wide path, with MY enemy, to hell.

You think you are good. Only MY Blood, which I shed on Calvary for your sin crimes against GOD, can erase your guilt. I can wash your sin away if you only come to ME now. Admit your guilt to ME and surrender everything over to ME. Partial surrender is NO surrender.

Do not give ME your lukewarm commitment. I won't have it. You will be sent to hell when you face ME if your relationship with ME is cool, lukewarm. You can't imagine this or believe that GOD could do this? Well, I, GOD can do it, I will do it, and I have done it. Eternal damnation is the destination of the lukewarm. Wake up O' dead church, church of the living dead. You believe you are alive in ME. You are lost and far from ME, far away. Your contentment with your lukewarm life is going to change soon when you find you have been left.

MY children, I want you to wake up and turn back to ME. I will save you. You are deceived. If you do not read MY Book, seek MY SPIRIT, and watch for ME, than how do you expect to know when I am returning? Are you relying on other men to guide you? This is a mistake. You must surrender to ME, repent, and seek answers from ME, your GOD and through MY precious Word. Only I have the answers to your questions. Seek ME. I am the WAY, the TRUTH, the LIFE. There is no alternative.

The hour is almost up. Make the most of your time. Make ME your LORD and SAVIOR. I will take you with ME when I come for MY bride. MY people, MY children, if you do not do this you will be left to face MY enemy. It will be horror.

Think this over carefully.

I, JESUS have spoken.

I, JESUS the Messiah have spoken.

After reading this letter, I can't help but to think of this Scripture from 1 Corinthians 2. and so I have included it:

1 Corinthians 2.

1And I, brethren, when I came to you, came not with excellency of speech or of wisdom, declaring unto you the testimony of God. 2For

I determined not to know any thing among you, save Jesus Christ, and him crucified. 3And I was with you in weakness, and in fear, and in much trembling. 4And MY speech and MY preaching was not with enticing words of man's wisdom, but in demonstration of the Spirit and of power: 5That your faith should not stand in the wisdom of men, but in the power of God.

6Howbeit we speak wisdom among them that are perfect: yet not the wisdom of this world, nor of the princes of this world, that come to nought: 7But we speak the wisdom of God in a mystery, even the hidden wisdom, which God ordained before the world unto our glory: 8Which none of the princes of this world knew: for had they known it, they would not have crucified the Lord of glory. 9But as it is written, Eye hath not seen, nor ear heard, neither have entered into the heart of man, the things which God hath prepared for them that love him.

10But God hath revealed them unto us by his Spirit: for the Spirit searcheth all things, yea, the deep things of God. 11For what man knoweth the things of a man, save the spirit of man which is in him? even so the things of God knoweth no man, but the Spirit of God.

12Now we have received, not the spirit of the world, but the spirit which is of God; that we might know the things that are freely given to us of God. 13Which things also we speak, not in the words which man's wisdom teacheth, but which the Holy Ghost teacheth; comparing spiritual things with spiritual. 14But the natural man receiveth not the things of the Spirit of God: for they are foolishness unto him: neither can he know them, because they are spiritually discerned.

15But he that is spiritual judgeth all things, yet he himself is judged of no man. 16For who hath known the mind of the Lord, that he may instruct him? but we have the mind of Christ.

PART 32

This was dictated by JESUS to Susan in the first letter for you. Then Sabrina received a letter from the LORD also for you. JESUS speaks of the stench the lukewarm church is to Him. He speaks of the path being narrow because it requires a full surrender which few are willing to give. In Sabrina's letter JESUS talks about the blood only being available in this world not the next life. HE talks about what happened on the cross and how this generation abuses HIS good name. The time of this mercy is running down.

December 31st, 2010.

This Part 32 was dictated by JESUS to Susan in the first letter for you. Then Sabrina received a letter from the LORD also for you.

The idea that the LORD is returning soon is about the furthest thing from many people's minds. Yet, we receive many messages from people who read these letters and who are reporting seeing visions and having dreams about end times topics. Many are hearing similar words from the LORD. Many of these are from children who are sometimes the best witnesses the LORD uses. We also receive many emails about incredible things going on in the world. The theme of these messages is about turning to JESUS, your only hope for being ready for what lies ahead.

Please Note: with this message below are different links put together by our friend Jude of the Philippines of the LORD's letters in brochure format for public distribution and also some of our linking partners and the LORD's letters translated into other languages.

All GLORY AND HONOR GOES TO OUR BLESSED LORD JESUS!

Shout HIS NAME on the rooftops!

Your friends in Christ, Sabrina & Susan.

Letter 61. December 29, 2010. Jesus dictated this letter to Susan.

Susan I will give you words.

Susan this is the final hour that I come before MY people and bring these words. I have tried to convince you. I have pleaded. I have reasoned. I have given you reason after reason to believe what I am saying. MY Words are clear. I am a truthful GOD. I tell the truth. I have come before you and I have spoken truth. You do not raise an eyebrow or bat an eye. You do not believe. You have your reasons: life seems so normal. Everything runs smooth. There is no reason to be concerned. No reason to change our patterns of living. No reason to shed a tear over our bad behavior, or humble ourselves before a HOLY GOD, repent of our worldly ways. No reason to think differently than we have always thought. Life goes on like always. We are just going along for the ride.

MY children, let ME tell you that I, GOD am fed up with this generation. I cannot stomach you anymore. You are a stench under MY Nose. Your preoccupation with every sin-ridden activity makes ME nauseous. I cannot tolerate this anymore. I cannot look on this world and its absolutely irrational evil doing any further.

You are nauseating. I cannot stomach this. What must I do to reach you? How can I reach a lost, dying generation that rejects GOD and loves evil so overwhelmingly? I do not want to hold up MY bride for this adulterous generation much longer. The people who have little or no part in their GOD are a stench to ME. I will spit you out. MY Word is clear about this. I do not want you to think that I, GOD do not stand by MY Word: I love, I bless, I provide, I heal, I give, but I am consistent in truth and when I tell you, MY people, I have no time for your lukewarm commitment to your CREATOR, I am truthful. You will depart from ME for eternity when you finally come face to face with ME. I cannot take you with ME to MY beautiful Home in Heaven. You will not enter in or even be part of it. You will never witness the magnificence of the heavenlies. You will be in outer darkness, in torment, far, far away from a loving, caring GOD. These are hard words to speak, but it is MY Truth and this is the way it will be.

MY Path that leads to MY Kingdom is very narrow. Very few find this path. Why, you ask? The path to MY Kingdom requires a full surrender. You must repent and give ME all your life plans and give ME everything. I must be the center-focus of your existence. This seems like an unreasonable request? I am GOD. I breathed life into your flesh and you now have your being. You exist because I deemed it. I know you better than you know yourself. So now, you believe MY request of a full surrender to your GOD too much to ask? If you really think I, your LORD am asking more than you can give ME, you may certainly have your life apart from ME. I will give you this freedom. You choose to go your own way, follow after MY enemy who lures you to the wide road to hell. This is your choice and you will have your choice. I will allow you to depart from ME and to have your decision to follow after MY enemy.

If you move in that direction, let ME tell you what will happen when you separate yourself from ME for eternity. All the things in this life that you consider to be good, will evaporate from your grasp. You will never know love, hope, peace, kindness, and MY Beauty. Instead you will receive terror, torment, and horror. This is hell. It is where most people go. Few find the narrow way. I am the narrow way. I am the way to the narrow path that leads to MY Kingdom of beauty, perfection, peace, love, hope.

MY bride knows the narrow road. She follows only ME and worships only ME, her LORD and MASTER. She will come with ME to safety. I will protect her, love her, and keep her safe for all eternity. She will never know regret. She will be forever satisfied by ME, her HUSBAND. I, JESUS am her love and I will love her always and forever. We will share in MY Kingdom for all time. It will be grand and wondrous. Very few come to this place, this place of MY Heart. Few look to find ME and put ME at the center of their worlds. Those who do, will never know disappointment. Their worldly loss is eternal Kingdom gain, MY Kingdom.

You are being given the opportunity to choose for yourself the outcome of your eternal existence. MY children, eternity never ends. Do not put yourself outside of MY World, MY Kingdom for all time. Surrender your all to ME NOW. The hour is swiftly disappearing. Find ME and find yourself.

MY Patience is wearing down. Soon the time will be up. I will leave without you if you choose against ME. I am always true to MY Word. I CHANGE NOT. MY Word is true.

Love ME and live. Hate MY Ways and live apart from ME for all time. You decide. I love you. Choose for ME. I am your MAKER and I created you for MY eternal pleasure. But you must want to be with ME.

I AM has spoken.

Words dictated to Sabrina of Belgium by JESUS on December 30, 2010.

"Listen to ME all MY people. I AM is speaking.

Why do you forsake ME? Why do you continue to live your lukewarm lifestyle? Why is it that I, GOD am not enough for you? You were good enough for ME when I died on the cross for you. You didn't even know ME. You were in existence, but not from this world. You were created by ME already, everything is created by ME. You did not know ME then. You got to know ME as soon as I sent you to this world.

You were a pleasure in MY eyes. Everything on you was perfect. I enjoyed every detail of each and every one of you. Yet, now, you turn your eyes to others. MY heart is hurt by this. Little by little you were falling away from ME, your CREATOR. You were like a love story for ME. The intention was to enjoy each other for eternity. Yet, I was losing you to this world and its attractions. You were enjoying it so much and I was standing on the side to see when you would turn your eyes on ME again, your CREATOR, the ONE who breathed life into your nose.

But you chose the pleasures of this world that was a way much better odour for you. Yet, MY odour, MY ways, MY instructions, MY plans, MY very Word, the Holy Word written by MY HOLY SPIRIT, who should be your guide in this life are not found pleasant in your eyes. This is the worst choice you can make: choosing against your MAKER who breathed life in you, is not a good thing to do.

Therefore, the Heavenly gates are closing in. The path is narrow indeed, like MY Word says, but the gate is closing in and those who have followed ME all the way with total love and surrender to their LORD, will enter in. They will be rewarded greatly. Their eternal life will be so overwhelmingly full of joy and peace and love, that it can never be measured. MY Place is a beautiful one. I have created all kinds of things so you could enjoy this for eternity together with ME your MAKER. I have thought out unique plans for every one of you. You would be so pleased, and the things you are running after now in this temporary world, are falling into pieces compared to what I have in store for you.

So here is the deal: Surrender it all, like MY Word says, like it is written, and live HOLY before your GOD in Heaven, or have your way in this stinking world full of sin and idolatry, leading you to the path of hell. Why do you think MY Words are so harsh and full of warnings? Because I know what hell looks like. Many souls are crying out in there to have another chance. They would do anything to follow ME now. They realize they were misled by their worldly activities led by satan. Now, they are in agony and pain forever, their torment knows no end.

They realize the power of MY BLOOD now when they see ME, as I visit hell often. MY BLOOD is only available for this world. If you reject it now, you make your choice for eternity. MY BLOOD cannot save you once you are lost, once you have chosen your destiny yourself. I gave you freewill. I died a horrible death for all of you, to give you life in abundance. This is meant for eternity. Yet you seek this abundance in the world away from ME, your GOD and CREATOR. This was never meant to be.

You know well enough MY people, when you wander away from ME. You know it in your spirit-being. That's the righteousness of GOD. I AM is a righteous GOD. So nobody would be lost. You still have a chance, but once the door is closing for good, there is little hope for you. MY bride will be with ME in Heaven celebrating her CREATOR and her victory through ME. Do you really want to let it come this far?

MY heart is broken, but I say, fine. What else can I do? You were created with freewill. But it is not MY will that anybody is lost and spends eternity in hell. You think: I will not go to hell. I remember MY GOD on Sunday, I go to church, and I harm no person. You violate MY Word and you harm no person? Love the Lord your GOD with all that is in you and your neighbour as yourself. Have you witnessed to your neighbours? Do they know and see in you that you are special, a different kind of breed, one who loves his of her GOD above anything else in this world? Do they see this kind of love flowing through you? Do they know? I have put you there, so you could be MY witness.

Everybody you meet should know I AM is your GOD. Yet, many of you are ashamed to even mention MY NAME. I tell you, I was not ashamed to carry your load of sins on ME, naked on a cross. I was not ashamed to endure the beatings of the whip for you. I was not ashamed to let MYSELF be humiliated by the rulers of that time, so they could mock ME and play a game with ME.

Yet, all you have to do is mention MY NAME and you can not get it over your lips. That means I AM is not in your heart. That means the pleasing of people is more important to you then pleasing your GOD, the ONE who created you. I will not be ashamed to take the ones when I appear in the clouds, who surrendered completely and gave their lives for MY NAME sake. However, I will turn MY FACE from the ones who have denied ME, mocked ME, made ME a joke to go along with their so called worldly friends, who abused MY HOLY NAME and who thought it was not really necessary to live by MY Word, MY HOLY WORD, so it would go well with you, so crime would not rule in this world.

Oh yes, the enemy is pulling at you, but you give him permission to do so. I am a righteous GOD, I gave you freewill, also in this. Every choice you make, is your own. So don't come with excuses when you stand before MY HOLY THRONE one day, I will not accept them. It's all or nothing. Everything in between I cannot accept, neither does MY FATHER.

Now is the time of grace. I made this all possible for you. So choose wisely. It's a choice for eternity, MY people. If I would not care for you, I would not have died for you. The way is open, the choice is yours.

I AM has spoken. Amen.

Ephesians 1:4. According as he hath chosen us in him before the foundation of the world, that we should be holy and without blame before him in love:

Isaiah 43:6-7. I will say to the north, Give up; and to the south, Keep not back: bring MY sons from far, and MY daughters from the ends of the earth; Even every one that is called by MY name: for I have created him for MY glory, I have formed him; yea, I have made him.

Isaiah 45:12. I have made the earth, and created man upon it: I, even MY hands, have stretched out the heavens, and all their host have I commanded.

Genesis 2:7. And the LORD God formed man of the dust of the ground, and breathed into his nostrils the breath of life; and man became a living soul.

1 Thessalonians 4:7-8. For God hath not called us unto uncleanness, but unto holiness. He therefore that despiseth, despiseth not man, but God, who hath also given unto us his holy Spirit.

Genesis 28:17. He was afraid and said, "How awesome is this place! This is none other than the house of God; this is the gate of heaven."

Joshua 23:16. If you violate the covenant of the LORD your God, which he commanded you, and go and serve other gods and bow down to them, the LORD's anger will burn against you, and you will quickly perish from the good land he has given you."

1 Samuel 15:24. Then Saul said to Samuel, "I have sinned. I violated the LORD's command and your instructions. I was afraid of the men and so I gave in to them."

Luke 9:26. For whosoever shall be ashamed of me and of MY words, of him shall the Son of man be ashamed, when he shall come in his own glory, and in his Father's, and of the holy angels.

Our friend Terry also sent us this note to add to this message: In China, the Bible is limited and often expensive. Often people have to rip out a chapter in the Bible and read just on chapter. Each person is allowed one chapter and they read that 1 chapter for a whole week, and get a new chapter when they exchange it every Sunday. This way, everyone is given a chance to read all the chapters within a year if it is 52 chapters. If you print one chapter on an 11 by 8.5 paper on both sides, and fold it three times, you can put it in your wallet without damaging the word printed. Did you know that if you read the same chapter the whole week, it will last sink deep into your heart because you have read it so much. Please visit: www.john316tips.com

These urgent prophetic messages are recorded at the website: http://end-times-prophecy.com

Sabrina's email is: jan.sabrina@pandora.be

and

Susan's email is: kidsmktg@sbcglobal.net